Walk with the Lord

Lent-Easter

SHARING THE CROSS,
SHARING THE GLORY

by
Fr. Anselm W. Romb, OFM Conv.

St. Paul Books & Media

Library of Congress Cataloging-in-Publication Data

Romb, Anselm W. (Anselm William), 1929-
   Walk with the Lord : sharing the cross, sharing the glory / by
Anselm W. Romb.
     p.   cm.
   ISBN 0-8198-8240-2
   1. Lent—Prayer-books and devotions—English.   2. Easter—Prayer
-books and devotions—English.   3. Bible—Liturgical lessons,
English.   4. Catholic Church—Prayer-books and devotions—English.
I. Title.
BX2170.L4R65   1990
242'.34—dc20   8949678
                                                 CIP

Printed and published in the U.S.A. by St. Paul Books & Media
50 St. Paul's Ave., Boston, MA 02130

St. Paul Books & Media is the publishing house of the Daughters of St. Paul, an international congregation of women religious serving the Church with the communications media.

1 2 3 4 5 6 7 8 9   98 97 96 95 94 93 92 91 90

This book is dedicated to all those priests and laity
who taught me to love the Word of God
and encouraged me both to preach and to write.
Generous affirmation and honest criticism
are the pillars on which the pulpit rests.

Contents

Lenten Season

Easter Season

Appendix

PREFACE

For those who use these Scriptural and liturgical reflections, I suggest reading the Bible texts on which they are based.

These reflections have multiple uses. They are principally for laypersons' daily meditations during the two liturgical seasons mentioned in the title. Secondly, those religious, clerics, and laypersons who pray the daily Office may wish to substitute these reflections for the second reading of the Office of Readings, although they derive from the weekday and Sunday texts of the Mass.

Preachers who are accustomed to preach every day, especially during the cycles of Lent and Easter, and who must preach every Sunday, may find this book a source of ideas. Because these commentaries would generally be too long, the preacher can readily choose those ideas which will generate a homily of suitable length.

Included also are some preparations for Penitential Services during Lent that may prove helpful for all readers.

Fr. Anselm W. Romb, OFM Conv.

Lenten
Season

Ash Wednesday

Joel's rousing text for Ash Wednesday is a real "call to arms" for the ascetic. He tells us to fast, weep and mourn. With rapid-fire verbs he stirs our imagination: blow a trumpet, proclaim, call, gather, notify, assemble! Infants, children, elders, bride and bridegroom, priests—none are exempt from the call to penance.

This sense of spiritual urgency is reinforced by Saint Paul in his letter to the Church at Corinth. *"Behold, now is a very acceptable time; behold, now is the day of salvation."* For at least 1500 years the Church has heeded this call and has reminded herself of how swiftly life passes, by marking our heads with ashes. These ashes are a sacramental productive of grace according to the degree of faith of the person who accepts the ashes and his or her spiritual "readiness." Hence even non-Catholics may receive the ashes.

The immediate and obvious meaning of ashes derives from one of the formulas used for the rite, namely, that we are only dust and shall return at death to the dust of the earth. These ashes come, of course, from burning palms blessed and distributed the previous Palm Sunday during the liturgy in memory of Jesus' tri-

13

umphant entry into Jerusalem. But this moment of glory was truly empty, truly transitory. The Lord gave no signs of gladness in the Gospel, because he would be crucified with the same crowd present a few days later. How untrustworthy is the praise of this world!

That the ashes are imposed on the head suggests that vainglory is foolish and that one's spiritual appearance remains paramount. Some ascetics of past centuries sprinkled ashes even over their food to kill any good taste that may have escaped the monastery cook's hands. (This is not encouraged today since researchers have discovered ashes may be carcinogenic!) Nevertheless the small amount of mortification with regard to food serves as a small symbol of the greater self-denial required to avoid sin and practice virtue. Ashes and fasting are exterior, physical, visible signs of Lent and conversion. Less apparent, but more significant, of course, is the interior motive and spiritual change of heart.

Too often we remain content with rituals and ceremonies and think they are enough. Even the ashes which the saints sprinkled on food was merely symbolic. To destroy the good taste of food which is God's gift, was not of itself of great spiritual value. The point was to consider the Bread of Life come down from heaven, celebrated in the Paschal Mystery, and containing all sweetness and delight. The ascetics were declaring their preference to await the imperishable joy and glory that were yet to come!

What is the principal "energizer" of corporal mortification is brought to light by the words of Jesus in the Gospel. He decries merely external observance, which is performing *"righteous deeds in order that people may see...,"* whether giving alms or reciting prayers in public. He does not refer to public, official liturgy, but private prayers assumed for public notice. The admonition of

Jesus to pray in privacy to the Father implies the meaning of genuine prayer: being present to God, cutting away distractions, and being totally engaged in communication, speaking and listening. If the essence of heaven is God's presence, then whenever we consciously place ourselves in his presence, day or night, in the church or car or kitchen or shopping mall, we already have one foot in heaven. We do not enjoy the vision of God, but at least perceive his actions "through a veil, darkly." The ancient monks had a Latin expression they applied both to prayer and death: *a cella in coelum,* "from (our) cell into heaven."

The importance of interior attitudes and heartfelt sentiments is emphasized by Joel. *"Rend your hearts, not your garments."* This is an allusion to the Jewish practice of appearing tattered and unkempt as a sign of penance or mourning. Joel's call to prayer and penance was a response to the fact that Israel had just suffered a catastrophic plague of locusts. Their change of heart might move God to relent in the punishment from this natural scourge.

We are sometimes told that "giving up" material comforts is merely negative and not very profitable spiritually. This would be true if our fast were motivated by dieting or a "health kick" in giving up candy or alcohol or tobacco. Yet such practices do have value according to the motive. It is far better for the believer to attend weekday Mass, make the Stations of the Cross, and read the Bible daily, if these acts of piety have not been one's custom already.

When a parishioner archly told his pastor that he avoided coming to church "because of so many hypocrites" that go to church, the pastor gently replied, "Then by all means come; there is always room for one more!"

Thursday
After Ash Wednesday

Dt 30:15-20;
Lk 9:22-25

The Lord clearly does not approve of wishy-washy, lukewarm spiritual "wimps." In Deuteronomy he tells his beloved people to stop straddling the fence. Whereas compromise is an important key to maintaining successful interpersonal relationships with our fellow human beings, compromise is an obstacle to our relationship with God.

Choose between "life and prosperity" or "death and doom." God offers "the blessing and the curse," that is, national strength and material prosperity for fidelity to his covenant or destruction under foreign domination. How much greater is Jesus' promise of eternal life! But his words are equally without compromise. *"If anyone wishes to come after me, he must deny himself and take up his cross daily and follow me. For whoever wishes to save his life will lose it, but whoever loses his life for my sake will save it."* For our initial conversion and response to our Christian vocation, Jesus does not present us with a body of doctrine, but asks us to accept him in a personal way: follow in my steps and lose your life for my sake.

The key words of Lent recur almost stridently in our ears: do penance, make reparation, rend your hearts, give alms, pray unceasingly. How do you "lose your life"? Be honest in your business dealings; care for the orphan and widow, the homeless and disenfranchised; restrain your tongue; be patient, forebearing and tolerant. This is how you die to yourself. When you multiply your prayers during this season, you should be moved to multiply your charities, too. You are to fast not merely from food and drink, but from abusive language, from impatience, from sarcasm, from angry words.

The best and easiest way to avoid compromise in faith and religion is by clarifying your goals and setting your priorities in order. Because "getting into heaven" is the bottom line of human existence, what is essential and necessary to salvation?

First, allow the Lord to enter your life. Be sensitive to his inner calls to avoid sin, and ponder the bible texts with Jesus' admonitions. Second, trust God, who has brought you to the present point of your spiritual development, to carry you further. Understand that he will bring good out of the evils that often afflict you. Realize that setbacks are temporary for a faithful believer. Third, cast your cares on the Lord. Do not preoccupy yourself with worries about which you can do little or nothing. Live more simply, without anxiety and the desire to accumulate. Fourth, listen more during prayer. Do not rush just to "get through" the prayers you generally recite. Penetrate the meaning of even such common prayers as the "Our Father" and the "Hail Mary." Find quiet time to meditate on the law of the Lord, who tells us in today's Gospel, *"What profit is there for one to gain the whole world yet lose or forfeit himself?"*

Do not spare yourself in formulating an honest answer without compromise. Abandon the illusion that there is always time left to change your life. Compromise is the signpost to hell.

Friday
After Ash Wednesday

Is 58:1-9;
Mt 9:14-15

Every liturgical season can be defined as a mini-experience of one's entire spiritual life, but the Lent-Easter Cycle is the clearest distillation of human life. Suffering and death, rising and joy constitute everyone's spiritual résumé. As we follow Jesus as he "goes up to

Jerusalem to die," we recognize our own pattern. We immerse ourselves in Jesus' own relationship with his Father, in obedience to whom he laid down his life for us. Our likeness to the Master is the goal and meaning of our spiritual journey.

We begin, like Jesus, in delivering up all that we are and all that we have to the Father. He wants our past memories, to heal us of sin, that we might be freed from anxiety. He wants our present, so that we may accomplish the works of holiness. He wants our future, so that we may be guided to fulfill our purpose in the divine plans.

Today's Gospel suggests that there was some rivalry between Jesus' disciples and the Baptist's disciples who saw the ascendancy of Jesus over John and his growing popularity. John's disciples criticized Jesus for not fasting as they and the Pharisees did. In answer Jesus applied the metaphor of marriage, which appears often in the Jewish Testament. The disciples of Jesus, who are the nucleus of God's new people, are guests of himself, the groom—which is the title God reserves for himself in the Scriptures. Then Jesus alluded to the proximate time when he would be absent and his wedding guests would be plunged into mourning and fasting.

Criticism of another kind surfaces in Isaiah today. The Jewish people had evidently been complaining that God ignored their fasting and self-discipline. The divine retort is a censure of their "contract mentality," that is, they wanted to "make a deal" with God, who points out, *"They ask me to declare what is due them, pleased to gain access to God."* In other words, those who fulfilled the externals of the law thought they deserved automatically God's blessing on their projects. They were, in fact, trying to manipulate God in favor of their own needs.

God tells them through the mouth of his prophet that on the very day of their most sacred ritual acts they drive their employees and quarrel with their associates. External acts of religion are pointless—to bow and scrape to God, to wear burlap sacking, and sleep on a board for a mattress. Instead they should loose the shackles of those who are unjustly in bondage, free the oppressed, share their resources with the hungry, shelter the homeless, clothe the naked, avoid quarrels and malicious talk. This is a call to social justice!

Isaiah's enumeration is actually our Christian social program, the works of mercy. How often Jesus preached against the perils of wealth and its pursuit! How clearly the saints opted for poverty and dependence upon Providence! Generous almsgiving remains an important expression of Christian asceticism. Even the understandable desire of some parents to provide an inheritance for their children "to make life easier for them" should cede to the exigencies of the poor who need help at once. In this way those parents win for themselves a spiritual inheritance from the Father. In imitation of the Lord we are called to look squarely into the faces of the embarrassed poor, the criminal, the mentally disabled, the senile, those who are marginal to our comfort-seeking society.

The disadvantaged in turn give us a gift: liberation from our ego, from building our reputation, from clinging to phony values, from insisting on our supposed or real rights, from being possessive and arrogant and demanding. By serving them we can see what it means to be trapped; the poor cannot very easily make their demands heard—despite the confident assertions of the demagogues. Often the poor are the closest to the kingdom of God and are our best models.

Saturday
After Ash Wednesday

Is 58:9-14;
Lk 5:27-32

Levi, who invited Jesus to dinner, is thought to be the Apostle Matthew. It was natural for him to invite his only likely friends, other tax-collectors, so that the dinner looked like a Jewish IRS party! The gripe of the Pharisees was not exactly that they were sinners for being tax-collectors, but for being agents of the Roman army of occupation. The Jews paid Temple taxes and tithes themselves, hence this was a legitimate duty. But they considered these publicans—another name for tax-collectors—as collaborators, who from Gentile contacts were corrupted, fell often into ritual impurity, did not observe Jewish traditions, and probably did not even serve kosher food!

Jesus' retort is most comforting: *"Those who are healthy do not need a physician, but the sick do. I have not come to call the righteous to repentance but sinners."* Thus he admitted implicitly that Levi and his friends were not observers of the Law, but that it was better not to lose contact with them and harden their attitude by nagging criticism. Even in the then existing Jewish Bible the Lord said, "I do not desire the death of a sinner, but that he be converted and live."

Observance of the Law, particularly the Sabbath, is the evident theme of today's readings, perhaps meant as a preparation for tomorrow, Sunday. Isaiah, speaking for God, tells his people to *"hold back your foot on the sabbath"* by not engaging in business, manual labor and journeys beyond a short, permissible distance (called a "sabbath day's journey"). They are to *"call the sabbath a delight and the LORD's holy day honorable."* To keep the Lord's day holy is still a requirement of the devout

Christian, but the definition of "keeping holy" has changed over the centuries.

Manual labor (with one's "hands") or servile work (proper to a serf or slave) was forbidden explicitly at one time, but mental work (reading, writing, bookkeeping) was permissible. Then the theologians taught that manual labor such as gardening and woodworking were really hobbies and a "break" in one's routine. Shopping was once forbidden, but later fell into the categories of the recreational (especially buying a car or home) or even the necessary, when both husband and wife worked during the week. Finally, washing and drying clothes was considered moral if machines did most of the work! No wonder people got confused, especially if they received no instruction from the pulpit!

The following norms can be your guidelines: It is not the amount of exertion and exhaustion that violates Sunday worship, otherwise even athletics would be forbidden, as Sunday football and baseball games! The point is to interrupt the work week and not do the things by which we earn our living nor do what occupies us with chores during the week, as for a wife and mother. Necessary work such as cooking or providing public services are exceptions. Yet all of this is merely pharisaical if we limit our idea of Sunday to what we must avoid.

Besides participating in the Mass we should make Sunday a time of rest and physical relaxation. We should make time for family and friends, common recreation, and visiting especially the sick and lonely and housebound. To make Sunday "holy" we should spend time in quiet prayer, reading the Bible, studying our religion, reciting and meditating on the rosary mysteries, particularly within the family, and perhaps attending Benediction where it is available.

Keeping the Lord's day "honorably," as Isaiah puts it, gives us a foretaste of Paradise—and that is the main point—when we shall know God and love him, associate with the saints, converse with Mary, speak with our deceased loved ones, and plumb the mysteries of God. Sunday is the day to ponder the wonderful works of God in your life and give him thanks and praise!

FIRST WEEK OF LENT

First Sunday
of Lent, A

Gn 2:7-9, 3:1-7;
Rom 5:12-19; Mt 4:1-11

The three Jewish Testament readings for Cycles A, B and C center on man's sinfulness and how God responded with his successive covenants—to Adam, to Noah, to Abraham. The three Gospels from Matthew, Mark and Luke all point out how at the beginning of his public life Jesus, the one who was sinless, accepted likeness to us in all things but sin, yet allowed himself to be tempted by Satan, in order to teach us how to reject sin.

In Cycle A the story of Adam and Eve falling into original sin, however, stops short of the covenant whereby the offspring of Eve will overcome Satan and his wiles. The message of the text from Genesis is that mankind wanted to determine its own destiny, to be godlike by knowing experientially the difference between good and evil. Upon eating the forbidden fruit, they at once sensed that their passions could be inflamed by their nakedness; so they fashioned loincloths for themselves! Thus our race was first exposed to the kind of temptations to which it was to become most

23

vulnerable, that is, all kinds of sensuality, every kind of indulgence, not only the erotic.

St. Paul in his letter to the Church at Rome, his masterpiece about sin, death, justification and grace, reiterates the fall of our first parents. Then he cites the covenant in Jesus, whereby grace abounds more than sin, and he calls Jesus a "gift," that is, something—or rather, Someone—whom we receive, yet to whom we have no right of ourselves. The only qualification to receive this gift is to accept Jesus precisely as our Savior and to graft ourselves into his life—which implies that we accept and live by his values—and so achieve eternal life.

The conversion process begins with our being "convicted of sin," that is, recognizing our fallen and deprived nature, our proclivity to sin, and our general spiritual weakness and inability to live under God's law without his help. This applies even to saints and relatively sinless persons. Their sin may not be measured only by the enormity of some act, but also by the grace rejected, given the spiritual sensitivity they had already achieved with God's help! The very word "contrition" and its weaker expression, "attrition," comes from the Latin verb which means "getting broken." A contrite person, convicted of sin, is "broken-hearted" because sin detours the person on the journey to God.

The Liturgy of the Mass clearly outlines the pattern of prayer that begins with sorrow for sin: The penitential rite leads us to regret sins we cherish the most, we must confess the most, and which are the most embarrassing. The orations go on to ask God to second our efforts to stay in his good grace. We marvel at his wonderful works during the readings and responsorial psalm. We pray for the needs of the world, the Church and ourselves during the general intercessions. During the Eucharistic Prayer we remind the Father of how Jesus gave us his Body and Blood, and finally unite ourselves with Christ directly in Holy Communion. Thus our sinfulness, which divides us from God, is turned into union with him already on this earth. The Mass is, therefore, the perfect model for our private prayer! It is the same process.

Even so perfect a human being as St. Francis of Assisi, at the height of his earthly sanctity when he was pierced with the very wounds of Jesus, was convicted of sin and felt the need to repeat this prayer, "Who are you, O God, and what am I, but a poor little worm?" It seems necessary at times that love speak foolishly (as all lovers know) and even disparagingly of itself. At the same time the lover knows that only by loving can it make up for sin and indifference and coldness. Love alone provides the fire that can weld a heart together if one gives God the broken pieces.

Writers who are fond of using Greek jargon, that is, theological terms derived from the Greek language, have added another word that resonates with conviction of sin, contrition and sorrow. It is metanoia, which suggests a "change in the way of (your) thinking." Physicians who treat heart disease know that medications, diet and abstinence from salt, caffeine and tobacco are not enough to prevent heart attacks. Patients must reverse their thinking. They may have been competitive, impatient with trivial problems, self-destructively ambitious and easily angered. Now they are told to deliberately stand and wait in long lines at the supermarket, drive in the rightmost, slow lane of traffic, play bridge with the intention of losing, and force themselves to perform dull and boring routines! Their new mindset will affect their heart condition. The parallel in the spiritual life is obvious.

Jesus did not have to change his mindset, but I think he wanted to set the record straight about his priorities in his ministry. As always, what he did, he did for us. His desert experience lasted forty days and nights; this is meant to summarize the forty years the Chosen People were led through the desert towards the Promised Land. (Some scholars are of the opinion that the Exodus lasted closer to one hundred years.) It will help us understand what Jesus was expressing in rejecting Satan's temptations if we look at what the Jews experienced and learned during the Exodus.

They were separated from foreign elements. They depended on God for sustenance. They stepped out in faith to follow a pillar of cloud and a column of fire. They had to trust God to defend them from pagan rulers. Their fidelity was tested by thirst, famine and idolatry. Non-believers were purged from their ranks. They experienced intimacy with God, especially through their leaders, who presented divine law to them. The Jewish prophets went out into the desert to recapture this series of events, and Jesus himself, led by the Holy Spirit, allowed himself to be similarly tested. He depended on God's ministering angels to provide food. He isolated himself from the distractions of the company of others. He stepped out in faith and sought intimacy with his Father in constant prayer.

Recognizing our sinful nature, convicted of sin, yet determined to change our mindset and seek first the kingdom of God and his justice, we enable ourselves to resist temptation. The same Spirit teaches us that our food must be the Word of God, that we must not "test" God by making deals with him, and that we shall serve and adore him alone.

First Sunday of Lent, B

Gn 9:8-15; 1 Pt 3:18-22;
Mk 1:12-15

We are reminded by today's readings that tradition-
ally Lent has been the Church's communal preparation
for the Baptism of her neophytes and a time for all believers to renew their own baptismal promises. Noah's
sign of God's approval was a rainbow, and every rainbow
for the rest of time was supposed to remind human beings of God's promise never to destroy the world again
by a general flood, no matter how threatening the appearance of storm clouds in the sky. To primitive minds
it was necessary for God to demonstrate his control over
human life by natural manifestations.

St. Peter in his first letter compares those who are
saved to the family of Noah: *"This prefigured baptism,*
which saves you now." He tells us that original sin is not
a physical stain, but some lack or emptiness of grace.
Baptism supplies the pledge *"for a clear conscience,*
through the resurrection of Jesus Christ." By his rising Jesus
overcame sin and death—a victory he shares with us!

But before that great day of victory Jesus had to fall
into line behind the earlier children of Adam and Eve,
and teach us by his words and example. The bare-bones
description of Mark today shows Jesus, inspired by the
Holy Spirit, meditating and praying to his Father about
his coming ministry. His message would be moral,
rather than doctrinal at the beginning. Mark merely
takes note of the desert experience of Jesus without describing it in detail as do Matthew and Luke. John does
not advert to Jesus' temptation at all.

Forty days seem an inexplicably long time to fast and
pray unceasingly. Yet this period of time has great mystical significance. "Forty" days as it appears in the Jewish
Testament, therefore, has its ultimate fulfillment in the

acts of Jesus. It rained for forty days after Noah sealed himself and his family and the creatures in the ark. The flood was a symbol of Baptism, as mentioned above, and Jesus was to begin his public life by being baptized in the Jordan. He was also to show his power as God over the elements, as when he quieted the raging sea, a biblical symbol of chaos. In Exodus 24, Moses stayed on Sinai forty days and nights. Jesus, the new lawgiver, stayed on the mountain of temptation for the same length of time to outline the parameters of his ministry, as Matthew and Luke explain in some detail. Moses delivered a covenant; Jesus is the covenant of the New Testament in the blood. Jesus' teaching was the law written on the fleshly tablets of our hearts. In 1 Kings 19, Elijah went on a forty- day pilgrimage to Horeb, the mountain of God, to encounter God who manifested himself only interiorly. Elijah was to use this communion with God as the authentification of his prophetic ministry. Jesus, too, derived his message directly from his experience of his Father. Noah, Moses, Elijah were "types" or figures of the Savior to come. So we learn to look beyond the simple narration of events to discover their mystical meaning when we read the Bible.

A final reference to "forty days" completes the use of this mystical number. As we read in Acts 1, Jesus spent forty days as a visible risen Lord, but he was able to be seen only by those who had faith in his divine mission. During that time he announced the final epiphany of God that appears in the Bible: the descent of the Holy Spirit, who would teach his disciples all things, strengthen them, and be their advocate. We need this Spirit so we can say that "Jesus is Lord." In fact, it is the operation of the Spirit that forms us to the likeness of Jesus.

The central teaching of Lent is Jesus' passion and glorification. We must await the crack of doom to rise to glory, but we can share in the death of Jesus as long as we are alive on earth. During Baptism, originally by immersion, we are "buried with Christ" and rise to new life in him. This phrase is repeated during the funeral Mass. We "help" God to complete redemption by our share in teaching others and in suffering. We must fill up in our persons "what is lacking in the sufferings of Christ for the benefit of his body, the Church."

Lent is the time to die to the world. Jesus says in today's Gospel, *"This is the time of fulfillment. The kingdom of God is at hand. Repent, and believe in the gospel."* If your renewal of baptismal vows on Easter Sunday is to be relevant and fruitful, not just another ritual, then you must take the words of Jesus to heart. Make this a time for healing and achieving inner peace. Be reconciled with others with whom you are at odds. Strive for greater intimacy and union with God by fervent prayer. Make a sincere resolution to do battle with sin, especially your favorites. Scrutinize yourself for the last vestiges of self-love. Get ready for a complete and sincere confession. Read the Bible and study your religion. Dare to stand up for Catholic values before others.

One of the beatitudes reads, "Blessed are the pure of heart, for they shall see God." Purity of heart here does not refer to chastity, but to integrity: being single-minded, undivided, focused on God. Without such an attitude we cannot "see God," that is, know and love him, any more than a blind man can imagine what different colors are like. He has no point of reference.

If your heart is divided, then you need heart surgery, perhaps repeatedly; indeed, you may need a whole transplant! We cry out in the psalm, "Create a clean heart in me, O God." And in the words of his prophet, God answers, "I will give you new hearts to replace your stony hearts." Like pure water, which is not polluted, and pure gold, which is not alloyed, so a pure heart is not polluted by sin nor alloyed with other values than God's. God will have no rival for our love. Human nature of itself is incapable of this. It takes God's grace, his helps, to love our enemies, pray for those who persecute and calumniate us, and overcome the desires of the flesh.

With grace we can kill the base affections of our hearts whereby we cling to forbidden persons, places and pleasures. We can destroy envy and hatred and lack of charity. We can uproot our "hidden agenda" of manipulating others and forcing a change of behavior on them. Instead we should free others, affirm them, and lift them up to God!

First Sunday
of Lent, C

Dt 26:4-10;
Rom 10:8-13; Lk 4:1-13

Luke records the inner urgency of Jesus to enter his "desert experience"; he was led into the wasteland. Pilgrims who travel near Jericho are shown the Mount of Temptation, jutting out over the valley which today is irrigated and fruitful even though the mountain is barren and arid. No eyewitnesses were recorded; Jesus was alone. Did Jesus tell his disciples about his experience, or did the evangelists "theologize" after the fact, from what they inferred from the life and teaching of Jesus?

The meaning of the three temptations of Jesus is a kind of summary of Christian values. As the Sermon on the Mount is a collection of special sayings of Jesus that sum up his moral teaching, and the beatitudes are a job description of a Christian, so the temptations are not about Jesus only, but about us and the parameters of our spiritual journey! In general, of course, the Gospel is not simply about the life of one Man, but about all of human life as one person, Jesus Christ, lived it as a point of reference for us.

In isolation on the mountain Jesus learned about his vocation, which was to become a "nobody" or *anaw*, to use the biblical expression—a humble person who trusted God to bring him to his destiny. I do not think that Jesus permitted himself to be tempted just to show solidarity with us ("like us in all things but sin"), nor to show that temptation is unavoidable and "normal" in our lives, yet ultimately superable. I think his temptations symbolize the final days of the world, with victory over Satan on the Day of the Lord. To thwart Satan, Jesus quoted from the Book of Deuteronomy, the Jewish book of laws. This is important. Satan is routed by law and order—something often forgotten in our days of lawlessness and "doing your own thing."

We see that Jesus was not tempted by evil things— bread, civil authority, and trusting God to save him in personal danger—but was tempted to establish his spiritual enterprise by secular means. But the Master will not alloy his gold with the base metals of this world's values. Testing whether Jesus might, indeed, be the Son of God, Satan suggests that Jesus turn the stones into bread. But Jesus refused to use his power for personal advantage and for satisfying his hunger, even though one might view that as legitimate. In a wider sense, of course, Jesus could have fed all the poor of the world by changing rocks into bread. In fact, the Church's hands have always been busy for the poor and disadvantaged. But Jesus' refusal is a reminder that evangelists are not primarily social workers nor fund-raisers. By their preaching and example they should motivate others to change the lot of the poor first of all interiorly by bringing them the message of Jesus. Otherwise we would be in danger of making "rice Christians," as some early converts to Christianity in China were called, because they had accepted Baptism to get a handout from the missionaries! We are in danger of falling prey to the world's advertisement, "You go around only once, so grab everything you can," as a child grasps for the golden ring on the carousel.

Satan's second temptation was more blatant. He offered power over the world's kingdoms, if Jesus would only worship him, that is, accept his worldly values. But Jesus refused to force his message down anyone's throat or ally himself with any clique or political party—which also serves as a warning to those who hatch revolutions and plot in the name of religion! Sometimes you hear someone say, "If only I could be president—or Pope—for a day!" Maybe they mean to say, "If only I could be God for a day!" The danger of authority is that we would attempt to remake others according to our will, even in our own image and likeness—which is making oneself into an idol! Jesus warned us in Luke 22 that the kings of the Gentiles lord it over their subjects, but that that should not be our way—that he was in our midst as one who serves. He washed the feet of his disciples and "emptied himself out and took the form of a servant."

Satan's third temptation was to have Jesus make a "grandstand" play to test God's care for him and simultaneously impress the populace around the Temple. He would surely attract them to his teaching as a wonder-worker, yet it could also be an ego-trip to win applause, which Jesus taught us to avoid. He said it was an evil and adulterous generation that looks for signs and wonders; he wanted his hearers to notice his teaching and accept his message for its own sake. Faith in him had to precede the wonders. He could work no miracles in places where he found no faith; in other villages he said, "Your faith has made you whole." Jesus warns us that giving God a "dare" is an attempt to manipulate God and perhaps take satisfaction that we are somehow "special" and have the inside track with God!

Evil always seduces by appearing to be good and desirable, as in the temptations of Jesus by Satan. Our signs of spiritual success are not social work, political alliances, and unrealistically waiting for God to accomplish our tasks when we have not nearly exhausted our own efforts. Nor is it our academic degrees, preaching ability, social skills, balanced books and grand churches and institutions that are signs of spiritual success, but a humble and contrite heart in one who does not live by bread alone, one who adores the Lord his God only!

Monday of the First Week of Lent

Lv 19:1-2, 11-18;
Mt 25:31-46

Since Ash Wednesday we have been poised, as it were, on the lenten "launching pad"—ashes to remind us of the transitoriness of life and bible readings about fasting and prayer and almsgiving and other kinds of social justice. Remember, however, that the Lord spoke to us outside the context of any organized charities. Hence it is not enough to toss a few dollars into the poor box or missionary collection or diocesan development fund. Whereas without funding many Church projects would come to a halt, money can never be a substitute for face-to-face contact with the poor, for smelling the noisome odors of old-folks homes, for hearing the clanging of jail gates when you visit prisoners, for visiting the sick and housebound.

The reading from Leviticus today is a "second statement" of the ten commandments in greater detail and with practical notes. Instead of the first three commandments, which refer to the worship of God, the Lord simply says to Moses, *"Be holy, for I, the LORD, your God, am holy."* What can this mean? How can we be holy as God? It is a help to examine similar passages in the Bible, by which we discover that "holiness" and "justice" are much the same with respect to our relationships with our neighbors. But the "holiness" of God in relationship to us is that he is the Totally Other, the completely different Person (or three Persons). He is eternal, infinite, non-material, the repository of truth, goodness and beauty. On the other hand, we are contingent, mortal, sinful and plagued by confusion and error, the absence of truth and goodness!

In a word, we are able not-to-be, whereas God must be, so that everything else can be by his creative and sustaining power. "Being holy," therefore, is easy to understand a little, and impossible to understand completely. This call to holiness is a mystery which we cannot comprehend, but which we can apprehend. (Philosophers make this distinction between comprehension and apprehension!)

God himself explains "holiness" in the continuation of this passage. His theology is simpler than ours and provides an examination of conscience: Don't steal, lie, swear falsely, profane God's name, defraud, rob, withhold wages, harass the incapacitated, render dishonest judgments, show partiality, spread slander, disregard those whose lives are in jeopardy, bear hatred, reprove others in anger, take revenge, or hold a grudge. And the Lord didn't even mention sins of sexuality! This is because his purpose in the present long enumeration describes his attitude towards us, of which sexuality has no part. God does not deceive us, harass us unjustly, show partiality or take revenge on us poor sinners. Thus when we act like God in these practical ways he sets before us, we become "holy" in the biblical sense of possessing "justice."

Further, we become part of the Totally Other when we participate in the Truth (which is all the truths in the universe as God sees them, otherwise they would be false); in the Goodness of God (which is all the rightly-ordered love and mercy and honesty as God presents these virtues to us); and in the Beauty of God (which is the harmony and clarity and human artistry as God conceives the glorious and marvelous and uplifting in human hearts). That is how we become part of the life of the Trinity, which we call grace in a human being.

In today's Gospel, Jesus goes beyond the "don't" of Leviticus and tells us about the positive side of participating in the Goodness of God. The "sheep" on his right hand fed the hungry, clothed the naked, visited the sick and imprisoned, and so forth, whereas the left-side "goats" are condemned to hell for failing to see Christ in the suffering and deprived. "Whatsoever you did (or did not do) to even the most insignificant of my brothers is what you did to me!"

Now you know what to pray for today: to be holy as God, to share in the Totally Other, to perform the works of mercy. Pray for these insights, act them out, and live forever!

Tuesday of the First Week of Lent

Is 55:10-11;
Mt 6:7-15

We have the help of Jesus' own words about prayer in today's Gospel. He tells us not to blah-blah endlessly like the pagans of his time, who thought they pleased their false gods by long rituals of endless words. He tells us to be direct, succinct and honest and to pray for spiritual needs. This does not exclude material and physical necessities, but we should set our priorities clearly. "Seek first the kingdom of heaven, and all these things will be given you besides."

The text of the Our Father is given here as part of the Sermon on the Mount; in Luke it was taught by Jesus on the side of Mount Olivet, overlooking Jerusalem. Whatever its history, it is an eschatological prayer, which means it refers to the end-time of the world, the final period of its existence. (Basically the world ends for us with the end of our lives, after which there is the particular judgment, hell, purgatory, or heaven.) Thus we must understand the petitions of this prayer in the light of how tentative our lives are.

We ask that God's kingdom come upon us as individuals and all over the earth, that his will might be accomplished. The best translation for the next phrase is "Give us bread enough just for today." Tomorrow will bring its own problems, which may include the end of the world! If the end comes upon us, we won't need to store up bread anyway. Thus we ask to live tentatively and depend on divine Psaloniansrovidence. And if the world will end, we had better set our accounts straight and forgive our debtors to the degree that we expect God to forgive our sins. Finally we pray to be saved from the trial and delivered from evil, that is, the evil at the end of the world, when, as Jesus foretold, perhaps even the just will be seduced! In 2 Thessalonians, the writer refers to the "great apostasy" of the end-time. Every age thinks it is the worst of all centuries, yet there is reason to think ours may be the worst.

We can take strength from the first reading from Isaiah about the effectiveness of God's Word in the end. My Word *"shall not return to me void, but shall do my will, achieving the end for which I sent it."* Even our most useless human words have become important in this age when the explosion of information causes them to be stored in the memory banks of computers. Having ruled out God's intervention, however, statisticians make incredible claims about words and the mindless development of this universe and intelligent life in particular! Even monkeys, they say, could in time type out a Shakespearean sonnet! One scholar computed that it could take one trillion monkeys, randomly striking typewriter keys at the rate of three letters per second, eight hours a day, a trillion years just to type out the name of William Shakespeare! The odds are not very favorable—which drives one to the conclusion that our complex world follows the plan of a mastermind whom we call "God." This implies that the universe as we know it may have an end, too. The predictions of the Bible ensure that this will be the case. The Our Father is Jesus' prayer to prepare us for that event.

The words taught to us by God's own Son will be effective in our lives. The coming of God's kingdom will not be a random event, like a trillion monkeys trying to type a name for a trillion years. God chooses the events of human history to guarantee our salvation. When the end-time arrives, it will be "timely," that is, according to God's time line and in his way. Pray the Our Father carefully and sincerely. Just like it's "not nice to fool Mother Nature," it is foolish and even dangerous to try to make a monkey out of God and his divine plan.

Wednesday of the First Week of Lent

Jon 3:1-10;
Lk 11:29-32

Today's readings have to do with signs. The sign given to the people of Nineveh was Jonah's preaching. In today's Gospel Jesus reiterates what he says in several places: an evil age seeks for signs. Sometimes God provides a reassuring sign to the world to uplift the good and warn the wicked. Yet we are warned by Jesus not to manipulate God nor test him by demanding or expecting a sign, an extraordinary phenomenon, an unusual event, a miraculous occurrence. So the Lord refuses to give his fellow Jews anything but the "sign of Jonah." As Jonah was in the belly of the huge fish for three days, so Jesus would remain for three days in his tomb, then rise alive. (Actually it would be about forty hours, spread out over parts of three days.)

On the other hand, the sign of Jonah was essentially his prophetic mission, not his unusual mode of travel! So Jesus' prophetic mission, his teaching, was the thrust of his three years of public life—although his resurrection was to be his chief miracle and proof of his teaching. Yet the Lord declared himself a more important preacher than Jonah and a greater teacher than Solomon.

Nineveh converted upon hearing Jonah, yet he was reluctant to fulfill his errand. When the fish vomited him on shore, he went to Nineveh, hoping that the Assyrians would ignore him, so God would be justified in destroying their city. They were, after all, mortal enemies of the Jews anyway!

Surprisingly, Nineveh converts to God's ways. Even the animals are covered with sackcloth and ashes. (This last line is one of many in the Book of Jonah that lead scholars to point out that Jonah is a mythical figure, by whose comic antics God teaches us a spiritual lesson. If a proud and pagan city of sin changes its way of life and is forgiven, then how much more can those of good will depend on God for mercy! The point is that cattle wearing sackcloth and ashes is meant to be humorous. What would be your reaction upon seeing a barnyard of cows wearing burlap slacks and blouses as a farmer threw shovelfuls of ashes in their faces?)

The Assyrians repented and then God in turn "repented of the evil he had threatened." Actually God cannot repent nor change his mind, because he cannot be the recipient of a creature's action. Nothing, no one, can impinge upon or change God in any way. Then, you logically ask, why should we pray to him who is unchanging and unchangeable? The answer is easy, given the countless times the Bible encourages us to pray. God foresees eternally how we will be disposed or pray or turn from sin and so forth. Thus he arranges our lives and destiny according to his divine foreknowledge. He anticipates our good actions, which in any case are the result of the prompting of his graces.

The story of Jonah centers on the fact that God cares about us. The Chosen People sensed this deeply throughout their history. The psalmist wrote, "What is man that you should be concerned for him or the son of man that you should care for him? You have made him little less than the angels; with glory and honor you have crowned him." Jesus made this point even more concretely: that not a bird from the air nor a hair from our head falls without God knowing and willing it. (Many of us wish that God had not willed quite so much hair to fall out—or provided a method of reversing the process!) We do not always easily see the hand of God at work; we do not fathom his design. Although the details of his plans are beyond us, we can faithfully acknowledge in retrospect that his hand was at work. From our rich experience of his care for us we can extrapolate to the future and feel secure that God is busy in heaven and so all is well!

Thursday of the
First Week of Lent

Est C:12, 14-16,
23-25; Mt 7:7-12

The Book of Esther is a short but lovely story, like a costume drama or an opera from the past. The background of today's reading is this: A large group of Jews were in exile in Persia. One beautiful young woman, Esther, was taken into the harem of the king, who was called the Lion of Persia. She learns about the pogrom by a coalition of Persian nobles against her people. The courtiers were going to use the unwitting king as a pawn in their plot.

Just before the scene in which we find Esther at prayer, she had replaced Vashti, her predecessor, as the king's favorite. Now her fellow Jews urged her to use her charms to reveal the plot to their sovereign. But as in every good story there is an obstacle and an element of danger. A woman's place was definitely not in government; she could not even gain access to the king without being summoned. To invade, as it were, the private operations of the empire could even merit death! At this point we hear Esther pray not to use her feminine wiles on the king, but to trust in God's help.

Esther calls God, "My Lord, our King," recognizing him as the only sovereign of us all. She asks God to protect her and keep his promise to make Israel his "lasting heritage." She feels helpless and cries out, *"Help me, who am alone and have no help but you."* Note the qualities of her prayer: her humility, her confession of helplessness, her confidence in God as her deliverer, her resolve to carry out her dangerous mission.

The words of Jesus in the Gospel express different, but equally important qualities of prayer: persistence (ask and seek and knock), and childlikeness (*"how much more will your heavenly Father give good things to those who ask him").* Both readings express the fundamental attitude of one who prays: a heart which is emptied out of itself and hands which lack effectiveness. We lift up our hearts and hands and ask God to fill them with his gifts.

It is long-range fidelity that makes a saint, that is, the "long haul" of sometimes years of perseverance. This applies particularly to prayer. Only when we keep asking do the answers surface and our resolve increase. We don't stop seeking, because the pursuit is really the same as the discovery of God in our lives. If we continue knocking, the door will open; in fact, God never locks his doors!

The biblical model of prayer is repeated often in the prayers we find in both Testaments. Esther is a good example. When we are at a loss for words when we begin to pray, we can advert to the biblical mode. First, we cite our own unworthiness and past history of sin, against which we have been helpless. Second, we recall the wonderful works of God in history and in our own lives. Finally, we ask him to continue his beneficence towards us and those for whom we are interceding. Contrition, thanks and petition—these are the outline of biblical prayer. The same elements appear in the liturgy of the Mass. Although we tend to think of prayer as activity, in fact prayer is rather receptivity. We stand before God and ask him to change us into better persons. It is God's pleasure to uplift the lowly, meek and poor in spirit and those who count the blessings they have already received from him. Mental and verbal activity are useful to begin our prayer, but prayer should end in quiet peace of soul and in a sense of being filled with God. Mary's hymn of praise, the Magnificat, exemplifies this attitude in a peerless way. We have received all our potencies already at Baptism, and as we empty ourselves out, God actualizes them through the Holy Spirit. Poverty of spirit is not a "pious species" of craven cowardice; it means that we let God move in on us. As the aphorism has it, "Let go and let God," that is, "Let God be God" in your life!

Friday of the First Week of Lent

*Ez 18:21-28;
Mt 5:20-26*

The attitude of God towards us is found in Ezekiel today: *"Do I not rather rejoice when he turns from his evil way that he may live?"* In Matthew's text Jesus is uncompromising: *"you will not be released until you have paid the last penny."* He warns us to go beyond the external religious actions of the scribes and Pharisees, who thought that merely avoiding murder fulfilled the command of God. Jesus tells us to make up with our brother, which means anyone who is hostile towards us, particularly before we come to pray before God's altar—which the Church applies to the greeting of peace before Holy Communion. "Peace" is the message we share, but "love" is the issue!

Peace is more elusive than ever in our century of conflict. We may well wonder whether modern inventions have been such a blessing. Instead of creating more abundance, there is more exploitation and suffering. Science can improve human life by such helps as plastics, fertilizer, sources of energy, automobiles, kitchen appliances, and so forth, yet who can forget the horrors of atomic annihilation and the weapons of destruction? Some governments make plans to alter the atmosphere to open the ozone layer to allow death-dealing radiation to fall on the enemy; to start forest fires, bomb dams, poison water supplies, trigger volcanic eruptions, and somehow melt the polar ice caps—which would cause the oceans to rise 230 feet and flood every coastal city in the world! These gruesome plans come from "think tanks" of the warlords. They would be willing to destroy the fragile ecology and delicate balance of nature to win wars, after which we would all be losers and victims.

But Jesus tells us today to avoid even abusive language and settle with our opponents while we have time—and even pray for our enemies and those who harass us. St. Augustine wrote that the only sure way of destroying an enemy permanently is by turning him into a friend, even our brother! Nor can you ration your love, which should be universal, and love only some persons or races or nationalities. You cannot say that you love Jesus our King unless you love all his subjects.

God's "love plan" is enunciated throughout the Christian Testament, although it exists equally in the Jewish Bible. God inspired the sacred writers to use the phrase "one another" repeatedly. If we considered each use as a tiny candle, what a light we could bring to our war-torn world! In the Letter to the Church at Rome we read: Depend on one another; be devoted to one another; outdo one another in showing honor. Weep with one another; be of the same mind toward one another; don't judge one another. Admonish one another; receive one another; greet one another.

Galatians, Ephesians, Corinthians, Thessalonians, Colossians, as well as the letters of Peter, James and John, return to this theme of concern for our fellow humans. A spiritually useful "homework" would be to read these letters and copy the "one another" phrases: "Love one another as I have loved you." Thus Jesus provides the motive and the model for loving. One of the incredible aspects of the lives of saints was their ability to forgive and to love as Jesus did from the cross. Saint Maximilian Kolbe urged his Franciscan brothers to pray even for the Nazis who destroyed their apostolate in the City of the Immaculate in Poland in 1939. In the concentration camp he himself prayed for their conversion.

Jesus said, "Father, forgive them, because they do not know what they are doing."

It is therefore not enough to refrain from external acts of hostility, such as fighting and verbal abuse. Jesus calls our attention today to our interior dispositions. After all, our thoughts are father to our actions; we must uproot the sources of violence that are within ourselves and in our way of thinking. When you take the hand of another during the liturgical greeting of peace, let it be your sign that you are at peace with all the world and wish to be reconciled with anyone who holds a grudge against you.

Saturday of the First Week of Lent

Dt 26:16-19;
Mt 5:43-48

In the first reading Moses tells the Jews to observe their "agreement" with God, to walk in his ways, and observe his statutes, commandments and decrees. The importance of law is quite clear; these words are used to reinforce the idea that the Lord guaranteed his support. *"You are to be a people peculiarly his own.... You will be a people sacred to the LORD, your God."* His people were not only to "hear" and do more than "listen"; they were to "hearken," that is, be alert and at the ready to receive the messages of the Lord.

Ultimately the purpose of God in choosing the Jews did not derive from any merit or skill or talents of their own. God rather used them to keep the promise of the Messiah alive in their hearts—which was to be their great gift to the believing world. From the Jews would come the Son of God and the Savior of the world. St. Bernard wrote that God does not change his mind; the Jews will always be the "apple of God's eye." Other nations have perished from history. Even the Greeks and the Romans are not the same entities they were in antiquity. Nevertheless the Jewish nation deserves the protection of God to the degree that it is faithful to its covenant. In point of fact, God loves all mankind with an eternal love: *"he makes his sun rise on the bad and the good, and causes rain to fall on the just and the unjust."*

As for us, loving mercy is beyond our natural abilities because it goes counter to our sense of justice, to our desire for revenge, and to our defense of our reputation and ego. (Yet we prefer God's mercy to his justice; otherwise who would escape a whipping?) We are not yet worthy of the name of "Christian" until we are ready to love the unlovable, to forgive the unforgivable, to accept the imperfect, to cherish those whom we find offensive in some way.

There is a subtle development between the Deuteronomy text and today's Gospel. There was a suggestion of Jewish self-glorification in those days: *"he will then raise you high in praise and renown and glory above all other nations he has made...."* So they were always to beware of aliens, foreigners and Gentiles. The perfection of God as Jesus preached it in today's Gospel is the universality of his love, even for the unjust and wicked, for whom he provides sun and rain. That universal loving mercy led Jesus to his immolation on the cross—and a theologian wrote that Mary would have nailed him to that cross herself, if that were necessary for our salvation! Although only God the Son could fully atone for the offense against God the Father, it was not his sins, but ours that led to Calvary.

You can love the good, psychologists say, only to the degree that you also hate evil and renounce it. You can appreciate health only after you have experienced illness and physical pain. You can perceive the truly beautiful only as much as you are sensitive to the crude and ugly and demeaning. So Jesus had to feel the full weight of our sins and "become sin" to experience for all mankind the nobility of suffering for others and the triumph of the resurrection. Similarly those who suffered abuse in childhood or the horrors of a concentration camp or the helplessness of being in the control of merciless persons—yet have risen above their suffering— hopefully learn the power of mercy and love. Forgiving those who offend us more than anything else likens us to God himself. Remember that Jesus was accused in this way: "Who but God can forgive sins?" This is another meaning of the closing line of today's Gospel: *"So be perfect, just as your heavenly Father is perfect."*

The command of Jesus is to pray for our detractors and persecutors, and love those who do not love us. Perhaps our example will lead to their conversion, although our motive must be independent of even that objective. We love and forgive because Jesus has done so to us, and therefore it is the right thing to do! God's mercy is often ineffective for the hardhearted; they are not open to the action of God. On the other hand, good persons do not keep demanding their "rights" in life, in the courts, in their families. How terrible it would be if we received full justice, especially from God! We are called to strive for conditions of justice in this world without always demanding our own rights. When we seek first the kingdom of God and his justice, everything else will be given to us in addition. All morality is reduced to this: be worthy of love by striving to love all the world!

SECOND WEEK OF LENT

Second Sunday of Lent, A

Gn 12:1-4; 2 Tim 1:8-10;
Mt 17:1-9

In the readings for this Sunday the Church outlines a progressively deeper call to intimacy with our heavenly Father. In each case there is considerable sacrifice entailed. Abraham was seventy-five years old when the Lord God called him to leave Haran. He had already left Ur in Chaldea and had migrated along the Fertile Crescent up into southern Turkey. Now he had to uproot himself and his wife, Sarai, and take his flocks and possessions further south into Canaan. God promised, *"I will make of you a great nation."* Abraham had to live with and for that promise for another quarter of a century until his son, Isaac, was born when his father was a hundred years old! Few of us have to live on promises and hopes for that long. Yet how important was Abraham's fidelity. From the nation he was to father would come the Anointed Savior of the world.

Answering the call of the Gospel requires sacrifices of us, the spiritual offspring of Abraham. (Pope John XXIII called us "spiritual Semites.") In his Second Letter to Timothy, St. Paul wrote, *"bear your share of hardship for the gospel."* God has saved us and called us to a holy life to fit into his master plan, which began with the patriarch Abraham—or rather, "before the world began." In other words, God has waited for each of us who are predestined to glory to appear on the scene to carry our burdens and our tasks for the kingdom. Paul tells the bishop, Timothy, whom he himself had ordained, to be faithful to his ministry; in any case, effectiveness would depend on God's grace, not on any merit of his own. This is difficult for us to understand, because we are so accustomed to "do our own thing" and "get our act to- gether." We are taught to be competitive and make something of ourselves. Yet God alone can make some- thing of us in the spiritual realm. As Abraham we are on pilgrimage with God setting the route, the resting places and the goals. Our amazement should derive not from being called to do this or that for God, but from being called at all in the first place! As a matter of fact, it is a mystery why God chose a particular man to start his Chosen People, why he chose Paul and Timothy, and why he chose us. We are not only pilgrims, but also strangers in this world, our primary citizenship being in heaven.

We must never think that by our Christian call we "possess" the truth, the life of God, and the kingdom of heaven. Rather all this possesses us. We are grafted into something and Someone greater than we; we are part of the eternal movement of God in history; we are lifted up into the very life of God, which we call "grace." Hence we are possessed. God is the musician; we are the strings of his harp—or today we might say "guitar." Each string must be tightened just so much to be in tune to carry the melody and be in harmony with the other strings.

The Gospel of the transfiguration today was sup- posed to be comforting to the disciples who witnessed it, a reinforcement to their vocations; yet the closing words of Jesus contain also the prophecy of his death: *"Do not tell the vision to anyone until the Son of Man has been raised from the dead."* So this was a bittersweet vision for them and a warning not to congratulate themselves too soon. They wanted to erect a memorial to their experience and to signalize their transitory intimacy with divinity. Their excitement was understandable, but perhaps a little tainted by pride in having been chosen to witness this epiphany of God. They could not foresee their own betrayal of Jesus and their martyrdoms.

When we examine our lives, we can clearly see that, despite the many small miracles of grace we have experienced, we often betray the Lord through our sins and hang-ups. When we examine the statistics of contemporary Christianity we are less tempted to congratulate ourselves. After two thousand years of evangelization the world is barely one-third Christian, and it is divided into over twenty thousand denominations! The Gospel is being preached in seven thousand languages and the Bible is printed in one-fourth of these languages, yet only about one-fourth of Christian believers actually attend weekly worship! Therefore the record is not encouraging, but rather "bittersweet"! Nevertheless we have to remember and "live on" the epiphanies and transfigurations that God grants us.

The story is told of a missionary who was working in a rural village in India. An old woman accepted the faith and at her baptism marveled that it took nearly two thousand years for the Gospel of Jesus to reach her village. "What took you so long?" she asked. We might well ask that same question of ourselves. Has it been our laziness and indifference, or lack of expertise and absence of conviction? The worldly, whom Jesus called the children of this generation, know how to propagate their doctrines, whereas we are the "children of light," to whom has been given the full revelation of God in Jesus Christ.

Perhaps we have tried to serve two masters, the Church and the world. The world is not evil, but worldliness seduces by the applause it gives to the famous, the powerful, the money-makers. The world is older than the Church and serves its own values. We are easily persuaded by the importance of living in the high-rent district, going on a fancy vacation, owning a prestigious car, and having a key to the executive washroom. It is admittedly no easy task to reconcile our Sunday mindset, such as humility, chastity and charity, with the attitudes necessary during our work week, such as money, power and clout.

Soren Kierkegaard observed that when the world and the Church make peace with each other, it will be either the end of the Church or the end of the world. The only alternative is to baptize the world as we detach ourselves from it and allow God to fill us with what we can never fully possess—himself, whose design it is to possess us!

Second Sunday of Lent, B

Gn 22:1-2, 9, 10-13, 15-18; Rom 8:31-34; Mk 9:2-10

The transfiguration is an important story about Jesus. All three Synoptics describe the scene, even Mark today, who is so often skeletal in his narratives. In 2 Peter the writer emphasizes, "this is not a contrived myth." It was deeply embedded in the consciousness and memory of the disciples. The transfiguration appears about halfway through the Gospels of Matthew, Mark and Luke, when the enemies of Jesus have already begun to orchestrate the design to bring him down, even to kill him. The disciples were getting edgy; some of his followers were urging him to establish his kingdom at once.

The readings for today are not meant by the Church to be triumphalistic, but foreboding. As St. Paul points out in his Letter to the Church of Rome, God *"did not spare his own Son but handed him over for us all...."* The figure of the young Isaac, of course, represents Jesus. Emphatically and somewhat ironically God told Abraham to sacrifice *"your son Isaac, your only one, whom you love."* In the nick of time God's messenger stayed the hand of Abraham from stabbing his child. What an unbelievable test, unbelievable obedience, then what a promise—to give the old man offspring as numerous as the stars in the sky and the sands of the seashore! Abraham represents God the Father who did not spare his Son. The "countless descendants" are the believers in Jesus, his followers and disciples. Thus the promise to Abraham has had a double fulfillment—granted that it was stated in the hyperbole of the Bible!

We may consider the transfiguration as the self-disclosure of Jesus, who had several messages to convey. 1) Jesus wanted to clarify to his three special friends, Peter, James and John, that he was going to give up his life voluntarily. He not only predicted his death, but he had the power of his Father behind him. 2) Jesus did not want his moment of glory to draw attention from his proximate suffering. As he stood on this mountain of his transitory glory, he was already looking ahead to his mountain of shame, Calvary. 3) To the Jews Moses represented the Law given to them during the Exodus, and Elijah represented all of the prophets who spoke of the Messiah to come. Jesus stood in the middle of them, the position of eminence, to show he was superior to the figures and symbols which flanked him—indeed, the fulfillment of all their hopes. This subtle lesson was not lost on the first disciples, who were all Jews and needed such a theological statement at the time the Gospels were being written, a time when they were being harassed and thrown out of the Jewish synagogues. 4) For all of us the Transfiguration is the feast of temporary glory, a flicker of heaven, a flash-forward. Anyone who has seen movies is familiar with flashbacks: a scene from the past is inserted into the plot to explain something about the actions of the characters. The transfiguration is a flash-forward to Jesus' future resurrection. Or in the idiom of movie advertising, the scene on the mountain is a preview of coming attractions, the rising and ascending of the Lord. In many small ways God gives us moments of comfort such as the apostles received: unexpected victory over sin; the feeling of God's closeness in prayer; a warm smile or letter of support when you are in a depressed mood; someone's gratitude for even a small favor; being told by someone, "I love you." Some of these moments are only on the natural level, yet they help our spiritual lives as well.

As the down payment on his resurrection, the transfiguration is an indicator to us, too, that humanity will share in the glory of God through resurrection. The Father spoke from the cloud, *This is my beloved Son. Listen to him.* The Father is revealing the divinity of Jesus, just as Jesus reveals his Father to us. "No one knows the Father except the Son; no one comes to the Father unless the Son draw him." We the baptized are adoptive heirs of heaven by belonging to the family: the same Father, Mother and Brother. Although this gift of God is gratuitous, unable to be earned, it is not kept without proportionate investment in the life of Jesus. In the same chapter 8 from which the second reading today is excerpted, in verse 17, St. Paul writes, "We are heirs of God and fellow heirs with Christ, provided we suffer with him in order to also be glorified...." Those who think that there is any other way to follow Jesus other than in his own bloody footsteps are mistaken. If they reject suffering outright, they end up rejecting the message of Jesus altogether. "Unfortunately, many go about in a way which shows them to be enemies of the cross of Christ." They fall into idolatry: "Their god is their belly, and their glory is in their shame."

The cross can be terrifying, but love makes it tolerable. Whoever loves God needs to fear nothing else; whoever does not love God needs to fear everything else. When God judges us, he does not put the measuring tape around our head—to see how large our brains are; nor around our muscles—to see how strong we are; but around our hearts—to see how much love we have. He gives each of us a vision to follow; he gives us a personal mountain to climb; he allows us to build a shrine to him for our quiet and private worship as we wait for his coming. The writer of 2 Peter makes a final allusion to the importance of the transfiguration: "You will do well to pay attention to this (the transfiguration) as to a lamp shining in a dark place, until the day dawns and the morning star (Jesus' return to earth) rises in glory in your hearts."

Second Sunday of Lent, C

Gn 15:5-12, 17-18;
Phil 3:17—4:1; Lk 9:28-36

From Almighty God the patriarch Abraham had been hearing about his innumerable offspring for many years, so when the Lord brought up the promise once more, the old man thought he should "hedge his bet," and so asked the Lord for a sign. After all, he had proved his obedience by the near sacrifice of his son Isaac on Mt. Moriah; he had been a "wandering Aramaean," as God had asked, for many years; he had twice uprooted his life at God's command—from Ur and Haran. Just a little sign was all he asked!

God always accepts us generously where we are and brings us to where we ought to be. He used a ploy with Abraham that was used commonly for contracts or agreements in the days of old in Canaan between royal persons or simple businessmen. Abraham prepared a blood sacrifice whereby both sides implied that, if either broke his end of the bargain, the same bloody fate would overtake him—of being cut in two! Of course, not only did God keep his promise, but there was no one who could bring down God if he altered his divine plan! So the animals were cut in two and placed to form a "corridor" through which each party would pass. During sunset a terrifying darkness and a trance fell upon the patriarch, during which God, symbolized by the smoking brazier and flaming torch, passed through the sacrificed animals. Abraham was the pioneer in the "Holy Land Project" of God—simple, of low estate and uncultured—so the Lord indulged his wish and communicated with Abraham in familiar terms!

Note that God represented himself by smoke and fire. This visible presence of the Lord is called *shekinah* in Hebrew, which is virtually untranslatable but it can be described. Shekinah is the palpable glory of the Lord, his unspeakable and terrifying presence. Later during the Exodus, he was to manifest himself as a pillar of cloud by day and a column of fire by night to guide and protect his people in the desert experience. That same divine "force" attached itself to the Ark of the Covenant in the Holy of Holies of Solomon's Temple.

The writers of the Gospels and the first readers were mainly Jews, steeped in Jewish lore and history, to whom the shekinah was a reality. So they easily understood the transfiguration as a manifestation of the divine presence. Jesus' face was changed in appearance and his clothes became dazzlingly white. Moses and Elijah also appeared in glory; they were heavenly beings. The overshadowing cloud and voice recalled similar events of Jewish salvation history. Jesus himself was the shekinah of the Lord; he is divine! When the two Jewish Testament figures disappeared, Jesus was left standing alone. The implication is that he superseded and replaced Moses as the lawgiver and the prophets as God's mouthpiece in the world.

Jesus did not need nor seek to have a shrine to himself built by human hands on the mountain. He looked to the day when true believers would worship him in spirit and in truth. Yet he does wish to be enshrined in our hearts. Thus his force and power will be active within us. But we must invite him into our lives to receive the effect of his salvation.

The three apostles who witnessed the transfiguration were not well educated by our standards, but were reasonably well educated by theirs. The Jewish leaders accused them of being unlearned in the sense of the rabbinical traditions and professional theology. Undoubtedly they attended synagogue schools and learned to read and write in preparation for their bar-mitzvah, their coming of age as sons of the Torah, the Jewish Bible. Peter, James and John were all businessmen in Capernaum, their fishing village which Jesus made the base of his Galilean apostolate; hence, they were not naíve in the ways of the world. Yet they often misread the Lord, vacillated, and later, except for John, deserted him. If the Gospels record the apostles' share in the Lord's glory, as at the transfiguration, they also record their failures. They were dedicated to promoting Jesus' cause, not their own justification. It was because of this humility and their own common sense that Jesus chose the apostles—plus their capacity to love God. Only slowly did they learn to depend on the power of Jesus instead of their own strength.

The experience of God by those first followers of Jesus was, at best, confusing. The God of the Jewish Bible demanded that men fear him, yet love him. "What nation has a God who approaches so close?" the sacred writer had asked. Yet God kept them away, as when Moses ascended Sinai and the people were forbidden to approach even the base of the mountain. He was a God of mercy; yet he ordered his armies to destroy every living being in the conquered cities—Saul lost his kingship for evading this mandate. He defined himself as the One Who Is, that is, "I am whoever I choose to be," totally free, who cannot be manipulated by human beings, yet he called Israel his "bride" or "spouse" many times. God's title of "father," absent from all the other major religions, was obscure for the Jews. Yet Jesus used this title more than any other in speaking of the First Person.

Conversely, the word, "son," appears in both Testaments more than 2,500 times. For the Jews, that word represented a metaphor, a figure of human speech. But in the mouth of Jesus it denoted a reality: God shares his nature with us, which we call "sanctifying grace." The Jews rarely used "father" in addressing God in prayer in the Bible; it is used about 170 times in the New Testament, especially in John's Gospel. Therefore the relationship of our heavenly Father to his children is at the heart of our spiritual lives. This relationship is one way of interpreting the whole Christian message. We can read this so casually, but it must have been an eye-opening revelation to the disciples. The concept was simple, but the reality was overwhelming. That is why the "unlearned" apostles did not need formal theological training that looked to the past. Jesus was not only the teacher; he was the very subject matter. As all fatherhood on earth is patterned after the fatherhood of

God in heaven, wrote St. Paul, so all sonship on earth is modeled on the Son, Jesus Christ. Therefore the voice from the cloud, the voice of the Father, proclaimed, *"This is my chosen Son; listen to him."* Scholar or drop-out, accountant or math failure, corporation executive or scrubwoman—all are unlearned until they learn Jesus; no one graduates from study until he/she hears the Word in heaven!

Monday of the Second Week of Lent

Dn 9:4-10;
Lk 6:36-38

Daniel plunges into an accounting of the sins of Israel and rehearses their wrongdoing, but appeals to the mercy of God at the end. The prayer from the book of Daniel is appropriate also for today, perhaps twenty-three centuries after it was written! One who abases himself and convicts himself of sin acknowledges God's justice, as Daniel does in referring to the dispersion of the Jews. Like Daniel, we have the confidence to appeal to God's "merciful covenant," as long as we have a change of heart.

Jesus used the same word with his hearers: *"Be merciful, just as [also] your Father is merciful."* He outlines further applications of the Golden Rule: Don't judge nor condemn, lest you suffer a similar fate. Because God is never outdone in generosity, he will return to you whatever you give to others, but with added measure. Jesus uses a homely metaphor: a woman holds her bowl or bag (to carry away a measure of grain) over a fold of her garment or veil or over her lap, to catch the stray grains that bounce out of her container. So God's mercy is also overflowing and super-abundant.

Jesus' prohibition against judging is difficult to apply correctly, especially if you are a parent or employer, an army sergeant or a religious superior or pastor! It is actually inherent in man's nature to judge, even in simple matters, as what to wear in chilly weather, what color combinations to choose, what friend to call in need, and so on. It is more difficult to answer such questions: Does my employee deserve a raise? Is my child watching too much television? Does the pastoral assistant provide adequate service to the Church? Yet it is necessary to make judgments about others. In a court of law, judgment goes even further: judge and jury try to assess the motives for actions, which ultimately only God can do with certainty.

But when one does not have the right or duty to evaluate motives, there sin may enter the picture. Such a duty exists, for example, when a bishop must assess the worthiness of a candidate for the priesthood; when a policeman judges whether to issue a traffic ticket; when a parent wonders whether a son or daughter is mature enough to drive the family car. Sin becomes a factor when a negative judgment may be too severe or prejudiced, not based on discernible facts, or when it invades the forum of conscience, to which God alone has access.

Even apparently charitable persons often, while withholding verbal accusations, criticize others internally. One of the last tasks to be accomplished in the spiritual life is to develop a non-judgmental charity, particularly towards non-productive persons, the psychosomatically ill, the person who craves your attention unreasonably and wastes your time. It is hard to distinguish at times between a bad will and a dull mind. Added to impatience with others is impatience with oneself when one is depressed, overworked, plagued by debts, etc. A religious person worries whether he or she prays enough, is doing the right thing according to God's will, or is too harsh and unbending. No wonder the saints universally said it is better to be subject to others than to command; safer for one's salvation as well as emotional equilibrium.

Pray today for those who have authority, especially over you in some way, in the business world, in family life, in the Church. May God grant them patience with others, correct judgment, and especially patience with themselves.

Keep the divine mercy before you as the measuring stick of your own actions. Without a relationship with God we soon degenerate in our social relationships. Whereas it is true that some rare souls can maintain their moral integrity and spiritual sensitivity without faith as such, yet how much more effective they might be with belief in God and his moral code! Sinful as we can be with religion, imagine how low we might sink without prayer and brotherly love and generosity! *"Forgive and you will be forgiven."*

Tuesday of the Second Week of Lent

Is 1:10, 16-20;
Mt 23:1-12

The prophet Isaiah seems to be addressing the long-dead wicked cities, Sodom and Gomorrah, but he is in fact speaking to his own contemporaries in a manner analogous with St. Peter who would write centuries later from "Babylon," but would mean "Rome,"— the contemporary center of power and corruption.

Despite Israel's evil, Isaiah prophesies that it will survive if it turns to deeds of humility and justice.

Jesus calls for humility and justice in today's Gospel. The Pharisees laid heavy burdens on others by their teaching, yet did not show by word or example how to fulfill this teaching. *"They widen their phylacteries and lengthen their tassels."* An explanation here would help to

explain this Jewish custom, which still binds the Orthodox Jew today. When I was traveling by bus between
Cairo and Jerusalem, two Orthodox Jews stood up in the
aisle as the sun rose over the desert horizon. Assisted by
their wives, the two men took their prayer paraphernalia out of suitcases. They tied thongs around their fore-
heads with small boxes containing Bible passages
dangling over their eyes. With the help of their wives
they tied similar thongs and boxes around their biceps.
The point was the Law of Moses with God's imperative
to keep his law before their eyes, in their minds, and
upon their arms, so that all they did would conform to
God's command. As do all conservative Jewish men,
especially in Israel today, they wore an undergarment
with strings and tassels coming out over the belt and
hanging at their sides. Finally the Jews put on their
prayer shawls; they were already wearing their *yarmulke*
or *kipa*, the skull cap. Then they began bobbing back and
forth, reciting prayers from the books they held in their
hands.

In one sense I admired them for their devotion and
unashamed keeping of tradition—which moved me to
take out my breviary and rosary for the long ride to
Jerusalem. In another sense I thought such a public display was a little theatrical, although virtue or vice must
be measured by the context in which it appears! But I
saw no reason to doubt their sincerity. What the Lord
was criticizing was praying in order to be seen, especially
with more ostentatious tassels and boxes.

Pride is certainly a vice we dislike in others, yet
rarely can one find a truly humble person. A humble
person would be surprised to be so named, because he
or she simply does not think thoughts of self. Even if one
"generically" admits to pride, probably he could not or
would not point out any specific instances of acting
proudly! Every sin has some dimension of pride in it. It

was the devils' sin: "I will not serve." When it comes to visibility in prayer, the following is a good guideline: Don't pray in order to be seen, but don't stop praying just because someone is watching you!

When Jesus directed that his disciples should not seek titles of "rabbi," "teacher," or "father," he was not telling students and children to put down their superiors; rather he disparaged those who were anxious to have applause and recognition. *"They love places of honor...."* The lesson is that those who are in authority—bosses, parents, superiors—should not impose on others the limitations they do not apply to themselves.

Wednesday of the Second Week of Lent

Jer 18:18-20;
Mt 20:17-28

Today's Gospel shows how Jesus handled the pushy mother of James and John. He turned from her and addressed her two boys directly. They were adults and should have been loosed from her apron strings and have spoken for themselves. With overweening self-confidence they assured Jesus they could drink from his cup of suffering. When the other disciples learned of this exchange, they were understandably irate.

Jesus therefore gave them and us a lesson about the nature of Christian authority as service and humility, and cited himself as our model. The Son of Man has come to serve and even to give his own life as a ransom for all. How often we see that pride is the root of the other sins. Lucifer's sin was a sneer that he would be expected to worship God in the form of a man (Jesus) and to accept as his queen and superior a mere human creature (Mary). Adam and Eve wanted to be "like gods" and know the difference between good and evil. Cain's injured pride led him to kill his brother, Abel. Always pride!

Whenever and wherever there is an attempt to become superior and dominate, sin proliferates. Applying this notion to superiors and bishops in the Church, we say that a man should not seek the office, but the office should seek the man. The mother of James and John did not see this. Nor can we be so sure that James and John sinned through pride, because who would not want to be closely associated with this wonder-worker and healer, this popular preacher and—as they hoped—the very Messiah? They did not realize clearly that Christ's success and his authority derived from suffering service: "Because of this, God exalted him and gave him the name above every other name." In fact, Jesus did not care for authority so much as influence over the hearts and minds of men and women. He did not give orders and make threats so much as use persuasion and affirmation.

The two apostles wanted to get in on the ground floor, so to speak. They made their mere association with Jesus the basis of their preferment; Jesus' test was rather their share in his passion. It was his death, in fact, that proved Jesus genuine from our human viewpoint; he was willing to accept the dire consequences of his preaching and criticism of the religious leaders, even to die for the values he proposed to the world.

G. K. Chesterton wrote that a person should be like a window. The simple and direct purpose of a window is to admit light and allow you to see through it clearly. When you start "prettying up" a window with blinds and drapes and valances or even putting in stained glass, then you decrease the light available and obscure your own vision. The best thing you can do with a window, he wrote, is clean it and forget about it. So the disciples of Jesus should simply clean themselves of sin, then forget about themselves so the light of Christ can shine through them without impediment!

The pride which is acceptable to God is that which comes not from our efforts but that which comes from the grace of God. We deserve no credit for what we do not control. The spiritual peril enters when we take pride from our own efforts: making money, winning academic degrees, even performing works of charity and prayer (all of which are good in themselves). The strange contradiction is that when we achieve something apparently by our own efforts, we are tempted to become independent of God, trust ourselves, bask in self-made glory, and put our piety on parade, as did the Pharisees. Soon we fancy we can save our own souls, whereas only Jesus can save anyone. So when you think of God and survey the grandeur of the universe, you will find little cause to applaud yourself. When you praise God the safest ground to stand upon is no ground at all!

Thursday of the Second Week of Lent

Jer 17:5-10;
Lk 16:19-31

Trust in this present world, Jesus says, is a "killer," that is, the world kills the soul, as the rich man experienced and as Jeremiah warned in the first reading. If you want to be successful according to worldly standards, then just collect the sayings of Jesus and do the opposite! It is not by accident that just half of Jesus' parables dealt with the perils of wealth and the necessity of giving an accounting for it. Jesus said, "Go sell what you have, give it to the poor and you will have treasure in heaven, and come follow me." "Take up your cross daily." "If someone wants your coat, give him your shirt, too." "Turn the other cheek." "If you wish to rank first, then serve everyone else." No one ever became a millionaire, rose to be the chief corporation officer, chairman of the board, or a political power by following these maxims of Jesus. Typically, perhaps always, the opposite holds true.

Jesus lays out a cardinal principle of the relationship between rich and poor, between Dives (from the Latin, "a rich person") and Lazarus. All of us are only stewards of what we possess; God's reckoning will be severe for the miserly and grasping. Jesus implies that the reason for the rich man's torment is precisely because he ignored Lazarus, covered with sores, begging at his door—not because of simply having been rich. There is a Yiddish proverb that if, in fact, the rich could hire other people to die for them, then the poor could make a good living!

Jesus put these words into the mouth of Abraham: *"If they will not listen to Moses and the prophets, neither will they be persuaded if someone should rise from the dead."* The reason is obvious: Jesus was teaching with greater authority than Moses and the prophets, yet the religious leaders ignored him. He predicted that not even his resurrection would be persuasive to them.

Jeremiah points out, *"More tortuous than all else is the human heart, beyond remedy; who can understand it?"* How can we identify the poor and realistically help them, and still live successfully in this world and contend with its values? As in most areas of the spiritual life, there are levels or gradations of involvement with the poor. (The following is based on "Service of the Poor," by Albert Nolen, O.P.)

First we become sensitized or aware of the sufferings of the poor, their hunger, lack of shelter, education and health care.

You try to see the suffering Jesus in them: "Whatever you do to the least of my brothers, you also do to me."

So you do relief work, collect food or money, give up your own luxuries, if only a few dollars.

Then you realize from reading and perhaps television that poverty is an institutional or structural problem, the result of exploitation, political or economic policies created by the controllers of our society here and abroad: tyrannical dictatorships, apartheid, migrant worker harassment. In most of Latin America 90% of the land and means of production is owned by 10% of the nation's citizens! You react with indignation at such discrimination, so you work on behalf of causes to help the poor and against such policies. You vote your conscience, picket, write to public officials, embark on campaigns of social activism.

The next level of involvement is to make face-to-face, one-on-one contacts with the poor who are near you, especially to empower the poor and help them to be self-reliant. God loves the poor in a special way; they are his anawim, the helpless, humble and disenfranchised. You become a missionary, a social worker, a doctor or lawyer who aids the poor directly.

The final stage is solidarity with the poor. Even though you may see the mistakes of the poor, perhaps their ignorance or laziness, you still can love them and help them. Perhaps you decide to live as a poor person in a poor neighborhood to identify with their lot. Then you realize that they in turn give you a gift: to understand real helplessness, defenselessness, and being trapped in poverty.

Most of us remain in stage one, giving a few dollars we can easily spare and making a few sacrifices. But if you read the prophets and Jesus carefully, perhaps you will be motivated to enter more deeply into the human problem of suffering!

Friday of the
Second Week of Lent

Gn 37:3-4, 12-13, 17-28;
Mt 21:33-43, 45-46

So often our lives seem twisted into odd shapes, confused pathways, strange relationships. Yet God is quietly behind the scenes, as the proverb goes, writing straight with crooked lines. His divine plan has its goals, but don't be surprised by the detours. For example, from Abraham, receiver of the covenant and promise of future greatness, to Joshua, who led the Chosen People into Canaan in triumph, five hundred years passed! Along the route comes the fascinating story of Joseph and his fancy technicolored tunic, which is, to my mind, the best piece of literature (as such) in the Jewish Bible. Joseph passed through more perils than a sci-fi hero and yet carried the day. He was the slave who became the master, the victim of sibling rivalry who overcame his brothers with love, the poor immigrant boy (in Egypt) who struck it rich, the employee who succeeded in business without really trying (because God was busy in the wings), and he probably married the boss' daughter, the child of Pharaoh!

"Israel," another name for Jacob, had twelve sons, progenitors of the twelve tribes of Israel, by two different wives and two concubines. His last partner was his favorite, Rachel, who died giving birth to the youngest son, Benjamin. She was also the mother of Joseph, the protagonist in today's text. As a sign of affection, his father gave him this special tunic. No doubt he was spoiled. He appeared rather narcissistic and told his family of his dreams in which his parents and brothers were bowing down to him—an idea which they resented! No wonder his half-brothers wanted to do him in, but finally decided to sell him into slavery for twenty pieces of silver. Yet in retrospect God drew good from this evil deed. Later when Joseph became second in command in Egypt, he saved his starving family, which began a sojourn of four hundred years in Egypt. Thus we do not always see the purposes of God, but his design will never be frustrated.

God is continually bringing salvation history to its close, exactly by choosing events that also include our personal histories. To the person of faith nothing happens by chance or accident or luck. It seemed a terrible tragedy that Joseph was sold to an Ishmaelite slaver and that he was falsely accused of seduction by Potiphar's wife. He had to sit in prison for several years—galling to anyone who has been framed, but especially a young man—but in God's good time he was exonerated. His meteoric rise to power led to the increase and prosperity of his family, who were being forged into a nation, first through glory, then in tribulation—ultimately to become the matrix out of which rose Jesus Christ, Savior of the world.

The connection of Joseph to Jesus is apparent, even apart from the ancestry of the Lord. Joseph was sold by his brothers for twenty pieces of silver; Jesus was betrayed by his apostles, of whom one sold him for thirty pieces of silver. The parable Jesus used in today's Gospel points clearly to himself. God's vineyard was the arena of salvation; the vines were the truths God revealed to this world. The Jews were the tenants, but they mistreated, even killed the prophets sent to them to "collect the rent." They did not respect the son either. So others were destined to become the tenants and caretakers of religious truth—the Gentiles, the *other tenants who will give him the produce at the proper times.*

Today is a good day to examine your life, consider your past blessings and deliverance by God from spiritual dangers, and identify the hand of God in the events which are bringing you to the kingdom of heaven. "He who perseveres to the end will be saved."

Saturday of the Second Week of Lent

Mi 7:14-15, 18-20;
Lk 15:1-3, 11-32

The parable of the prodigal son is familiar to practically every Christian; the story has been repeated in many families. The word "prodigal" means "wasteful, over-generous, open-handed to a fault." The prodigal was the second son who, from the evidence of the story, did not get on well with his older brother. When he left for a "far-off" land, he bought the affection of his friends with his inheritance. When he was flush with money and paid for the parties, he was very, very popular. When his money ran out, so did his "friends."

This is reminiscent of the story of the Irishman Matt Talbot, who fell into a pattern of drinking early on and became an alcoholic. On payday he would walk up to his favorite Dublin pub and would soon be drunk. His "friends" greeted him, clapped him on the back, told a joke or two, and got a free drink. They sang the old-time songs to the point of oblivion. Matt, too, was very prodigal with his salary. After many years of "lost weekends," after which he nevertheless made it back to work on Monday morning, one Monday he just couldn't make it, so he lost his job.

When payday came around again for his drinking buddies, he crawled back to his favorite bar—but suddenly nobody knew him anymore. The bartender refused to "put it on the cuff." Like the prodigal of the Gospel, who longed to eat even the swill of the hogs, poor Matt got only the D.T.'s.

The prodigal son told himself he was foolish for starving when, by comparison, the least employee of his

father was well-fed. Matt Talbot reached the same conclusion; only by the grace of God he began to hunger for
spiritual food and drink. He dumped his fair-weather
friends and came home to his heavenly Father. With
Luke's customary sensitivity the Gospel notes that the
prodigal's father kept looking for his boy from afar,
hoping for his return, and finally ran out to meet him,
hugged and kissed him, gave him a change of clothes,
and threw a party!

What a marvelously touching and comforting story.
An alcoholic once told me that sometimes you have to
hit bottom before you bounce upward again; you have to
experience the worst before you're ready for the best;
that you have to fall—he was quite graphic—into a gut-
ter with your face in your own vomit and maybe be
arrested and thrown into jail, before you realize you
can't escape this disease by your own efforts. Similarly
we cannot arise from our sinfulness by our own power
and strategies.

How stupid we become when we put a great distance between ourselves and God. The young in particular want to prove their adulthood, sow their wild oats,
become independent and the life of the party. The
prodigal certainly had no right to half the inheritance,
yet he felt the world (and his father) owed him a living.
Like the father in the story, God does not force his will
on us. When we leave our spiritual home, the Church,
we are soon bankrupt. Pleasures no longer please, our
money can never buy enough, our shallow friendships
turn sour.

Yet we are never abandoned by our heavenly Father,
who always runs to meet us more than halfway by his
graces. If we make the smallest effort to reach out to
God, he throws his arms about us and kisses us. But we
have to invite God into our lives, step out in faith that
we can be healed. Realize today the great inheritance

you have received—heaven itself—and the dangers of squandering the graces that will bring you to this destiny. Come to your senses so you can reach your homeland, forever to celebrate with your Father, Jesus, Mary, and the saints and angels. If you have been dead, then come back to life.

THIRD WEEK OF LENT

Third Sunday of Lent, A

Ex 17:3-7; Rom 5:1-2, 5-8;
Jn 4:5-42

The first reading and the Gospel correlate today on the theme of water. The Jews were on Exodus across Sinai and grew weary of the arid desert with only occasional oases. When they complained to Moses, remembering the green valley of the Nile and its abundance of water, God instructed his prophet to strike a bare rock and sweet water would flow out of the crevice. God overlooked the complaints of the people and demonstrated his providence one more time.

In the lengthy Gospel from John today, Jesus encounters a Samaritan woman. The people of Samaria were most unfriendly to the Galileans and Jews. Sometimes they waylaid and even murdered them, especially when they were on their way to pray in the Temple of Jerusalem. The Samaritans had intermarried with foreigners centuries earlier and were thus considered partly "Gentile," hence they were not allowed to share in the building of the Temple nor were they allowed to worship there. Jesus' disciples were amazed that he was talking with a Samaritan woman at the well. The woman was equally amazed to be addressed by a Jew.

Jesus used the occasion of this meeting to teach a theological lesson. The dialogue itself is very human and interesting. Jesus asked for a drink from Jacob's well. When the woman expressed her amazement and hesitated, Jesus told her he could give her a drink of living water, which meant flowing, not stagnant water. This drink would never leave one thirsty again, but would be a fountain of eternal life. Jesus told her to fetch her husband, so they both could drink, that is, learn from him. She replied that she had no husband, with which Jesus agreed, saying that she already had had five husbands! She neatly side-stepped the marital issue and proclaimed him a prophet. Nevertheless she aired the Samaritan grievance that everyone but them was supposed to worship in Jerusalem. Meanwhile the Samaritans worshiped on Mount Gerizim—as they still do two thousand years later. So Jesus responded that neither place is where the Father desired to be worshiped, but in spirit and in truth, because God cannot be confined within walls! Then he openly admitted what he concealed from his fellow Jews, namely, that he was the Messiah. She ran off to get the villagers to meet Jesus. The disciples, who had gone off earlier to buy food, asked him to eat something. He told them he had another kind of food: doing his Father's will. He stayed with the Samaritans for two days and taught them, so that many believed in him. As Moses gave his people living, flowing water for their physical thirst, Jesus gave his people the living water of Baptism for their spiritual thirst. And later he called himself the Bread of Life.

God's providence extends to the smallest details of human life and, in fact, to the care of the whole universe. Starting from the "Big Bang" of creation, he sorted out the galaxies and prepared this earth for mankind. He still cares about babies and oak trees, caterpillars and specks of dust, and every molecule of water. He keeps track of every change in the universe and sustains every part of the process.

Take two atoms of hydrogen and one of oxygen, and you have a molecule of water. Suppose that lightning and thunderclouds caused a heavy rain a million years ago over Minnesota. A raindrop crystallized into a snowflake that landed on the nose of a deer. The deer plunged its face into a stream for a drink and the molecule of water passed into the stream that disappeared underground and began its many-thousand-years' journey through the limestone in the bowels of the earth. It finally reached a well in southern Wisconsin, where a farm woman drew a bucket of water for her geraniums. But the farmer came in for a drink and swallowed our molecule. When he milked the cows that evening, he really worked up a sweat, and the molecule evaporated off his brow into the atmosphere, where it was swept by the wind onto the surface of Lake Michigan. The water-pumping station sucked it into the water supply. And God was still taking note of its movements!

The sacristan drew water from the tap for the ablution cup during Mass. Afterwards he threw the used water, containing our molecule, into the drain, from which it passed into the sewer system. After purification it traveled into the Chicago river, Illinios River, Kankakee River and Mississippi River down to the Gulf of Mexico. Carried by the Gulf Stream, the molecule reached the Straits of Gibraltar, hesitated, then entered the Mediterranean Sea, where a fish drank it. And God was still watching its movements!

A Sicillian fisherman caught a sea bass with the molecule in its tissues. The fish was sold in Rome and bought in the Vatican delicatessen for the Pope's dinner. He ingested the molecule of water and went to bed. And God gave the Pope pleasant dreams. By this time the molecule might be in outer Mongolia! But the point of this modern parable is that God follows the movements of every molecule of water on earth, all of which are subject to the natural laws he established. He conserves them in being. Then how much more does he care for us! His wonderful works stagger our imagination.

Every drop of water that flowed from the rock that Moses struck, every drop of water in Jacob's well, every drop of water used in thousands of baptisms all over the world since Pentecost is known by God. So we can pray with confidence to such a Father and worship him in spirit and in truth. Does he not know your wanderings and keep track of your spiritual journey? Will he not continue to supply the fountain, *"welling up to eternal life"*? Our heavenly Father holds us in the hollow of his hand!

Third Sunday
of Lent, B

Ex 20:1-17; 1 Cor 1:22-25; Jn 2:13-25

The responsorial psalm provides a theme that binds together the three readings for today: "Lord, you have the words of everlasting life." The first reading is about the commandments. This is not the simple list of prohibitions and negative statements ("Thou shalt not..."), but a more comprehensive interpretation. One can see the hand of the priestly redactors of the text, because of the fuller condemnation of idol worship and their giving of the reason for the sabbath rest, namely, that God himself rested a day after completing creation. (Of course, God would not be God if he had to rest after the "work" of creation!)

The most significant event of Jewish history is the Exodus, the deliverance from Pharaoh, the preservation and purification as a nation in the desert, and the covenant of Sinai. The ten commandments were to be considered part of the covenant. Acceptance of the Law won eternal life. The "words of everlasting life" were all the events of the Exodus and all of the divine messages through Moses.

When we use the phrase, "most significant," we are aware that the word significant means "sign-making." The Exodus generated the chief sign for the Jews; the death and resurrection generated the chief sign for Christians. That is why Jesus proclaims in today's Gospel to his adversaries that the sign he would give them was to raise up the temple (of his body) in three days after its destruction (his death at their hands). Another time he referred to the "sign of Jonah" with the same meaning.

In his first letter to the Church at Corinth, St. Paul refers to the signs sought by the Jews and Greeks. The former wanted a divine endorsement of anyone who might claim to be the Anointed One, the Messiah—miracles, healings, wonders and heavenly locutions. As a matter of fact, Jesus did provide all these things, yet his people did not accept his message, which was essentially himself! The Greeks vaunted themselves as the sages and sophisticates of the ancient world, the people of great literature and political ideas and especially systems of philosophy. As St. Paul learned in the Areopagus of Athens, they expected Christian preachers to be eloquent on noble themes of divinity, some new philosophy, some proposal for a new worldwide system of government (for the Greeks, too, were under Roman domination). What the Jews and Greeks got was the folly of the cross. This was a "stumbling block" for Jews, that God's Son was crucified; this was an "absurdity" for the Greeks, that apparent failure was actually the great victory of mankind. Jews wanted to see power and control, but the cross was weakness on display; Greeks wanted to hear lofty wisdom, but the philosophy of the crucifixion reversed this world's values. Beautifully, Paul suggests, *"The foolishness of God is wiser than human wisdom, and the weakness of God is stronger than human strength."*

The typically tranquil and mild Jesus surprises us by his vehement zeal for the honor of his Father's house, which he said was being used as a marketplace—not a "den of thieves," as in a parallel text. Yet the entrepreneurs were necessary to the liturgical life of the Temple. People, who came from afar for the Passover feast (when this scene took place), had to buy animals for sacrifice nearby. They were not allowed to give money to the Temple in foreign coinage, which often carried graven images of pagan gods and rulers, forbidden by the Law, but they had to make their offerings in Jewish shekels. Jesus' hard line had a deeper meaning. As he told the Samaritan woman at Jacob's well, the time was soon coming when people of faith would worship God neither on Mount Gerizim in Samaria nor on the Temple Mount, but in spirit and in truth. Of course, Jesus himself had the Spirit of God and even called himself the Truth. All men would have to worship God in and through him. He would be liturgy, celebration and the solemn feast of nature and grace. That is why he called his own body a "temple" in this Gospel. Eminently in the Eucharist does his prophecy hold good. In the Mass we re-present his death in a mystical manner, but we have also the living, resurrected Christ who sits at the right hand of the Father. All signs and wisdom, all power and knowledge come to focus in the Catholic liturgy. In John's Gospel the cleansing of the Temple takes place early in Jesus' public life. In the parallel passages of the other Gospels, this event transpires after the raising of Lazarus and Palm Sunday. In the latter case the prophecy of his death is closer to the fact itself. It was ironic that not a stone would be left on a stone less than forty years later, when Titus and Vespasian and the Roman legions would destroy Herod's beautiful edifice.

Even though many came to believe in him, *"when they saw the signs he was doing,"* their faith did not include the acceptance of Jesus himself and his teaching, just the signs. But the master did not trust them; he knew their hearts. He *"did not need anyone to testify about human nature. He himself understood it well."* At this very moment he still knows what is in our hearts, what we think of him, the degree to which we accept him, how we look for signs even after 2000 years of Church history, how we reject the folly of the cross, how we desire a worldly philosophy about morality and permissiveness and sensual indulgence. Yet he still loves us, feeds us, slakes our spiritual thirst, and forgives us when we repent. Come to him today and every day and tell him, "Lord, you have the words of everlasting life."

Third Sunday of Lent, C

Ex 1:1-8, 13-15;
1 Cor 10:1-6, 10-12;
Lk 13:1-9

There were no such things as business cards with name, address and function in the time of Moses when God called him to attention by the unconsumed burning bush. At first, God identified himself as the "God of Abraham, Isaac, and Jacob," which had been his standard title for centuries. "No, no," Moses protested, "Pharaoh is going to demand more than that! What is your real name?" To know a god's name, it was thought, gave you a measure of control. It was more likely that your prayer would be answered because of the implied intimacy.

"What's in a name?" Juliet asked herself. "A rose by any other name smells just as sweet." Nevertheless we have the feeling that a name should fit the person or place or thing. Remember the Hollywood actors who fabricated names to describe their movie personality:

John Wayne, Rock Hudson, Marilyn Monroe. (They are all dead now and practically forgotten, and their names don't matter anymore.) Some peoples, for example the native Americans, have three names: a given name, a nickname acquired during life, and a third secret name, known only to themselves, never to be revealed, but used when they identified themselves in prayer to the Great Spirit. We all know how devastating a pejorative nickname can be, particularly if it follows us through life: Fats, Dumpy, Skinny, Baldy, Pear-Shape! In religious orders until recently novices were often given a new name to signify their change of life and status. That sense of control by knowing a name is seen when we are confronted by a snarling dog; it may be ferocious, but if you call its name and command it, it is likely to become more docile. Names are important.

One of the plainest, yet maybe the most moving, of war memorials is the one in Washington, D.C., in memory of the soldiers killed in the Vietnam War. It is simply a chevron-shaped, polished black marble wall with the names of all the dead incised in columns on the marble face. There is no majestic figure of nobility or suffering or triumph of the human spirit. Yet after all is said and done, the names of all the "small guys" are the most important, so those who knew and loved them could come to look, mourn and weep that an unpopular war destroyed them in the prime of life.

So the Lord God revealed his own name; it is doubtful whether the unsophisticated Jews of that time could comprehend it. "I am who am," or "I am the IS," or "I simply exist." We would say, "I am the boss," or "I am Bill," or "I am the owner," or "I am yours truly." God told Moses, "I am just plain AM! Not like those phonies, Baal, Hathor, AmonRa, Astarte, Beelzebub. I really exist!"

"I am. All existence flows from ME. I am the summit and fullness of being, a fountain overflowing into your created existence!" He preserves us in being, continues our existence. If he momentarily withdrew that metaphysical support, we would disappear and the molecules around us would rush in and fill the vacuum! We are totally dependent on his will for our ability to act, even when we choose to sin! (This certainly gives a more profound meaning to our free will.)

The Jews may not have understood the philosophical implications of "I am," but they did grasp the awesomeness of the Deity. For example, in a passage of the Bible where the Hebrew word "Yahweh" appears, the devout Jew would cover his eyes and cheeks with his hands and simply substitute, "the Name"—as, "the Name said to Moses." This is done even today by the Orthodox.

Jesus not only did the works of God, like control the unruly sea, change the law of the sabbath when the disciples were hungry, work miracles, forgive sin, and speak with divine authority, he called himself by the same name God revealed to Moses: "Before Abraham was, I AM." The present tense is used in both instances to underscore the timelessness of God, without past or future.

Names not only confer control and right of access, they suggest function. "Peter" became the Rock of the Church. "Jesus" means Savior, or God-saves. As Isaiah wrote, "They shall call his name 'Emmanuel,' which means 'God is with us.'" "I AM," however, does not exactly describe a function, but rather gives the basis for all functions.

Every name has a meaning in the language from which it was derived. Bible names are heavy with meaning. Your name is part of your personhood, your self-disclosure, your self-esteem, your principal communication, and generally the opening ploy of your personal encounters. When you introduce yourself, you don't want anyone to ridicule or mock your name. You are saying, "Handle with care. This is ME!" The name God revealed to Moses was his great self-disclosure, his principal communication up to that time. He, too, expects to be "handled with care" and respect and, of course, adoration.

In Philippians 2 we read that God gave Jesus the name which is above every other name, so that at his name very knee in heaven, on the earth, and under the earth should bend in adoration. St. Peter stated, "The only name by which we are saved is Jesus Christ." Because you know his name and are, in fact, on a first-name basis with Jesus, you have access to him, can call on him, address him most intimately. Love his name. Do not use his beautiful name ("God saves") as a profanity. "I AM" is God's name as it appeals to our intellect; "JESUS" is God's name as it captivates our heart.

Optional Mass for the Third Week of Lent

Ex 17:1-7;
Jn 4:5-42

Use the commentary on page 71 for Cycle A of the Third Sunday of Lent, which contains the readings for this optional Mass.

Monday of the Third Week of Lent

2 Kgs 5:1-15;
Lk 4:24-30

In today's Gospel Jesus was preaching in his home territory of Nazareth. He managed to rile the hometown folk by pointing out that no prophet finds acceptance on his home ground. Comparing himself to Elijah and Elisha, he added fuel to the flames of their indignation when he pointed out that the prophets snubbed their noses at the Jews and took their prophetic and therapeutic gifts to the Sidonian woman and to a Syrian general. So the "downhome" citizens took Jesus to the brow of a cliff of Nazareth with the intention of throwing him to the rocks below, but he gave them the slip.

It is still possible to visit the site of the former synagogue. A building there, which was once a Catholic church, is now empty except for occasional pilgrims and tourists. The local guides show you the *Saltus Domini* cliff nearby. This means the "leap of the Lord," but Jesus eluded the crowd's grasp. Because Nazareth is built on a low mountain with many limestone buttresses, murder was planned for Jesus. But his time had not yet come.

In his sermon Jesus referred to Naaman, the Syrian general whom Elisha cured. This is one of the most fascinating stories that punctuates the sometimes dull history of Israel. The captive Jewish girl told her mistress, Naaman's wife, that Naaman should visit the prophet in Samaria for a cure of his leprosy. His king, in turn, the Aramean, or Syrian, ruler, sent Naaman with a load of gifts to the king of Israel. The latter, however, saw this as a pretext to invade the weaker Israel, because, of course, he had no healing power. Elisha heard of the king's plight and instructed the king to send Naaman along to see him. When Naaman arrived, ready for a little magic or some exotic potions, Elisha told him simply to take seven baths in the Jordan River.

Naaman was outraged. Weren't the rivers of Damascus better than the trickle of the Jordan? But his servants pointed out that, if he was ready to obey some difficult ritual, then why balk at the easy solution? Now we know that "leprosy" covered many kinds of skin diseases and blemishes in ancient times. Maybe Naaman just had to learn a little hygiene! And they all lived "happily ever after."

Two lessons emerge. The first is that you never know when you are going to bump into a prophet. Beware of rejecting him as the Nazarenes did to Jesus. Just listen whether your personal prophet is telling you the truth— perhaps a neighbor, an in-law, a bank teller, or maybe even a preacher! The second point is that spiritual healing is rarely the result of grandstand plays and production numbers, but comes from quiet, consistent and generally repetitious actions: regular spiritual reading, especially of the Bible; consistent prayer; joyful performance of the boring tasks of making a living or making a home; putting up with "rain on your parade," noisy kids next door, rock-and-roll in the middle of the night, phone callers that waste your time, and so on and on.

With respect to consistent prayer, remember that nothing much happens from the best of prayers—no sweetness, no uplift, not even much satisfaction. As today's responsorial psalm reads, the best thing you can do is "thirst for the living God"—that is, wait for his visitation. You are often closer to God when the right words don't come, the feelings don't flow, and you have the "blah's." Don't be worried about doing something; just wait for God to disclose himself and his will. In other words, don't pray because you "get something out of it" (although that may be comforting), but because praying is the right thing to do!

Although it is essential and important to interrupt your busyness to remember God, the best prayer occurs when you are ready to "waste time" with God, that is, prepared to be non-productive and simply to rest in the Lord. We do not see the Lord face to face in this life, but we can always long for the next life: "My soul is thirsting for the living God: when shall I see him face to face?"

Tuesday of the
Third Week of Lent

Dn 3:25, 34-43;
Mt 18:21-35

The text from Daniel represents once more the classical model of biblical prayer. The narration of God's wonderful works in the past, confession of one's unworthiness, and a plea for God's mercy are also the heart of today's Gospel. In imitation of our heavenly Father, we must likewise forgive 490 times, 7 times 70—which really means endlessly.

Many, many times does the Bible call us to forgiveness. There is today's Gospel about the servant who did not reciprocate the forgiveness he himself had received. In the "Our Father" we pray to be forgiven our debts to the degree that we forgive our debtors. We have the example of Jesus who forgave so many persons whose physical ills were coupled with moral failures. There was the accusation hurled against Jesus, "Who but God can forgive sins?" We in turn become "godly" by forgiving those who offend us. Then when we are offering a gift before the altar (as attending Mass) and we remember our brother has some hostility against us, we are to find him and be reconciled before offering our gift to God.

We often make mistakes in life that are not sins, because they have no moral dimension, yet we are erroneously burdened with guilt because of those actions. When I make a mistake in addressing an envelope and rip it out of the typewriter, I inevitably think of the lessons we were given in elementary school by the sisters about wasting paper—which I had crunched up and had thrown in the wastebasket at the rear of the room. When those castoff papers began to uncrunch and straighten out in the basket, making crackling noises, Sister told us it was the poor souls in purgatory coming back to look for the paper they had wasted when they were pupils, probably in that very classroom! This phony guilt stays with me until today, albeit not the terror!

Another time Sister patriotically pointed out that good old Abe Lincoln as a boy had to do his sums with a piece of charcoal on the back of a shovel. (Thankfully, I never chopped down a cherry tree; otherwise I would be spitting cherry pits into holes for the rest of my life!)

Of course, the Lord was never referring to unreal or childish guilt that was imposed on us, but real moral guilt that comes from our sins. We have enough real sins that we don't need to add phony guilt to our burden. As we pray to be delivered from God's severe judgments, our plea gains credibility by our willingness to forgive those who have wronged us.

How many families squabble for years over trivialities! How many brothers and sisters argue over their inheritance, for which they never worked a day in their lives! How many business partners have a falling out that drags through the courts for years! How many neighbors join battle because an innocent child hits a baseball into their yard or a tree sheds its leaves over the fence! How many youngsters develop an unhealthy rivalry over grades or sports, boyfriends or girlfriends! How many religious resist authority by becoming "passively aggressive" over real or supposed infringements on their "rights"!

Shakespeare observed that if we all got our deserts, no one would escape a whipping! So make up for your own sins by readily forgiving those who make a sarcastic remark about you in public, those who tell a joke at your expense or hang an unpleasant nickname on you, those who reveal a secret about you, those who ignore your greeting, those who don't invite you to their party. These are minor things and we have inflicted them as well on others, whereas God has forgiven us major offenses!

Wednesday of the Third Week of Lent

Dt 4:1, 5-9;
Mt 5:17-19

Liturgists point out that during this week of Lent occurred the first of the "scrutinies" or examinations given to catechumens who were preparing for Easter Baptism. After the readings of today's Mass they were tested on the commandments and their practical meaning and application.

Although catechists today generally frown on manuals and memorization, probably all those thousands of early catechumens had the ten commandments both memorized and correctly interpreted. Every teacher knows that, while it is more important to understand the content of a lecture or textbook, nevertheless there are many useful tools that require the work of memory: the multiplication tables, the periodic chart of the atoms, formulas in physics, and the morphology of word-endings in language study.

So we, too, are greatly aided by knowing memorized definitions of terms and theological formulas of our religion. Even after years of preaching and teaching, I find myself returning to the lessons of childhood to place a concept into proper context, e.g., sacrament, grace, person, nature, matter, form, the Trinity, Hypostatic Union, Transubstantiation. Such words, canonized by centuries of tradition, are the building blocks of doctrinal statements, dogmatic definitions, and even popular preaching. Persons who claim that it is not important to define theological words so painstakingly are saying analogously that it is not important to plot the trajectory of a rocket in great detail, or mix a medical compound with accuracy, nor does it matter if we use a clock that loses only three minutes a day!

When God revealed religious truths to mankind in the ancient days, he appealed not only to the mind, but to the whole person, as when he inspired these words in today's text: *"For what great nation is there that has gods so close to it as the LORD, our God, is to us whenever we call upon him?"* There was a progression in the faith of the Jews with respect to the Deity. At first the "God of Abraham, Isaac and Jacob" was only one of many gods. Later he became the strongest god, then the only God. The great self-disclosure of God to Moses showed Him unique and the Totally Other: "I am who am"—or "I simply exist; I contain all being; I am responsible for all existence; I am singular; I am alone; I am who am!"

In the Christian Bible, wherein Jesus said he came to fulfill the law and prophecies, his self-revelation as God the Second Person and the sending of the Holy Spirit as God the Third Person completed God's communication of himself in the Trinity, the central doctrine of Christianity. Yet the concept of Deity began when God walked with Adam and Eve in Paradise in the cool of the evening.

We sometimes think that the Lord simply set aside the Law univocally with its centuries of sacrifice and whole-burnt offerings. On the contrary, he knew that the Old Law would be displaced by the New Law and his personal holocaust on Calvary. Still he applauds the Law of Sinai, the desert experience, and the institutions of past prophets. When Jesus said, *"until heaven and earth pass away,"* he was speaking with Semitic hyperbole and exaggeration. In fact, he calls us to spiritual greatness by adhering to God's Law: *"Whoever obeys and teaches these commandments will be called greatest in the kingdom of heaven."*

In the spiritual life we must dare to dream great dreams and look for great visions of suffering and glory. Imagine the mother of Einstein telling him, "Albert, you think so much about mathematics and yet you flunked the last three arithmetic tests! Why don't you learn something practical! You're half-blind from all that squinting." These are facts in Einstein's life and the spiritual lesson is clear: see the possibilities with God's help and not the limitations from your own weakness. There is no limit to the beautiful things you can do and become with positive thinking and grace. You will probably not be an astrophysicist, but you are not prevented from becoming a saint!

Thursday of the Third Week of Lent

Jer 7:23-28;
Lk 11:14-23

Both of today's readings have a succinct and appropriate "bottom line," that is, their final verses sum up the message of the whole text quite neatly.

The very name of Jeremiah has become synonymous with complaints, gripes or laments; the English language has been given a new word to describe this frame of mind: jeremiad, or a sad tale of misery. It applies to those baggy-eyed pessimists who enjoy being miserable and are happy to share their sorrows, point out what's wrong with virtually everything, and bring you down or put you down. They are the kind of persons who "enjoy poor health" for years, and of whom you should never inquire, "How are you?" because you will get the full report from falling hair to ingrown toenails and everything else in between!

At least Jeremiah had ample cause to complain after centuries of Jewish infidelity to God. He sums it up in his "bottom line": *Faithfulness has disappeared; the word itself is banished from their speech.*

Jesus' dialogue with his enemies, who accuse him of exorcising by Satan's own power, cuts through logic and the rules of argumentation and says (also to us), *"Whoever is not with me is against me, and whoever does not gather with me scatters."*

Not everyone criticized Jesus, but there was that persistent knot of his enemies who followed him right up to Calvary, never at rest until they downed him completely. Nevertheless, sometimes it seems that Jesus is quite abrasive or, as Madison Avenue advertisers would put it, Jesus did not "package" his Gospel very attractively. Of course, he was precisely challenging the seductions of this world and its values. He deliberately used the "basics," as advertisers put it, or "generic packaging."

Supermarket packaging is an art unto itself. "Generic" products are supposed to look unattractive, in order to give the impression that no time or money was wasted in packaging! Factually, however, the cost of fancy and colorful packages is exactly the same as plain black and white boxes. *"Whoever is not with me is against me, and whoever does not gather with me scatters."* You cannot be both a sheep and a goat. You have to make a choice, then live by it with all your heart!

Friday of the Third Week of Lent

Hos 14:2-10; Mk 12:28-34

Each of the Jewish prophets is distinguished by a descriptive adjective: Isaiah the poet, Jeremiah the pessimist, Ezekiel the moralist, and—today—Hosea, the tender prophet of God's love and forgiveness. His book is short enough to read easily in one sitting to get the full effect. Today his words read, *"I will heal their defection, I will love them freely.... I will be like the dew for Israel: he shall blossom like the lily.... Again they shall dwell in his shade and raise grain; They shall blossom like the vine...."*

If Hosea expresses the love of God for humanity, then Mark's Gospel expresses what the love of mankind for God should be: we are to love him with all our faculties and love our neighbors as ourselves. Although the scribes were typically the enemies of Jesus since they added complexities to Jewish law, there were—as in all groups of people—men of good will, like the scribe in today's Gospel. He saw that the double command of love supersedes all ritual sacrifices and burnt offerings. So the Master commended his insights: *"You are not far from the kingdom of God."*

To love someone whom we don't particularly like seems to be a complex spiritual assignment. For example, there are those whose personal habits of life (like hygiene) or jokes (like puns) or lack of finesse (like insensitive remarks) or insatiable curiosity (like asking prying questions), may prevent us ever from liking them. Yet our Christian chore is to love them! Liking is based on an attraction you sense towards another person; loving is based on God's having loved that unlikeable person first—as well as ourselves. As St. John wrote in his letter, God sent his Son to redeem that person, and graced him or her with a thousand gifts we probably cannot even identify or of which we are unaware. Yet we are not yet a Christian unless we love the unlovable, forgive the unforgivable, and cherish the ugly.

If you want to see a rainbow, you have to put up with inconvenient showers and rainfall. If you want to see butterflies in your garden, you have to tolerate crawly, hairy caterpillars who wrap themselves in gauze and "die" as they change into beauties. If you want someone to love you, you have to tolerate—or rather accept—that person's sometimes being a nag or a grouch. If you want to prevent your enemies from controlling your feelings of anger, then stop hating them; your very hostility empowers them! If you want to prove your love for God, then love your neighbor.

Perhaps the scribe in today's text did not yet deserve another comment of Jesus elsewhere in the Gospel: "The kingdom of God is within you." He was "not far," yet not "within." As many of us, he had an intellectual understanding of the precept of love, but he had not internalized it yet; he had not experimented with loving actions. I suspect that most of us know the answers to our problems, but we have not internalized those answers. We have not put them to work; they are not operative in our lives. Often a counselor or spiritual director has an accurate insight into another's problem and the probable answers, but it does no good to express them, because they would remain only an idea in the intellect, a cerebral concept. The other person has to discover his or her solution. Then you see that person's face suddenly light up, hear a sigh of satisfaction, and see him or her lean back comfortably in the chair—a kind of "new creation" in the human sense.

Jesus talked incessantly about love, but his hearers could not pull their feet out of the swamp of the laws. Perhaps they were more secure in fearing God than in trusting him. The parameters of fear are clearly set, but love is shapeless and more of a mindset of generosity, giving, easy communication and sacrifice. We do not know whether the scribe ever took the next step, from being not far to getting inside the kingdom of God. But for him as well as for ourselves the only way to find out is to test our ability to love without expecting to be loved in return, but only because it is the right thing to do!

Saturday of the
Third Week of Lent

Hos 6:1-6;
Lk 18:9-14

The story of the Pharisee and the publican (or tax collector) takes me back to my childhood, when I saw a lithograph of this scene of the two men at prayer. The Pharisee bragging at the front of the Temple, elegantly dressed, looked like a "fat cat," but the publican was depicted in rags, cowering in the rear. I did not have the foggiest notion of what a "publican" might be. After studying the Bible I realized that probably the publican, a tax collector for the Roman government, was the "fat cat!" In the ancient world public officials were generally wealthy.

The question of their clothing, however, is irrelevant; their mindset is the point of the story. The tax collector knew he was disliked because of the rapacious system of tax collection in the Roman provincial system. A tax collector was a Quisling, a defector from his nation, a collaborator. Yet in the story of Jesus (who always forces our minds down unaccustomed avenues) he was the hero, because God looks not to your profession (as long as it is honest), your social contacts, or your clothing, but looks squarely into your heart. Hence the tax man was "justified," which in biblical parlance means that his sins were forgiven, or that he was acceptable to God. The lesson for Lent is transparent: you can fast three days a week, you can be generous with your bucks to the Church, and be as pure as the driven snow, but if you consider yourself "holier-than-thou," you are taking your spiritual meaning from your own efforts and trying to become the architect of your own salvation, rather than relying on God's help!

Thus the tax collector who kneels humbly before the Lord is like patient Job who sat without true friends on the dungheap outside the town. The publican was out-cast and friendless. He and Job both experienced a radical aloneness, an emptiness. They were alienated from their fellows, felt abandoned, perhaps by God himself, and shattered by their experiences. Yet only in this state of mind could they touch the mystery of God.

In our frantic world where we catch a bite, catch a movie, catch a plane and catch a bus, where our minds are diverted by novelty and fantasies, our hearts encapsulated by pleasure and self-seeking, we need to slow down and deal with our radical aloneness before God—because that is the truth, whether we will it or not! It is, in a sense, like the Last Judgment, at which, despite the millions appearing before the Lord, each person stands without the trappings of money, power or clout; without good looks, athletic prowess, high grades, two cars in the garage, academic degrees. Not even the priesthood or religious vows can shield us from the powerful scrutiny of God. Yet we need not fear that moment of truth if we have experienced that same radical aloneness beforehand in our prayer.

I have often said that no pleasure, no stimulation, no experience in this life is superior to standing on the vantage ground of truth and understanding whatever is in our view. There may be two sides to a story, but only one posture of truth. This is particularly true when one stands, like the tax man, on the vantage ground of self-knowledge with one's head bowed down in worship and sees everything with God's vision. "He who acts in truth comes into the light, to make clear that his deeds are done in God."

FOURTH WEEK OF LENT

Fourth Sunday
of Lent, A

1 Sm 16:1, 6-7, 10-13;
Eph 5:8-14; Jn 9:1-41

God is subtle and sometimes humorous. One of God's delights (from our human vantage point) and a constant theme of Scripture is to detour our thinking down unexpected roads. He lifts up the lowly, chooses the nobodies, and uses the rejects of society: Mary Magdalen, a "woman of easy virtue," tax collectors, uneducated fishermen.

God "calls the shots." Abraham and Sarah were one hundred years old when they started the Chosen Race with a single son, Isaac. Hannah bore Samuel the prophet (who appears in today's first reading), and Elizabeth bore John the Baptist when she was well beyond the age of childbearing. Likewise in today's reading from First Samuel, God did not judge by the tall and manly appearance of the other sons of Jesse, but chose the boy, David, so young and inexperienced and unimportant that his father did not even call him from the field to be "reviewed" by Samuel for anointing. Yet God chose David to be king, from whose line Jesus would be born!

This was also true of so many saints whom God chose for his work. They were not always the most brilliant, most healthy, most eloquent, and so forth. God chooses those persons through whom his own divine power shows the most clearly. This brings to mind St. Maximilian Kolbe, the patron of our difficult century. He was physically weak from tuberculosis throughout his life, but a diligent student, although a poor writer and speaker. One of his seminary professors predicted, "He'll never amount to anything. Just let him teach, and he'll write a few boring books that no one will read. He'll always just be a dreamer." Yet in a few years he founded Niepokalanow, the City of the Immaculate, which reached the astounding number of 750 friars and seminarians by the time World War II began in 1939. He published books in ten languages, put out a magazine with a monthly circulation in Poland of over 1,000,000 (then a nation of thirty million), and a daily newspaper with a circulation of over 100,000, which was delivered by airplane all over Poland. He founded the Japanese mission of his Conventual Franciscan Order, which is thriving today as an independent province and publishing center. Many know how he was later arrested, abused in the concentration camp of Auschwitz, and offered his life in exchange for the father of a family—a man who had been condemned to death by starvation in reprisal for an escaped prisoner.

We see the same divine action in today's Gospel. Who was the man born blind? Why was he chosen? He was an outcast, despised by his fellow Jews, told that he was "steeped in sin" because of their theological viewpoint that physical or emotional afflictions were God's punishment for sin. Yet Jesus used him to teach that spiritual blindness is worse than physical blindness. His healing led to his belief in Christ. When we allow God to enter our lives, he takes the initiative, choosing us rather than we choosing him. In the second reading, St. Paul wrote to the Church at Ephesus, *"Live as children of light.... Take no part in the fruitless works of darkness. ...but everything exposed by the light becomes visible, for everything that becomes visible is light."* This light is to the spiritual blindness of sin what daylight is to physical blindness.

The dialogue between the Pharisees and the cured man and his parents is one of the most completely recorded in the Gospels. The humanness and the motivations of the characters appear in this drama: the arrogance of the Pharisees and their envy of Jesus, the fear of the parents and their evasiveness, the pointed sarcasm of the man born blind and his defense of Jesus and later his adoration of Him, and the honesty of Jesus in answering his adversaries. *"If you were blind, you would have no sin; but now you are saying, 'We see,' so your sin remains."*

In this text Jesus called himself the light of the world and the Son of Man. With divine irony and perhaps a little sadness Jesus explains to the formerly blind man, *"I came into this world for judgment, so that those who do not see might see, and those who do see might become blind."* Upon hearing this condemnation, the Pharisees were undoubtedly outraged. They boasted in being disciples of Moses, yet were envious of Jesus' popular success. Envy is "sorrow at another's good" (St. Thomas Aquinas). It is a species of pride; both are competitive and thrive on outdoing and putting down others. The first sin of envy is the second sin recorded in the Bible— Cain's envy over Abel's more acceptable sacrifice. Every sin of envy is a "small murder" of our neighbor. Genuine goodness shares itself, whereas envy bases itself on the idea that when another person increases, you automatically decrease in importance.

We even use the word, "Pharisee," as a description of being "holier-than-thou." They were subtly critical of the Romans with the pretense of patriotism. Actually they never had it so good! Of course, no one wishes to be under foreign domination, but the Romans allowed them freedom of religion, exempted them from military service, and maintained trade routes and roads protected from bandits and pirates. They kept the peace and brought sophistication to the backward nation of Palestine.

Nevertheless, in another place the Lord told his listeners to obey the Pharisees, for they inherited the teaching "chair" of Moses. He did not criticize all their teachings, only the unreasonable ones, as well as the attitude they conveyed. They fulfilled every detail of complex laws to force God, as it were, to give them his approval. They often did what they were supposed to do as devout Jews, but without humility. Their piety was always "on parade." They thought that they had all spiritual truth at their command, as well as the inside track with God.

We are all in danger of falling into Pharisaic ways. We must always question whether "our" truth is the same as God's truth and values and modes of operation. We must not be envious, but rejoice at the success of others and even help them to grow. If we receive graces and favors from God, we should praise him without boasting. When we bow our heads in prayer, let our posture manifest our inner lowliness and dependence on the Lord!

Fourth Sunday of Lent, B

2 Chr 36:14-17, 19-23;
Eph 2:4-10; Jn 3:14-21

Many persons take upon themselves Lenten penances, such as giving up this or that. Yet this season brings its own penances, such as spring flu, the need for spring cleaning after having the house closed up all winter, that spring fever which urges us to get out into the warmth of the sun. If we are able to handle these problems and anxieties well and without complaint, they can be spiritually very profitable. Self-imposed mortification is excellent, but better and more realistic are the unexpected, unsought, unpleasant penances.

Spring is also the season of Jesus' death. Spring is lovely in Palestine, especially in Galilee. There is new life in the soil and in the sheep pens; grain and flowers and lambs remind the people that this is a time for beginnings. The scarlet poppies are mixed in the grain fields, not by the design of the farmers, but by natural processes. (These are Jesus' "lilies of the field.") Whereas farming is generally done by machinery in the kibbutzes and plantations, one sometimes sees a poor farmer who scatters his seed as was done in the time of Jesus. The Lord must have seen such sights, which caused him to think of his own proximate passion and remark, "Unless the grain of wheat dies, it remains alone; but if it dies in the earth, it produces a harvest a hundredfold."

Each believer is asked by Jesus to go up to Jerusalem to die with him in a unique way. We ought to do our repenting early and so avoid the Easter rush! G. K. Chesterton wrote that repentance is very personal; no one can do it for you. Like blowing your nose or writing your love letters, you have to do repenting for yourself. Jesus refers in today's Gospel to the serpent Moses lifted up in the desert. Many Jews had sinned and God allowed in the camp an infestation of vipers which bit the sinners. Moses fashioned a bronze snake to wind on his staff—a symbol of Jesus on his cross—and the sick persons were healed by looking upon it. So sinners are likewise healed by looking with faith on the cross of Jesus. *"So must the Son of Man be lifted up, so that everyone who believes in him may have eternal life."*

Who needs to look upon the crucified Lord with faith and repent? 1) Those who have lost the certainty of faith by watering down their Christianity; those who say that all religions are the same; those who habitually miss Sunday Mass; those who justify themselves by saying that the Church is falling apart anyway. 2) Those who can't get their act together; their lives have lost meaning; they are depressed about an uncertain future; they can't forgive those who have offended them; their trust in God has all but disappeared. 3) Those who are self-centered, seeking the almighty dollar; those escaping into sexual excesses; drowning themselves in liquor, constant television or other diversions.

God stays involved even in a sinful person's history. The first reading describes the seventy years of the Babylonian Captivity. It was God who changed Jewish history by bringing Cyrus to power in Persia, and he decreed the Jews' return to Palestine. St. Paul in his letter to the Church at Ephesus tells us that salvation is God's free gift; he has entered history for our sake. *"This is not from you; it is the gift of God; it is not from works, so no one may boast. For we are his handiwork...."* In the Jewish Testament God had to keep repairing the railroad (to use an earthly metaphor) to keep the world "on track." But Jesus in the Christian Testament built a whole new railroad, the new Gospel Train. He did this through his death and resurrection.

Unlike us, Jesus knew the details of his death. There were the prophecies, especially in Isaiah, and his divine foreknowledge. In God's plan this awareness made it possible for Jesus to say "yes" completely. He did not use his divinity as a "cover"; on the contrary, by his divine nature he was certain of his painful demise. He also made a fully human decision: "No man takes my life from me; I lay it down of my own will." The seed must die for life to continue and for the harvest, which is ourselves. We in turn extend the effect of Jesus' death by taking up our cross daily and following in his footsteps. The apostles did not discover this until Pentecost, when they gave up their scheming. Even Peter did not become the Key Man—with "the keys of the kingdom"—until he embraced the possibility of the cross and died upside down on one in Rome.

What is the quality of your faith in God? Do you try to manipulate him, make deals with him, or remake others as you want them to be? Look at the submission of Jesus. To a pious Jew the cross was a horror. Crucifixion was considered unclean, and the punishment was carried out outside the city walls of the sacred city. It was shameful to be stripped and have cruel bystanders stare. Yet at the Last Supper Jesus prayed, "Father, glorify me!" We recognize that our spiritual life is bittersweet. On the way of the cross Simon of Cyrene was embarrassed and reluctant, yet his name is remembered today for that chance encounter. The daughters of Jerusalem heard a dire warning from Jesus, yet they remain symbols today of heroic compassion. The Magdalen saw her beloved beaten and helpless, yet Jesus appeared to her first in the written record of the resurrection. Mother Mary felt every blow of the scourge, every thorn, every pound of the hammer, yet we call her "blessed among women."

It is not merely recommended, but it is necessary that we accept sufferings as a part of repentance. We can't gamble that final grace will be ours if we have not prepared ourselves during life. No one suddenly downs the "cup of mortal sin." Big sin is always preceded by many small sips of little sins. Yet to carry our cross daily is worth it. We can die laughing and not be surprised on judgment day—nor scared!

Fourth Sunday
of Lent, C

Jos 5:9, 10-12;
2 Cor 5:17-21;
Lk 5:1-3, 11-32

It is said by scholars that Jericho is the oldest walled city in the world. Even today in winter it is crowded with tourists and those lucky enough or wealthy enough to own a home there. Today it is also a military outpost of Israel, because it is close to the Jordan. This ancient city was also the border town of Canaan, the Holy Land, and the first city of the Promised Land to fall into Israelite hands. After Moses died, when he had seen this land from Mount Pisgah, Joshua led the wandering Jews to the end of their exodus into the plains surrounding lush Jericho. There would be no more manna, no more miraculous springs of water. The Promised Land had it all! God provided for his people as he had promised!

The second reading is better than the first in correlating to the Gospel. St. Paul points out that God is rich in mercy, as was the father of the prodigal son. God did not count our transgressions, but saw rather the reconciliation Jesus provided by his cross. We know the familiar story line about the prodigal son: he was weak, he was dumb, but he was not so wicked. He had to hit bottom before he repented. He had to feel helpless. He wanted to show his independence from his father and probably didn't like his older brother very much. He arrogantly asked his father for what was coming to him! His father owed him nothing, so the son was very impertinent and demanding.

The older son did not have to worry that his brother's return might jeopardize his inheritance; whatever was left would be his anyway. Commentators explain that the older brother represents the Jews, jealous of being the Chosen People, and the younger son represents the Gentiles. The younger son won the affection of his father by his repentance for the pagan ways he assumed in that far off land. In fact, the older boy did not have a very loving relationship with his father. When the second son returned, the older son did not speak of his love for his father, but said that he had slaved for his father for years and had gotten nothing. He seems to have had all the virtues of dutifulness, except humility. That made him hard-nosed and unforgiving toward his brother. Yet which son proved the better man—the rigid son who failed in love, or the "easy" son who repented his foolish arrogance and openly proclaimed his guilt?

Note that it was not the ring and robe and shoes that counted in the end. It was not the fatted calf and the party that was important. Rather it was the son's father on the lookout for his return, looking for him when he was a long way off. It was his father who ran out to meet him and threw his arms around his neck and kissed him. Some parents try to give their kids the moon, as we say. They don't need the moon, but a kiss of love and a hug of understanding with forgiveness.

Cannot we all identify with the prodigal? We, too, have squandered our heavenly heritage and wasted the graces of our redemption. Yet we have also known the pursuit of our heavenly Father, his kisses and hugs! Our part is to be open to his interventions and meet him half way on our journey home. We like to be judged on our status in society: whom we know, what we possess, where we've been. But if we want to know our real value, we need only to look at the cross. That was the price at which we were purchased! Two formerly popular songs describe the egotist: "I Gotta Be Me" and "I Did It My Way!" That leaves no place for trust in others and the simple belief that children possess.

A behavioral psychologist researched status symbols in our culture and noted that one aspect of "status," which symbolizes our importance, is the amount of cubic feet we live or work in. Important people live in bigger houses, such as castles, palaces, mansions, the White House. Wealthy people have bigger bedrooms and dining rooms and gardens. Higher executives have bigger offices, sometimes with private bathrooms, exercise rooms or showers.

Now that there are more and more white-collar workers, office space is at a premium. As workers climb the corporate ladder there are fewer cubic feet of that status of space to surround themselves with. Actually, you do not need much space for a desk, some chairs, a file cabinet and a work table. No longer are original works of art provided by interior decorators. The new executive can choose his office furniture from thirty kinds, from traditional to ultra-modern. And everyone gets the same amount of space!

What is the point? Both the prodigal son and his brother tried to create their own space, design it and furnish it according to their own taste. The prodigal wanted a lot of room for his freedom and whatever contributed to his pleasure. His older brother, under the mask of dutifulness, was longing to be like his younger brother, surrounded by friends and enjoying a party in which he was the star. Meanwhile the father tried to understand them both and treat them according to their needs. God our father is like the top-drawer organizational planner, who places us equally on the same level of opportunity. In his "corporation" no task is more important than any other. Efficiency is not related to productivity, but to the love in the relationship that led us to the service of the Boss. External status symbols count for nothing. Our spiritualized bodies will not need cubic feet nor any space in heaven. Meanwhile God treats us according to our spiritual needs. When we turn in repentance to our Father, the only space we get or need is within his eternal embrace.

Optional Mass for the
Fourth Week of Lent

Mi 7:7-9;
Jn 9:1-41

Use the commentary on page 93 for Cycle A of the Fourth Sunday of Lent, which contains the Gospel for this optional Mass.

Monday of the
Fourth Week of Lent

Is 65:17-21;
Jn 4:43-54

The Bible often uses earthly figures of speech to define and describe spiritual realities. For example, the description of heaven is a case in point: mansions, crowns, gold and silver, alabaster and jasper, heavenly choirs. All this symbolizes the riches of God's house, its graciousness and happiness. Leaping from the known and familiar, we can attain spiritual knowledge from this comparison.

Isaiah speaks for the Lord: *"Lo, I am about to create new heavens and a new earth...."* No infant will die—we recall the sad statistics that about one-half of the babies born in the Third World die before the age of two. An adult who dies before the age of one hundred will be considered as if cursed! People shall live in the houses they build and eat the produce of their fields, because no wars will cut them down, destroy their homes, send them into exile, nor drive them from their homesteads. This is Isaiah's description of God's kingdom!

So it is thought that paradise will be restored on this earth. Some optimists think that the behavioral sciences and scientific technology is about to restore this Golden Age of the springtime of mankind. We do have new powers to alter genetic codes and manipulate the biological inheritance of our offspring. Nuclear power can either destroy us or give us incredible energy resources to better our lives. Psychology promises to heal our emotional instabilities and psychic impairments so the whole world can again love properly with no crime and no more institutions. But so far—nothing!

Our quasi-divine powers have taken us farther than ever from paradise! So the mythical time projected by Isaiah, the peace of Jerusalem, and the fraternity of all nations have eluded the human race. We must understand Isaiah only as a symbol; the "new heavens and the new earth" were fulfilled in the New Testament and the New Covenant in the blood of Jesus. That is why this text of Isaiah appears during Lent. Jesus became our brother not to tell us what we want to hear, but what we need to hear to enter his kingdom. He does not leave us "safe" nor "comfortable" in our self-delusion.

The Gospel today contains an anomaly. John says Jesus testified that a prophet is dishonored in his own country, but Jesus returned to Galilee where we read that the people welcomed him. Yet earlier a murder attempt had been made by his fellow Nazarenes. Some writers think that John was referring to Judea as Jesus' country, because he was born only a few miles from Jerusalem, where he had just suffered rejection by the Jews. On the other hand, Jesus loved his "north country," Galilee, so productive and green, even today. He was less threatened up north, far from the scribes and Pharisees plotting his downfall. In Galilee he told his loveliest parables and metaphors, and worked so many moving miracles, as in today's text.

This Gospel reading is a "reworking" of an incident reported in the other Gospels, wherein the "royal official" is actually a Roman centurion, who had built the synagogue in Capernaum. In the Synoptic version the sick person was a "servant," not his son. Of course, the meaning of the story comes from the miraculous cure, based on the man's faith. We need the trustful attitude of that official. Simply upon the word of Jesus, he returned home satisfied. He even ignored the complaint of Jesus that people were seeking signs and wonders; he was too preoccupied with the health of the child. Only in retrospect did the official discover that his perseverance in prayer paid off. He did not try to put it into a theological syllogism; he simply invited Jesus into his life and believed.

This is what has been missing from our "paradise-planting." We have not invited Jesus into our lives. Yet that is the only formula by which this earth can ever become a paradise and so fulfill its destiny!

Tuesday of the Fourth Week of Lent

Ez 47:1-9, 12;
Jn 5:1-3, 5-16

In the first text Ezekiel sees a vision which is "apocalyptic," that is, filled with symbols, metaphors and allusions to the future. Imagine the setting. The Temple Mount is the highest land for miles around. From the Temple flows water in every direction, becoming (from the prophet's reported vision under the escort of an angel) continually deeper. The meaning is transparent. In the arid land of Judah water means "life." Hence water signifies baptism and the graces of all our lives.

There is also a subtle allusion here to "paradise regained." From the Garden of Eden rivers flowed in the four directions of the compass, too. The Temple of Ezekiel's vision is the restored paradise on earth, because God is there. Instead of the forbidding angel that guarded the original paradise from the re-entry of Adam and Eve, the angel of the vision invited the prophet to enter and understand paradise regained. The rivers that were dammed up by the original sin now burst forth to irrigate the formerly unproductive land. The temples of both Solomon and Herod faced west to Mount Olivet, so that the first rays of the rising sun would flood the façade and sanctuary with golden light. The parapets of the temple looked out over the Kidron Valley, which, although typically dry, occasionally flooded with winter rains and might have suggested to Ezekiel the figure of water flowing from the temple foundations.

The rivers flowed mostly to the east and south, where the mighty powers of that day had had their strongholds, Egypt, Syria, Babylonia, Persia. The powers of this earth will finally be engulfed by the power of God. The fresh, sweet water from the Temple will be so abundant that it will reach the sea —either the Dead Sea, devoid now of all life, or the Gulf of Aqaba and the Red Sea—and turn the salt water into fresh! The trees will so flourish along this river of God that they will bear fruit not just annually, but monthly. Their very leaves will provide medicine and healing. Whoever lives close to the saving river of grace will be themselves fruitful and the source of forgiveness for others. The trees are a reference to the trees of paradise, the "tree of life" and the "tree of the knowledge of good and evil." The trees of the vision, however, bring life, not death.

This concept of the power of "living waters" is reiterated in today's Gospel about Jesus healing a man sick for thirty-eight years, who had sought healing in vain from the supposedly miraculous pool of Bethesda. "Bethesda" or "Bethsaida" means the "house of the double gusher." As the Gospel mentions, this double pool is near the Sheep Gate, where even now on Fridays the Arabs and Bedouins bring sheep and goats in their pickup trucks to sell and trade. Just inside the gate is the Church of St. Anne, a beautiful Crusader Church over the supposed home of Joachim and Anne, where Mary is said to have spent some of her earthly years. The pools are adjacent and, at the time of Christ, were very deep, fed by natural springs which from antiquity were thought to have therapeutic value. (There is a later addition, apparently an insertion not from the pen of St. John, which explained that the waters of the pools were stirred up by an angel and whoever was first to get into the water would be healed.) Actually the springs would occasionally bubble up some gases from an underground source, but Jesus did not comment on the veracity of the popular belief in the angel; he merely used the context for a miracle of compassion. There were many precipitous steps leading to the pool, and the sick man in today's Gospel never made it in time, after hanging around for thirty-eight years!

Jesus cured the man and told him to take his sleeping mat home. The Jews criticized Jesus for this "work" on the Sabbath: both the curing and the carrying away of the healed man's sleeping mat. Jesus felt that the one who had cured him had also the right to command his actions. Thus did Jesus slowly reveal that he was God incarnate, by implicitly asserting that he was Lord of the Sabbath. From Jesus' own mouth comes the lesson for today: if you want the effect of his living waters of grace, then give up your sins "...*so that nothing worse may happen to you*," namely, spiritual sickness or even death. Jesus' allusion to the sick man's sins leads us to conclude that here was some unresolved evil in his life. Perhaps he enjoyed the self-pity and possibly the alms for thirty-eight years; perhaps he liked being the center of attention; perhaps he really lacked the faith to take a risk to plunge headlong into the pools.

We may resemble the sick man in these three respects: self-pity, self-centeredness, lack of faith. Because Lent is the period of the Church's preparation of candidates for Baptism, these readings are appropriate for reflection on our own lives, as we, too, prepare to renew our baptismal vows on Easter.

Wednesday of the
Fourth Week of Lent

Is 49:8-15;
Jn 5:17-30

In today's reading we hear from Isaiah echoes of the first days of Lent, when John the Baptist cries out, "Make straight the way of the Lord. Every mountain will be flattened and every valley filled in." God promises through his prophet to cut a road straight through to their own territories. Even from great distances will they come: the north (Turkey), the west (the islands of Greece), and Syene. This last place was a few hundred miles down the Nile at the first cataract, where the Aswan-Nasser Dam has been built. At that location I looked out over the Nile from a hotel terrace; the river was filled with gigantic, treacherous rocks sculpted by swirling waters for many milleniums. Syene is an island in the middle, covered with the ruins of an ancient Jewish settlement and one of the oldest synagogues in the world. How strange that despite the slavery in Egypt and the problems of the Exodus, the Jews found refuge in Egypt—from Alexandria to Syene—as did the Holy Family when Herod was seeking the life of the Child.

Commentators often point out that Jesus did not suddenly proclaim the doctrine of the Holy Trinity. He performed the acts of God—miracles, forgiving sin, showing himself as Lawgiver and Master of the Sabbath. Later he spoke of the Holy Spirit who was to make his appearance on Pentecost. Thus his hearers were led to the conclusion of the Holy Trinity. It is said that one sign of the mature mind is the ability to keep opposed ideas in one's mind simultaneously—like today's Gospel. Jesus declares his equality with his Father; both are "at work." The Jews understood clearly that Jesus was "making himself God's equal." They both grant life, and to honor one is to honor the other.

Yet as a human being Jesus places himself in a sub-ordinate role: *"...I do not seek my own will but the will of the one who sent me."* These contrary ideas co-exist in the minds of believers. This is the mystery of the God-Man and his Incarnation: a son begotten by a Divine Father in the Trinity; a son given birth by a human mother. Fully divine, fully human, yet he is a single Person, so Mary may correctly be called the Mother of God. We enter the family of God as adopted children, the broth-ers and sisters of Jesus—which is not a mere figure of speech. "Adoptive" does not mean "second-rate" nor "second-best." First of all, we tell adopted children that they were specifically chosen by their parents. The true parents are those who nurture, cherish and love them. All this applies to our heavenly Father, too.

When Jesus retorted to the Pharisees that the Son can do only what he sees the Father doing, this is not humility, but theology. Although we attribute specific actions to each Person—as the Creator, the Redeemer, the Sanctifier—this Divine Community of Three acts upon the world outside itself in concert, never sepa-rately. In this sense we speak of one God, but three Persons. Jesus spoke quite simply, but theologians, wary of the possibly erroneous spinoffs of every statement, seem to make doctrines more complex!

Jesus points out how he and his Father act together: giving life, judging, receiving honor, being the source of life, assigning heaven or hell to sinners or saints. Nev-ertheless the Godhead is less fearsome in Jesus Christ. We approach one like ourselves "in all things but sin." He was born and died—but he rose to a new life to share his divinity with us who believe. The Gospels are silent about so much of Jesus' life on which we can only spec-ulate. I wonder whether Jesus, as a boy, went fishing with his foster father, skipped flat stones on the surface of the Sea of Galilee; whether he bruised his knee or cut his finger on a sharp tool in the carpenter's shop; whether Mary had to call him more than once to supper. I wonder whether he, as a young man, excelled in sports, who his closest friends were, whether he enjoyed parties. (After all, his first public miracle was changing water into good wine at a wedding party, and his enemies, as in today's Gospel, accused him of going to too many dinners with "sinners," who were probably more fun than the rigid Pharisees.) Did Jesus like a second glass of barley beer, the common table drink of the Palestinian poor? He was "like us in all things but sin."

Thursday of the Fourth Week of Lent

Ex 32:7-14;
Jn 5:31-47

Throughout the Jewish Testament we hear the patriarchs and prophets argue familiarly with God. (Like Tevye in *Fiddler on the Roof* who complains, "Why me, Lord? Why didn't you choose someone else?") A beautiful example of this familiarity appears in today's text.

While Moses is parlaying with God on Sinai as interlocutor between heaven and earth, God points out the golden calf the people fashioned, their feasting and rising up to play—and it wasn't Bingo! Fired up, he tells Moses, "I'll zap them all and start over with you, and make you into a great nation." God could do that, of course, because that is what he did with Abraham, who was nearly a hundred years old. With consummate diplomacy Moses answered that the Egyptians would laugh and say, "We told you so! You Hebrews wanted the desert experience, and you sure got it!" Moses reminds God of his past promises, and the Lord relents. We can imagine the Second Person, not yet incarnate, observing the salvation history of the race from which he was to be born! So God "changed his mind"—which is an imprecise statement, because with his knowledge he makes every decision perfectly. But the Bible, of course, is written according to our perception of God.

Thus the fickle Hebrews were forged into the cohesive Jewish nation on the anvil of the Sinai with Moses as the hammer in the hand of God. He is the giant of the Jewish Bible, the major prophet, the principal lawgiver, the greatest leader, and the main intermediary with the Lord God! Moses' leadership ended before the entry into the Promised Land, but Jesus' kingship continues after his Ascension—forever. Moses was changeable; Jesus remains constant and the same.

Today's Gospel continues the text begun on Monday and correlates nicely with Moses' dialogue with God on Sinai. Jesus tells his adversaries that Moses himself will accuse them on doomsday, because they do not obey Moses just as their ancestors in the desert did not obey him but rebelled.

Although he did not need any witnesses, Jesus nevertheless calls upon several testimonials. John the Baptist testified to him. The works given him to do by his Father testify. The Scriptures testify. Moses testifies to Jesus in prophecy as the promise to come. Jesus could not be intimidated by being ostracized from the Temple. Even those who are not fearful of physical violence against themselves nevertheless fear social ostracism—to be thrown out of the neighborhood, off the bowling team, from the carpool, or out of work.

We tend to take our meaning from significant persons in our lives—friends, family, bosses. But as Jesus said today, he already had all those other testimonies in his favor, yet he was being rejected. This world accepts and applauds narcotized musicians, sex symbols, corrupt athletes, spurious movie stars, and self-serving politicians, and parades them as heroes and heroines.

But it does not forgive saints or even those who simply try to live decently, because such persons are a living accusation against the world. Like Jesus, they are called fanatics, pious fools, abnormal celibates, holier-than-thou hypocrites, and so forth. As a matter of fact, saints called themselves "fools for Christ." Unfortunately most of us are not good enough to be harassed for the sake of Christ.

Take heart, however. If you were in the midst of a universe of darkness, even a single match you struck could be discerned from a distance. So even a little goodness shines clearly in a universe of evil. Perhaps that is why the Church appears stronger in anti-religious, totalitarian and repressive countries than where the Church is "free." Never feel surprised by intolerance or hostility against you when you try to do the right. Be surprised when you don't get criticism, then start to wonder why! Nevertheless, the final blow to evil will occur when we believers, like Jesus, love the world which has not loved us!

Friday of the
Fourth Week of Lent

Wis 2:1, 12-22;
Jn 7:1-2, 10, 25-30

The first reading from the Book of Wisdom easily applies to Jesus. Evil persons plan to test a good person, whose conduct is a reproach to their sins. *"Let us beset the just one..."* they say. *"...he holds aloof from our paths as from things impure."* These words were fulfilled in Jesus. In fact, Wisdom was compiled probably less than a century before Jesus lived. Because it was written in Greek, the Jewish scholars did not consider it "canonical" or inspired. The book was written by men who made their claim to fame in being "friends of Solomon," who were writing in his memory and honor. With Solomon's famous name attached, the book was guaranteed both readership and preservation. Perhaps Wisdom was written too close to the time when the Jewish Council was establishing the "canon," or official list of inspired Old Testament texts, to allow them sufficient perspective. The Catholic Council of Trent in the sixteenth century, however, declared Wisdom inspired and authored by God through human writers.

In today's Gospel Jesus sneaks into Jerusalem for Succoth, the Feast of Booths, *"not openly but [as it were] in secret."* His enemies were careful not to say that Jesus was evil, because his actions would have belied their words. Instead—and this is an old ploy—they said Jesus was not "acceptable," not "appropriate" in his behavior, not "in conformity with traditions." Jesus upset their safe and comfortable and predictable behavior. They just wanted to offer a sacrifice for this or that favor from God, a sin-offering for some offense against God without their change of heart, a ritual purification for each legal impropriety—this was the legalistic approach of the Pharisees. This contractual mentality did not alter their behavior.

It is as if Jesus said, "I've got some good news and some bad news. First the bad news: repent, you sinners, and give up your adultery, cheating, lying and injustice. Now the good news: take heart; God forgives you. He sent me to be your Savior, the Messiah."

A significant problem we face as Christians is knowing when to speak out and when to be silent, especially about religious matters. To follow the lead of Jesus requires that we defend the truth and the honor of God without worrying about our good name nor seeking our personal advantage. Remember that Jesus remained silent before the accusations of the Sanhedrin and Pontius Pilate. He spoke up for the truth loudly and clearly throughout his public life, but when he knew his "time had come," and the cards were stacked against him, and his death was, humanly speaking, inevitable, he was silent.

It is a rare person who can live by this standard because we all have enough pride to defend ourselves—our ego, name, title, position. We are hesitant to speak out against pornography, abortion, and the problems that beset the poor and aged. Yet we all develop solidarity in guilt when we are silent in the face of prejudice, bigotry and hatred of those who are somehow different from us. The most difficult of all communications is self-disclosure, revealing our weakness and sinfulness. In this we might take our cue from recovering alcoholics!

Alcoholics have a constitutional sickness that changes their metabolism. Yet they often do not recognize, much less admit their own affliction. They deny; they protest; they accuse you of "witch hunting." But once the alcoholic accepts the bad news, he is ready for the good news, which is contained in the Alcoholics Anonymous Creed of twelve steps. (It is a moving document.) These points are exactly what our Lenten pilgrimage is about! In summary: your life has become unmanageable, but after self-scrutiny you turn to a higher Power, God, to save you. You admit all this to yourself, to God, then to another human being and ask for help. In humility you reconcile yourself with those you have alienated and seek the will of God in prayer. Having learned this, you try to teach others!

Saturday of the Fourth Week of Lent

Jer 11:18-20; Jn 7:40-53

As Lent heads for the climax of Good Friday and Easter, the voices of the Bible—the prophets and Jesus—grow more insistent, namely, that the Just One will suffer and die. Poor Jeremiah in his book-long rehearsal of grievances complains to the Lord that he is like an innocent lamb led to slaughter. He momentarily loses his "cool" and asks the Lord to wreak havoc on his enemies and let him see God's justice by revenge. Of course, the Church applies the figure of the lamb to Jesus himself, a figure which is derived both from Jeremiah and from Second Isaiah.

Today's Gospel is a series of short and snappy dialogues and questions about Jesus. Imagine that you are there. You would certainly remember all the details about this famous rabbi, Jesus. (Everyone old enough remembers where he was and what he was doing when John F. Kennedy was slain, when Pope John Paul II was shot in Rome, and when the first man was seen walking on the moon.) Think of yourself in Palestine.

Throughout the dialogues Jesus maintains his meekness, a quiet dignity. His own demeanor is the best argument in favor of the beatitudes. It is easy to mistake meekness for cowardice, for being a "wimp." It is the mandate of the beatitudes to be poor in spirit, which implies neither being nor appearing inferior. Actually, a superior person such as Jesus—who could have destroyed his enemies in a second but preferred to convert them, or at least give them a chance to convert, and who also remained meek and humble of heart—is all the more impressive because of his self-control.

John Henry Cardinal Newman once defined a "gentleman" as one who never hurts anyone, yet Jesus was often confronting and abrasive. However he was not sarcastic, nor did he try to humiliate anyone. The beatitudes, which are the "job description" and "hallmark" of the believer, say that the meek shall inherit the land. This could not have referred to this earth, because the meek and unaggressive often lose everything, like Jesus appeared to do! It must refer to the "new earth and the new heavens."

The controversy surrounding the origin and identity of Jesus mounts. The Jews argue that Bethlehem is to be the place of the Messiah's origin—they did not know the facts about Jesus—yet Jesus is always referred to as a Nazarene. The temple guards declined to obey the command to arrest him, because he was so different from all other rabbis and prophets of the Holy Land. Even so, as Nicodemus pointed out, the Pharisees wished to condemn him without a trial or hearing. They arrogantly put down the guards: "You don't see the Sanhedrin (their Supreme Court) or Pharisees (strict observers of the Law) taken in." Only the "lower classes," the rabble, the mob, those who are ignorant of the Law, accept him. Besides they are all Galileans from the wrong side of the theological tracks!

Looking at the Pharisees, we see that affluence is the first thing that gets you into trouble with Jesus. (Get rid of most of it before you die!) The next is book-learning and education that indicates intelligence, but not wisdom. Yet both money and schooling are good and necessary to survive in our society. The problem arises when you let these elements become blinders, so that you lose the broader vision, the whole picture of the meaning of life. Possessions and knowledge (which is a "possession" of the mind) should bring us closer to God.

The beatitudes are only a few lines long, but they have changed the spiritual perception of generations of believers, even when they do not put them into practice. The great spiritual truth is that the whole Sermon on the Mount, the evangelical counsels, and the works of mercy are not meant to be answers, but rather questions about the meaning of human life and behavior. Always the bottom-line question is the most important: "Who do you say that I am?" We do not ask this question; it is asked of us! This applies to everyone, but eminently to the Jews of that day, because of their tradition that no one would know the birthplace and origin of the Messiah, seeing that David's royal line perished during the Babylonian Exile. Of course, this tradition was also partly true. Jesus did come from David's stock, but he also had a mysterious origin, a divine origin as the Son of God. The southern Jews from around Jerusalem looked down on Nazareth, because in the time of Jesus it had only two hundred or three hundred citizens; it was just an unimportant way station of the Via Maris, the arterial road that led from Damascus in Syria and ancient Babylon across the desert into Palestine, the western edge of the Fertile Crescent. Galileans also spoke with an accent. A maidservant said, "Your speech betrays you," to St. Peter when he denied Christ.

The one question, "Who do you say that I am?" leads to the second, "What are you going to do about it?" Jesus asks us to commit ourselves to his kingdom and not be scandalized by the cross, as were the Jews who could not see how the "Anointed One" could suffer and die as a sign of triumph and delivery. Nor should we find our crosses to be stumbling blocks to our spiritual service. We live on faith, uncertain of the future, fearing everything from tomorrow's headlines and headaches to the end of the world! But Jesus reproves and comforts us at the same time. "You of little faith! Are you not worth more than the birds of the air and the flowers of the field?"

FIFTH WEEK OF LENT

Fifth Sunday of Lent, A

Ez 37:12-14;
Rom 8:8-11; Jn 11:1-45

Because the ancient Jews were not very clear nor unified in their theology about life after death and immortality, it was important for them to have a long, productive life here on earth. Many will tell you even today that they achieve immortality by living on through their children, their business, the worthy social projects for which they work. Through the prophets God gradually taught the Jews about personal sin, reward and punishment. About three hundred years before Christ, Daniel wrote, "Those asleep in the dust of the earth shall awake; some shall live forever, while others shall be an everlasting horror and disgrace." The Jews, however, did not consider Daniel an inspired book of their Bible.

In the Gospel today Jesus develops and confirms the teaching about the resurrection of the body; all shall rise on the last day, some to be saints forever in heaven, others as reprobates in hell. When Jesus tells Martha, *"I am the resurrection and the life,"* he is saying that he is the very cause of our rising. Later he added that heaven is an eternal union with God and a share in his divine life. St. Paul adds, "If Christ has not risen, then our faith is in vain!"

In the second reading, the Letter to the Church at Rome, St. Paul remarks, *"But you are not in the flesh."* Then where are we? How can he say that? Further he says that those who live by the flesh cannot please God. "Flesh" has several meanings in his letters. "Flesh" may refer to mere physical relationships, as nationality and family and spouses. Commonly "flesh" means earth-bound because of our creatureliness. Then we have no spiritual effectiveness, because we judge according to earthly values and human prudence, whereas we need faith and the Holy Spirit. So he continues in Chapter 12 of Romans, "Do not conform to the standards of this age." Today he comments, *"if Christ is in you, although the body [flesh] is dead because of sin, the spirit is alive because of righteousness."* It is natural, therefore, for St. Paul to use these terms in the mystical sense of the Body of Christ, the Church, with each member serving a specific function for the good of the whole. Most obviously, of course, "flesh" or "body" refers to sexuality. But in today's reading St. Paul refers to earthly thinking.

In a nutshell, the spirit of Christ is opposed to the prince of this world, the prince of death and darkness. In fact, the Holy Spirit, who raised Jesus from the dead, will raise us also to life. In this Gospel, however, Jesus invokes, not that Spirit (who had not yet come upon the Church at Pentecost), but his heavenly Father to raise Lazarus from the dead. The Spirit is the spiritualizing power of God, who enables us to love rather than fear God. That is why only in the Spirit can we call Jesus "the Lord"—which is the recognition of his divinity; and cry out lovingly to the Father, "Abba!"—which is the recognition of the tenderness of our filial relationship. By this intimacy perfect love casts out fear, and we see God no longer as the Scorekeeper of sin. In fact, sin quickly loses its attraction when God is our Abba, our dear Daddy, so to speak. The Holy Spirit is the Vicar of Christ in indi-

vidual souls, because Jesus promised to send the Paraclete, the Strengthener, to teach us to observe whatever
he has commanded us.

We are all unique, the sum total of all our background: our personality, education, family life, prayer
life, career, etc. So each of us needs individual spiritual
direction from the Spirit. So easily does sin dull the
conscience: Through repetition an action does not seem
so bad; or "everybody does it"; or "I don't feel it's
wrong." When we walk with the Spirit, the criterion for
action is not convenience, not opinion, not pleasure, but
the sense of pleasing God.

Looking at the Gospel, we note how delicately John
records what Lazarus' sisters say of him: "...*the one you
love is ill.*" Elsewhere in his Gospel the same evangelist
refers to himself as the "disciple whom Jesus loved." The
operative relationship is being loved by Jesus, "more
than that we love him." Then Jesus' grief shows that
mourning is natural, because some part of ourselves dies
with those whom we love—that is, the experiences we
once shared can never be recalled together, but only in
loneliness. So Jesus was grief-stricken.

Nevertheless Jesus dallied after the report of Lazarus' sickness, because he planned to resurrect this
well-known friend of his. This was, in fact, the immediate prelude to his own death and rising just a few days
later. Jesus used this occasion for his great teaching
about the resurrection from the dead. He extrapolates
from Martha's assertion about the general resurrection
on the last day to refer to himself, "the resurrection and
the life." There was a clear distinction between Lazarus
and himself. Lazarus rose to his same, dull, old life, but
Jesus—with whose rising ours will be analagous—rose to
a different, glorified, painless state with the faculties like
(and superior to) those of Adam and Eve in their original state. Therefore it is important to keep the whole

Paschal Mystery before our eyes: not only death, but also resurrection. This is our goal, this is our objective, this is our hope, this is our desire.

Fifth Sunday of Lent, B

Jer 31:31-34; Heb 5:7-9; Jn 12:20-33

Jeremiah, prophetical author of the first reading today, predicts that God will make a new covenant with his people, not written just on their minds—some intellectual agreement to be God's people—but inscribed on their hearts, an agreement which was later to be the New Covenant in Jesus' blood. The new agreement would captivate his people's hearts, just as the death of Jesus would be so compelling an event that we would be drawn to him! *"And when I am lifted up from the earth, I will draw everyone to myself."* To be productive we have to die, otherwise the "grain of wheat remains alone." When a seed germinates into new life, its old being corrupts and vanishes, so Jesus is warning us we have to die to our old selves to release the power of the Spirit within us. In fact, Jesus gives us his mandate: *"Where I am, there also will my servant be."*

Even though Jesus was predicting his death, he knew it would be his moment of triumph and delivery: *"Father, glorify your name."* Similarly, although Jesus told us he came that we might have life and have it to the full, yet he tells us to die. Even though only some are called to actual physical death as the martyrs, in order to be Jesus' disciple none can escape spiritual death: killing our pride, our manipulation of others, our attempt to remake others as we would like them to be, to control!

The process of dying to self is always in relationship to others. We accept others, despite their shortcomings. In fact, we stop trying to judge their shortcomings. This implies forgiveness when they fall short of what they might have been or should be. This is the way God treats us. He forgives whoever repents, but we are obliged to forgive even those who do not repent and seek our forgiveness. But the real issue is our relationship with God, not another human being. Hence we pray, "Forgive us as we forgive those who trespass against us." Jesus warns, "The measure with which you measure will be measured back to you." The dope addict, the drunk who falls into his own vomit, the unwed mother and father, the uppity snob, the popular sarcastic wit, the deadly bore— they are all forgiven by God; we can do no less. His enemies called Jesus a theological illiterate, not "graduated" from any rabbinical school, a hayseed from Galilee who talked with an accent, whose best friends were smelly fishermen, who ate with collaborators and ladies of easy virtue. He would have accepted his enemies as readily as those "unacceptable" new friends of his.

He had difficulty in teaching this death to self to his own disciples. They were ambitious, disbelieving, self-centered, cowardly. When one of them got closer to Jesus, the others were jealous, instead of rejoicing at the other's good fortune. They claimed that they could even drink from Jesus' cup of suffering; then they ran away in the fracas. Jesus told them to die to their own perceptions: "If you want to be great in my kingdom, then serve the others; obey their needs, not your own." The hierarchy obeys the needs of the faithful by teaching clearly and forcefully. Parents serve the needs of and "obey" their children by providing parameters of behavior. Spouses obey the needs of husband or wife by affirming them, compromising with them, and satisfying the sexual drives of the other, rather than merely seeking their own pleasure.

Pride not only is self-destructive, but destroys others by harsh words, rigidity, competitiveness and arrogance.

We are asked to break wrath with gentle words, stop demanding real or supposed "rights" from others, compete with no one, except with the self-concept with which God has inspired you. This is dying to self, becoming sensitive to others' suffering, sympathetic to their struggles and generous in their distress. Think of someone whom you have difficulty loving. Are you willing to humble yourself for reconciliation, take a risk of being rejected or even ridiculed? Jesus warns us not to "save" our life in a miserly way, but spend it, invest it in others, give it away, as he did.

During Lent it is helpful to make the Way of the Cross and ask yourself in what role your particular lifestyle would fit. Do you wash your hands of Jesus like Pilate? Do you at least show compassion, as did the Daughters of Jerusalem? Are you reluctant to help bear another's burden, like Simon of Cyrene? Do you take the risk of stepping out with courage, like Veronica, against the shouts of the crowd? She appears nowhere in the Gospels, only in tradition, but symbolizes everyone who acted on inspiration to be brave, who refused to join in the stares and derision of the crowd.

Jesus stumbled; his vision was clouded from his blood, sweat, and tears, and the spittle of the brutal soldiers. Veronica saw a task to be done—and did it, because it was the right thing to do. She interrupted her life to make room for another in need. Perhaps she heard the shouts of the crowd from within her home; perhaps she was out shopping when she saw the Man being dragged along with a rope around his neck like an animal. But God is never outdone in generosity; she was rewarded with the Face she had just wiped appearing on her veil as a testimonial of her action!

The lessons from the Way of the Cross move us to action. We wipe the face of Jesus in the poor family, the terminally ill in the hospital, the bag ladies and street people, the vagrant beggars and the AIDS victim. It is not easy to see Jesus in the mugger, the rapist, or the drug pusher, but it is the Lord who is asking to be forgiven and loved. Yet if we step forward in faith, Jesus will imprint his Face not on a perishable piece of cloth, but on our immortal souls!

Fifth Sunday of Lent, C

Is 43:16-21; Phil 3:8-14; Jn 8:1-11

Our contemporary society tries every gimmick to catch our attention. One of the most interesting kind of ads is for women's perfume or men's cologne. Bound into a magazine is the inevitable envelope for making an order, plus a blotter or heavy piece of paper that is impregnated with the essence of the proposed fragrance. Like much of life's allure, the odor disappears in a few days, but as long as it lasts it has a great power to attract.

Many things catch our attention: a honking horn, a crying baby, an unexpected joke, a gunshot. But nothing is so startling or stimulating as sex! It can sell anything but chastity. When there is an auto show, a food show, a boat show, even a print show, shapely models demonstrate and advertise it all, including themselves. Unfortunately they lose their personhood and become "objects" like the items they sell—beautiful objects, to be sure, to be gaped at and used till they wear out with age and the buyer wants a newer model.

In today's Gospel the adulteress was herself the advertisement, not for sex, but because of it. The Pharisees used her to attract attention, because Jerusalem was a small town at best. In a town of about 10,000 she would be well known as a sexual sinner. No doubt the ladies of Jerusalem were indignant at this blight on their fair sex, and they felt justified in using scurrilous words. The

men were pruriently gaping at her, probably not thinking pious thoughts, yet voicing their "shock" that such
a person lived in the Holy City. The children, of course,
were sent home. All this was taking place during the
holy season of Succoth. The Pharisees were "using" her
as an expendable pawn in their game against Jesus.
They made themselves a "kangaroo court," a lynching
party, vigilantes who may well have been some of her
customers. They were using her to test Jesus' actions. If
he let her go, he would have gone counter to the Law in
Deuteronomy. If Jesus stoned her or urged others to
stone her, he could have been reported to the Roman
authorities; only the Roman officials could condemn
anyone to death. Further he would have lost his reputation for forgiveness and compassion.

The Lord turned the tables on his adversaries. Following up on the Law of Moses, he pointed out that the
innocent accusers should cast the first stone (Deuteronomy 17:7). Whoever casts the first stone could fall into
jeopardy with the Roman authorities. Meanwhile Jesus
bent and "doodled" in the dust; he scratched some
words or figures on the ground as his penetrating gaze
read their sins. None of them was concerned about the
poor woman's embarrassment; they slowly left the circle
in retreat! Jesus once again acts in the Person of God,
forgives her sins, admonishes her not to sin again, but
does not condemn her.

With the promiscuity of our times people often think
that sexual sins between consenting adults are justifi-
able, especially if the liaison is a "trial marriage" of
persons who are "in love" before the more permanent
commitment of marriage. Others say that sex is just a
harmless way of relieving tension and pressure. On the
contrary, the meaning and purpose of sex is precisely the
sign of commitment in a deep emotional and religious
relationship. In fact, within the context of marriage, sex

is "sacramental" in the sense of producing grace for the husband and wife to help each other to reach heaven.

Jesus showed compassion for the "marginal" person, the adulteress, perhaps because he saw her interior struggle. Maybe she was habituated to sin; maybe she felt unloved by anyone and therefore without value and was, in a sense, punishing herself. Maybe she was poor and needed the money. Maybe she just stopped caring. Chastity is, however, one of the principal ways of dying to self and conforming to Christ. Chastity also indicates our rejection of the values of this world, which feeds itself on so much sexual material. Chastity is another way of repeating St. Paul's words in today's reading: *"For his sake I have accepted the loss of all things and I consider them so much rubbish, that I may gain Christ...."* St. Paul gave up whatever called attention to himself in the Jewish world: his prestigious position, his teaching assignment, his rabbinical post, his status as a prominent Pharisee, his income, his friends, perhaps a wife, everything.

Why did St. Paul make such a move? His experience on the road to Damascus would not necessarily have moved him to such efforts on behalf of Christianity. But he knew he had to be conformed to Christ in order to be totally effective. Each of us must ask ourselves what we have to give up—wealth, sexual excess, bitterness—to be conformed to Jesus, in order to rise with him on the last day.

Optional Mass for the Fifth Week of Lent

2 Kgs 4:18-21, 32-37;
Jn 11:1-45

Use the commentary on page 119 for Cycle A of the Fifth Sunday of Lent, which contains the Gospel for this optional Mass.

Monday of the Fifth Week of Lent

Dn 13:1-9, 15-17, 19-30, 33-62;
Jn 8:1-11

Daniel was a prophet, a spokesman for God, and a judge, a leader of Israel. Today's "short story" is about his wisdom in rescuing the chaste Susanna. This is one of the many "folk tales" told about Daniel in the last centuries before Christ. In fact, they are part of a collection found at the Qumran Monastery among the Dead Sea Scrolls. The two elders represent what was corrupt in the Jewish leadership; Susanna represents what was noble and beautiful. Her name means "lily," perhaps signifying her chastity. Daniel tricked the elders into condemning themselves: one testified to having seen the girl with her lover under the mastic tree; the other elder claimed it was an oak!

Susanna's story correlates with today's Gospel. Jesus and Daniel are parallel figures as judges and prophets, but the girls are not exactly the same, because Susanna was chaste, unlike the lady of the Gospel. We do not know exactly why Jesus was doodling on the ground. Maybe he was giving the accusers time to think. Perhaps he was writing their sins in the dust of the street—or at least so they feared. Maybe he was writing the text of the Jewish Law which required the witnesses to the adultery to cast the first stone. Yet how could they have witnessed the adultery if they were not present or somehow guilty?

Remember the bottom line: *"From now on do not sin anymore."* As Pope St. Gregory once wrote, "God promises forgiveness to those who repent, but not a tomorrow on which to repent." We are all vessels of clay, fragile and prone to sin. We all like the feel of "skin on skin"—from babies being fondled and kissed, to old folks who need to be held when they are lonely and frightened and confused. Our human touch is for healing and comfort, as was Jesus' touch. The pleasures of the "skin," so to speak, are reserved for marriage, but anyone can be a true healer by his or her embrace.

Some persons will claim it doesn't matter if you "sin" by impurity, whether alone or with others; after all, it is only "natural," and it doesn't hurt anybody. Well, it may be "natural" in the sense that it is "natural" to kill your enemies or anyone who stands in your way. But it is not "supernatural," which is God's expectation that you rise above nature. The final appeal of morality is to the will of God. Secondly, it does injure others, in fact, the whole body of Christ (which we are). When one member is ailing, the whole body is miserable and "sore." If the liver or kidney or foot or eye is unsound, the whole body is considered diseased and becomes ineffective. The bottom line remains: *From now on do not sin anymore.*

Tuesday of the Fifth Week of Lent

Num 21:4-9;
Jn 8:21-30

The parallelism between the two readings today was well designed by the liturgists. The spirit of complaint by the Jews on Exodus merited frequent chastisements by the Lord and just as frequent intercessions by Moses to lift the punishments. This passage shows them complaining about the manna. It was a free gift from God, requiring neither work nor payment, but in time it became boring to the palate. God sent them an infestation of vipers, which crawled into their tents and under their blankets. Some died and some got very sick, and they had no cure. The remedy was for Moses to make a bronze snake, attach it to a pole, and carry it among the sick. Upon seeing it, they would be cured. (This is the logo for physicians today!)

This text and the Gospel are appropriate for Lent just before Holy Week. Jesus on the cross is the fulfillment of the Old Testament figure or "type." When he is raised on the cross for sinful believers to look upon, they are healed by the therapy of the cross! In fact, the Lord says, *"When you lift up the Son of Man, then you will realize that I AM."* (Elsewhere the text reads, "When I am lifted up on the cross, I will draw all men to myself.") This was dangerous for Jesus to say. His "I AM" echoes the words on the mount from God to Moses. He thus made himself equal to his Father.

John the Evangelist is always the subtle theologian. Not only is today's text about the bronze serpent's ability to heal a figure of Christ, but it makes the crucifixion of Jesus the very moment of his divinity being manifested: *"When you lift up the Son of Man, then you will realize that I AM."* Once more we hear the echo of the "I AM WHO I AM." More and more throughout the Gospels does Jesus make reference to the unity between him and the Father. *"I say only what the Father taught me. The one who sent me is with me."* At the Last Supper, the night before he was lifted up, Jesus told his disciples that the Father and he are one.

Then Jesus prayed for them and for all of us who will believe in him until the end of time, and suggested implicitly that we shall share in the name, power and glory of Christ: "I pray for those who will believe in me through their (the apostles') words, that all may be one, as you, Father, are in me and I in you."

Wednesday of the
Fifth Week of Lent

Dn 3:14-20, 91-92, 95;
Jn 8:31-42

Today's story from the Book of Daniel is derived from a collection of folk tales associated with the Babylonian captivity into which the Jews were taken as exiles after the fall of the kingdom. The three Jewish lads were unwilling to adore the idol of Nebuchadnezzar. The fiery furnace is an "exaggerated" reference to the large idols with big bellies, into which persons, especially babies, were thrown as offerings. The three boys were saved without Daniel's direct help, however, by an angel, who is termed a "son of God." From having been the court favorites they had been slated for execution.

On the other hand, the attitude of the three young men was proper: God can save them if he chooses. If not, that will be fine, too. They were going to disobey the king, because it was the right thing to do! They were considered guilty of civil, not religious disobedience. (Subsequently the king legitimized the Jewish worship of God.)

Jesus makes no reference to the Book of Daniel in today's Gospel, so we must look for the link between the readings in another area. The Bible contains many such stories of civil disobedience, because religion and the state were inextricably joined. The ruler's religion was imposed upon all the citizens, supposedly to foster unity and unanimity within the kingdom. The Jews in Egypt were guilty of civil disobedience; they asked leave to go into the Sinai desert to worship their God. They revolted against their slavery and exploitation, then became refugees as well—which shows why the Bible is so meaningful to political dissidents today.

Jesus, too, was accused of such disobedience. The leaders of Judaism told Pilate that Jesus made himself a king in disobedience to Caesar. Further, he preached a criticism of Pharisaic restrictions and opposed their spiritual domination of the nation. He continued to teach after they forbade him. The motive was jealousy, but the accusation was disobedience to the Law of Moses and to the law of Rome!

Sometimes our religious convictions lead us to disobey the civil laws, as in the case of conscientious objection to war and opposing abortion clinics. We have also seen the rise of the "sanctuary" movement in our country, giving aid and shelter to political and religious refugees.

All this is not as black and white as it sounds. But we must be sensitive to the fact that Jesus opposed the Sanhedrin which accused him of insurrection and revolution, for which he was crucified as an enemy of the state!

One lesson some insurrectionists have not learned from Jesus is that violence begets violence and "those who take the sword shall perish by the sword." You cannot pick and choose what to believe in Jesus' teaching. We should remain politically active, but remember that true and lasting peace is a gift from God, and he is moved to give us this gift by our prayers.

Today's Gospel seems to "telescope" two events. At the beginning Jesus addresses "...those Jews who believed in him." Yet a few lines down he says, "I know that you are descendants of Abraham. But you are trying to kill me, because my word has no room among you." As the dialogue continues, it centers on the contrast between Judaism and Christianity. Jesus was not advising his fellow Jews to abandon Judaism, but rather to see the deep spirituality of their religion. It is necessary for faith to be expressed in the concrete regulations of religion and morality, but not so as to obscure a person's progress towards God.

Similarly there is considerable controversy today in the Church. Be wise in seeking always the more perfect, more spiritual of two possible actions when you have a choice—which is not found in doctrines themselves, but in living out the consequences of doctrine!

Thursday of the Fifth Week of Lent

Gn 17:3-9;
Jn 8:51-59

We return to Abraham in the Genesis story. His former name, "Abram" means the "Father-God is exalted," whereas "Abraham" means the "Father of many." Christians call him "Father in faith," as in the first Eucharistic Prayer. Thus Jews, Arabs and Christians look to him as their spiritual ancestor. Jews entered the covenant through circumcision for men and through marriage to a Jew for women. Christians enter the covenant through Baptism. St. Thomas Aquinas wrote that circumcision took away original sin for the Jews, although, of course, heaven was closed until the ascension of Jesus into heaven.

In the earliest rite of baptism both infants and adults were immersed in the baptismal water, as Jesus was by John the Baptist. Rather than a baptismal font, there was a baptismal pool, called a *piscina* in Latin. St. Paul called this being "buried with Christ" and rising out of the water to a new life in Christ, which was like Jesus rising from his tomb into glory. We reflect this concept somewhat in the present rite of baptism, but even more so in the beginning of the rite for funerals, when the body of the deceased is sprinkled with holy water, recalling the waters of baptism. Thus we begin and close our earthly spiritual life with analogous ceremonies.

The presiding priest greets the casket-bearers and mourners, and says, "All who were baptized into Christ were baptized into his death. By baptism into his death we were buried with him, so that just as Christ was raised from the dead by the glory of the Father, we too, might live a new life. For if we have been united with him by likeness to his death, so shall we be united with him by likeness to his resurrection." Then the ushers place the white pall over the casket to remind us of the baptismal gown of white which we wore or had placed on us at Baptism. In fact, in the early Church, the newly baptized wore a white garment from the Easter Vigil Baptism until the following Sunday, which was called *Dominica in Albis* or "Sunday in White."

With each newly baptized person Christianity starts over again, or, at least because of the new configuration of persons in the Church each Easter, the Church is new! Each person brings his or her own talents, graces and charisms to the Body of Christ. Just as Abraham, our father in faith, was repeatedly tested for many years, every believer is tested in what psychologists would call an "integrity crisis." We are led by the Holy Spirit to review our lives and discern whether we have kept our baptismal commitment, especially since our last renewal the previous Easter. As Lent is the time for preparation of candidates for Baptism, all Catholics should be preparing during Lent to renew their baptismal vows on Easter. This is, however, typically done without much preparation or connection with the Lenten season!

Being baptized, confirmed, emitting religious profession and receiving ordination are only "initiations," as the Church calls her restored rite for adult baptism. To carry out our resolves requires study and graces throughout our lives. For example, in virtually all public issues there is some moral dimension: 1) Politics—the positions of candidates for public office, military aid to

Third World nations, intervention in other smaller countries; 2) Medicine—abortion, euthanasia, organ transplants, gene splicing, *in vitro* fertilizations; 3) Conservation—exploitation of our resources, conspicuous consumption and waste; 4) Economics—trading with countries which exploit their citizens, selling nuclear technology, controlling of poor nations by multi-national corporations; 5) Entertainment—salaciousness and pornography in the media, erotic lyrics of rock-and-roll, the bad example of cult heroes, certain athletes, actors and musicians, etc.

Jesus told us to be the light of the world, the salt of the earth, the city set on a hill, the yeast that leavens the mass of flour. The Church is not a collection of buildings, but people. Under the leadership of those who think with the pope, the laity must supply most of the practical applications of moral teaching—in the halls of Congress, the theaters, the marketplace.

Friday of the Fifth Week of Lent

Jer 20:10-13; Jn 10:31-42

It has often been repeated that there is no evil which mankind will not cheerfully perform in the name of religion. There were the centuries of religious wars, not only the Crusades, but the spread of Islam and Communism (which is a religion without God!). Between Iran and Iraq, within Northern Ireland and between India and Pakistan hostility has had religious basis. Both the persecution of Jeremiah, whose prophetic statements nettled his fellow-religionists, and the harassment of Jesus by the Pharisees were done in the name of religion.

Jeremiah was no doubt a kindly and concerned prophet, but prone to complaining and lamenting. His fellow-citizens were after him for the unpopular predictions of woes to come upon them. False "prophets" told of favorable events to come. So Jeremiah laid some curses upon them. *"Let me witness the vengeance you take on them,"* he asks God!

Jesus had lamentations of his own as his enemies prepared his downfall. Jesus, too, made unpopular predictions. Although he preferred the conversion of his enemies, he predicted the dissolution of the Jewish nation, the fall of Jerusalem, and the destruction of one of the most beautiful buildings of antiquity, the Temple of Herod, called the "Second Temple." Yet he proclaimed that he came not to destroy the Law, but to fulfill it. He set aside the temporary and transitory rituals of Judaism, holocausts and sacrifices, kosher foods and customs. The Pharisees were the right-wing traditionalists, not always evil persons, but closed to Jesus' new ideas.

There is nothing inherently evil in being traditional and conservative either. Evil arises when there is the implication that "liberal" automatically means "bad." As long as either position is acceptably Catholic, both should be allowed to co-exist. After all, "Catholic" means "universal," or "embracing everyone who accepts the creed of Jesus in obedience to the pope." The Church becomes a stronger alloy when all the components fuse together, with each contributing his or her own strength. The Church is enriched by its many-flavored, many-splendored aspects and personal gifts, so as to complete the image of Christ in the world.

The Jewish conservatives shouted against Jesus: "Let his blood be on us and our children!" Punishment, however, belongs to God, not to us. Nevertheless Christians have used this quotation of the Pharisees to persecute and calumniate the Jews for two thousand years. But God never forgets his promise, and they remain the "apple of his eye." Perhaps the establishment of the State of Israel signals their being allowed to pursue their own destiny unmolested. Of course, Israel may continue to suffer God's judgment—because they do have a mission in history—if they do not accept the Arabs as their brothers.

Jewish rabbinical lore is filled with great wisdom; one parable compares human beings with the topography of Palestine. The significant feature is the Great Rift, which begins under Mount Hermon in the north and plunges below sea level at the Sea of Galilee, then further along the course of the Jordan to the lowest place on earth, the Dead Sea or Salt Sea. Of the two great inland seas one is filled with sweet, potable water, a source of life to fish, animals, plants and people. It drains out the south end into the Jordan River. This, in turn, empties into the Dead Sea, in which nothing lives and which continues to get saltier because it has no outlet. The rabbinical statement is: if we not only receive love, but pour it out again, we remain "sweet" and a source of life to others. But if we hoard the love we receive and give it no outlet, then it turns bitter and useless, like the Dead Sea.

Saturday of the Fifth Week of Lent

Ez 37:21-28;
Jn 11:45-57

In the first reading Ezekiel predicts the restoration of the Holy Land to the Jews. After Solomon's death, his son divided the country into the northern and southern kingdoms. Divided, they were no match for any invaders. After most were dispersed into exile, the remaining Jews developed in Galilee, where Jesus was raised; and Judea, where Jesus was born and where Jerusalem was the political and spiritual capital. Some rivalry always remained between the two entities. But Ezekiel's promise that a descendant of David would rule in the land of holiness with an everlasting sanctuary remained to be fulfilled in Jesus.

In today's Gospel the curtain comes down on the first act of Jesus' trial, passion and death. All the rancor, harassment and accusations came to focus in this scene, and we saw the true motives of Jesus' enemies emerge— not zeal for the religious principles of Judaism, but crass envy and jealousy. Their self-serving criticism of the Master laid in the worry that "the Romans will come and take away both our land and our nation." They wanted to remain in control and power.

What was ironic was that only thirty-six years later the Romans came and did destroy the sanctuary and the city and disperse the nation. Again, only sixty years after that, the Romans returned to quell an uprising (ending at the famed Masada) that led the conquerors to erect pagan temples with their abominations on the site of Jewish and Christian sanctuaries.

The supine hardness of the Pharisees' hearts lies also in their disbelief of Jesus' message right after he cured the man born blind (chapter 9) and raised the well-known Lazarus from the dead (chapter 11). They admitted the validity and power of these signs and wonders precisely because they said, *"What are we going to do? This man is performing many signs. If we leave him alone, all will believe in him."* They resented the popularity of Jesus, which he in any case never sought. Popularity is such a seductive mistress, as we see in the teenage and adult idols today. These are the wealthy, those who live "in the fast lane," entertainers and athletes. Often their lifestyle is publicly sinful, yet we overlook their sins because they are "successful" and "celebrities." They, in turn, feed their egos from their fan clubs and adulation. Jesus saw how fleeting such popularity would be: the same crowds who acclaimed him on Palm Sunday called for his execution a few days later.

Although Caiaphas, the high priest during the year Jesus died, was the Lord's enemy, he nevertheless spoke with the grace of his office when he said, *"...it is better for you that one man should die instead of the people, so that the whole nation may not perish."* Then John the Evangelist editorializes: *"...not only for the nation, but also to gather into one the dispersed children of God."*

The Gospel clearly states that a person with the grace of his or her office may be speaking for God when they are spokespersons of God in some official capacity. From every teaching, spiritual lecture and sermon, one may cull a treasury of graces—that is, those who submit their minds and hearts to the word of God on the lips of his servants.

HOLY WEEK

Passion Sunday
(Palm Sunday)
The Procession with Palms

(A) Mt 21:1-11;
(B) Mk 11:1-10 or Jn 12:12-16;
(C) Lk 19:28-40

Today's readings accompany a double liturgy: the re-enactment of the triumphal entry into Jerusalem, which was begun by the first Christians of that holy city, and the liturgy of the passion, which we both read and effect mystically during the sacrifice. This is truly the "Holy Week" in celebration of the death and rising of Jesus, as well as in hope of our own. In his suffering and death Jesus manifests his humanity; we acknowledge his divinity in his resurrection.

We must not think that we are simply commemorating the events of the past. In fact, the disciples have no spiritual advantage over us! Just as in the Mass the Last Supper is commemorated and Jesus' redemption is made present on the altar, the point of the Scriptures and paraliturgy of the procession is to make these events present to us again with their saving graces. The Church—to say it theologically—calls the assembly together to make Christ's redemptive actions effective again. When we are assembled, he is among us, as he promised when two or more are gathered in his name.

The people carry palms and sing Hosanna to play the role of the Jews proclaiming their Messiah, even while some of them are plotting his death. Every liturgy is a crosscut of human life, a bittersweet mixture of pain and joy, success and failure. Jesus rode into the city on an ass, that is, in a lowly and non-militaristic manner—which was ironic, because the Jews were hoping for a revolutionary leader of an anti-Roman uprising.

The procession with palms symbolizes the restless journey of us all to God's kingdom, which appears over and over in the Bible: Abraham sets out from Ur in Chaldea, then from Haran into Canaan; Moses leads the people out of Egypt towards the encounter with God at Sinai for the covenant. The prophets lead the captives out of Babylon. Jesus goes up to Jerusalem to die and fulfill his destiny. Later the apostles take the Good News all over the known world. The liturgical procession is a symbolic journey with Jesus. We are a pilgrim people with no permanent residence here. We should be a Church on-the-move, a missionary assembly seeking converts. Thus our citizenship is in heaven, to which we look for the glory of perfected love, the place of the Beatific Vision!

Throughout Holy Week we must confront the mystery that God has suffered, that he has somehow allowed the power of his divinity to be abrogated for a time, as we read in Philippians: "He did not cling to his divinity, but emptied himself, and took the form of a slave...." It is necessary for theologians to speculate on this mystery, but faithful believers should simply immerse themselves in the mystery of his suffering.

Jesus was aware of the messianic prophecies, so he was terrified at the prospect of suffering, as his bloody sweat in Gethsemane and his despair on the cross indicated. Because of his willingness to undergo the passion, his death assumes the cosmic meaning of the universe redeemed for the glory of God. If we are to build up the kingdom, then we, too, must share in that same willingness. We, too, are terrified, resentful of suffering, tempted to bargain for time and to delay our commitment to suffer. But if we look on him who was raised up on the cross in order to draw all things to himself, we shall see beyond the blood to the triumph.

Passion Sunday (Palm Sunday)
The Mass A, B, C

Is 50:4-7; Phil 2:6-11; The Passion of Our Lord Jesus Christ (A) Mt 26:14—27:66; (B) Mk 14:1—15:47; (C) Lk 22:14—23:56

Jesus not only lived in a time of violence, but he was also a victim of violence. The Romans were an army of occupation, by the strength of which the Jewish people were exploited and kept in subjection by King Herod and the Jewish leaders, so that the people were longing for a revolutionary leader; hence they lived with violence in their hearts and tried to make Jesus their messianic hero-warrior. No doubt this led to terrorism and riots, provoked by memories of the Maccabees and their successful guerilla war against Antiochus Epiphanes, heir to Alexander's empire. We could even make an argument for racism, Samaritans against Jews—the point of the Good Samaritan story. To all this we can add the evils of widespread poverty and slavery.

We see daily violence in the real world of the newscast, as well as make believe violence in movies and television. So we take it for granted: That is how it is. We settle for the routine of criminals escaping justice, homes being vandalized, ghettos being terrorized, concentration camps being filled with political dissidents, exploitative governments torturing, and all the other acts of dehumanizing violence. We are so desensitized to this ongoing hostility, that violence—especially verbal violence—is routine in many American homes: squabbles and putdowns, insults and sarcasm. Jesus endured the violence of his passion like a lamb led quietly to the slaughter in order to lead us to reverse the pattern of violence in the world and interrupt the cycle of hatred by his act of love.

Practically everybody who professes Christianity rejects violence in theory, "unless it becomes the only answer." Such acts of violence may be the "non-violent" civil disobedience of protesting civil-rights activists, burning draft cards, the Quakers' conscientious objection to military service; or violence may take the form of revolution, terrorism, guerrilla wars. Even St. Thomas Aquinas taught that assassination of a tyrant is justified as a last resort to gain freedom! Each believer holds that his or her brand of Christianity is correct! It is helpful, on a day when we read the passion of our Lord Jesus Christ, to reflect on how he handled torture and violence when he was condemned as a revolutionary and seditionist against Jewish religion and Roman rule.

In the first reading of Isaiah the Church puts these words prophetically into the mouth of Jesus: *"I gave my back to those who beat me..., my face I did not shield from buffets and spitting."* In the second reading from Philippians: *"He emptied himself, taking the form of a slave,...becoming obedient to death, even death on a cross."* He could have invoked armies of angels, but he said his kingdom was not of this world. He told Peter in Gethsemane, who tried to defend him by force, *"All who take the sword will perish by the sword."*

All Jesus desired was spiritual influence over people; he rejected power and authority, riches and fame. He fled from the Jews who tried to make him a king, a political messiah and a military strategist. He reprimanded the apostles who wanted to sit at his right and left hand, and said that the last shall be first. When John was angry that the Samaritan villages rejected the Gospel and wanted Jesus to bring down fire and brimstone to destroy them with violence, Jesus scolded him.

Jesus tried to win others by love and gentleness; his plan for the social ills of his day was personal change of heart and sharing of the goods each person possessed. Far from violence, Jesus calls those "blessed" who are the peacemakers, for they shall be called the children of God. Indeed, we are to turn the other cheek, walk the extra mile, and surrender both tunic and shirt.

Each Christian should examine himself or herself regularly on the violence in his or her life—whether viewing it as "entertainment" or using it oneself, as in bickering and argumentation in one's home, putting down others with suspicions and accusations, or demeaning them with insulting language. A person should counteract such tendencies by doing violence to oneself: prayer, discipline, fasting, patience in trial and suffering.

Monday of Holy Week

Is 42:1-7;
Jn 12:1-11

A few days before his immolation, Jesus was visiting the house of his wealthy friends, Lazarus, Mary and Martha. They lived in Bethany, on the other side of the Mount of Olives across from Jerusalem and the Garden of Gethsemane. As usual, Martha is described as busy with the chores of hospitality—only in this text Jesus does not chide her for being "busy about many things." The tender scene of Mary anointing the feet of Jesus is reported in the other Gospels, which shows that it has an importance beyond the scene itself. Jesus points out that this is a preparation for his imminent burial. The wicked character of the scurrilous Judas is revealed by his venal remark.

Some scholars think that this Mary of Bethany was the same as Mary Magdalene, or at least the adulteress woman whom Jesus saved from stoning. (We shall have to wait until heaven to separate all these ladies!) Matthew and Mark also record the scene with different details. The reading has its surprises. It was the lowliest of servants who washed the feet of guests when they reclined at table, not the hostess. Older women and women of quality always had their hair piled atop their heads, often in an elaborate hairdo, except when they were in mourning, when they were supposed to look disheveled and unkempt due to their grief. Even today in the *souk* or bazaar of Near Eastern countries one can buy the essence of flowers. We are familiar with the "attar of roses"—which takes hundreds of pounds of roses to extract just one ounce! Other popular essences from fertile Egypt are poppy, jasmine and lotus. Mary used nard as her perfumed ointment.

Mary did not care at all about the opinions of the other guests as she bathed Jesus' feet when he lay upon the couch at the dining table; all her affection was for the Master. When Mary poured out the aromatic nard with a prodigal hand, Judas complained it wasted three hundred pieces of silver, which was exactly ten times the value of his betrayal of Jesus a few days later! Jesus' response is that the poor are always there, whereas he would not always be so available. In any case, Mary was anointing his body for burial. As a matter of fact, if the Bethany Mary is the same as Mary Magdalene, she was the one who came early on Easter morning to embalm Jesus for burial and merited to be the first person reported in the Gospel to whom the resurrected Jesus appeared! (They had not had time two days earlier to bury Jesus properly because of the Jewish Passover and they had hurriedly placed him in the tomb of Joseph of Arimathea.)

Mary's action provides an important lesson to all of us: the significance of an emotionally tender attachment to Jesus. See how it led to her indifference to the opinion of others, how it triggered her generosity and service, how it signified her turning away from sin in repentance! In order to profit from participation in the liturgies of Holy Week (indeed, in all liturgies), it is helpful to approach them with the mindset that you are actually present physically, not just morally, or in "spirit" at the historical scene. You smell the nard filling the house. You catch the upward loving glance of Mary to Jesus. You overhear the murmuring of Jesus' enemies. Then you shout "Hosanna!" and—unfortunately— "Crucify him!" (This is why the Church provides for the participation of the congregation in the reading of the Passion.)

All these events in which we share are rehearsals for our own sufferings and for our own resurrection on the last day, when we will hear the Savior, who has gone before us, say, "Come, you blessed of my Father. Receive the kingdom prepared for you from the beginning."

Tuesday of Holy Week

Is 49:1-6;
Jn 13:21-33, 36-38

During these last days of Lent (as during the last days of Advent) we turn to Isaiah and his poetical predictions of the Messiah. The four Suffering Servant Songs appear from chapters 42 to 53. For the greatest effect they should be read in one sitting. Although they appear elsewhere during the liturgical year, the Church singles out these four Songs for Monday, Tuesday,

Wednesday and Good Friday of Holy Week. Although the Church uses these texts to make explicit the redemptive suffering of Jesus and his ultimate exultation—comparable to Philippians 2:6-11—nevertheless, some scholars claim that the four Songs refer globally to all of Israel being called to suffer and to serve humanity, especially because it was thought when "Second" or "Later" Isaiah was written, the Messiah was long overdue!

For the convenience of this reflection let us highlight the four Suffering Servant Songs of Isaiah. (The parenthetical sections are added commentary.)

Chapter 42

vs. 1. *"Here is my servant...upon whom I have put my spirit"* (who descended upon Jesus when he was baptized in the Jordan).

vs. 3. *"A bruised reed he shall not break, and a smoldering wick he shall not quench"* (but he tries to heal the spiritually sick).

vs. 6. *"I formed you, and set you as a covenant of the people"* (the New Testament in his blood).

vss. 6 and 7. *"A light for the nations"* ("I am the light of the world"), *"to open the eyes of the blind, to bring out prisoners from confinement"* (which are signs of the Messianic Age).

vs. 8. *"I am the Lord, this is my name."* ("You will surely die in your sins unless you come to believe I AM.")

Chapter 49

vs. 1. *"The Lord called me from birth, from my mother's womb he gave me my name."* ("He shall be called Emmanuel, a name which means 'God is with us.'")

vs. 4. *"My reward is with the Lord, my recompense is with my God."* ("He who gives me glory is the Father, the very one you claim for your God.")

vs. 5. *"For now the Lord has spoken who formed me as his servant from the womb."* ("You shall conceive and bear a son and give him the name of Jesus.")

vs. 6. *"I will make you a light to the nations, that my salvation may reach to the ends of the earth."* ("A revealing light to the Gentiles, the glory of your people Israel.")

vs. 7. *"When kings see you, they shall stand up, and princes shall prostrate themselves."* ("At Jesus' name every knee must bend in the heavens, and on the earth, and under the earth.")

Chapter 50

vs. 6. *"I gave my back to those who beat me, my cheeks to those who plucked my beard; my face I did not shield from buffets and spitting"* (during the passion and torment of Jesus by the soldiers).

Chapter 53

vss. 2 and 3. *"There was in him no stately bearing to make us look at him, nor appearance that would attract us to him. He was spurned and avoided by men, a man of suffering, accustomed to infirmity, one of those from whom men hide their faces, spurned, and we held him in no esteem"* (scourged, spat upon, crowned with thorns, mocked for a fool in a royal robe, dragged to the scaffold with a rope around his neck).

vs. 4. *"Yet it was our infirmities that he bore, our sufferings that he endured."* (He became sin for us.)

vs. 5. *"But he was pierced for our offenses, crushed for our sins, upon him was the chastisement that makes us whole, by his stripes we were healed."* ("Once I am lifted up from the earth, I will draw all things to myself.")

vs. 6. *"We had all gone astray like sheep, each following his own way."* ("I am the good shepherd. I know mine and mine know me. They heed my voice.")

vs. 7. *"Like a lamb led to the slaughter or a sheep before the shearers, he was silent and opened not his mouth."* ("Behold the Lamb of God!")

vs. 10. *"If he gives his life as an offering for sin, he shall see his descendants in a long life, and the will of the Lord shall be accomplished through him"* (and his disciples throughout the ages).

Wednesday of Holy Week

Is 50:4-9; Mt 26:14-25

The Church interrupts her reading of St. John's Gospel in favor of a text from St. Matthew, who provides another account of Judas' betrayal. The formerly Catholic Church of England frequently gave a title to special days or seasons of the liturgy. Lent was said to last from Ash Wednesday to Spy Wednesday. Today is Spy Wednesday because Judas agreed with the Sanhedrin in today's reading to spy on Jesus to find a time when he would be vulnerable and able to be taken captive.

Judas was possibly the most talented of the apostles, a non-Galilean and so perhaps less attached to the Nazarene and his comrades from the north country. He was probably the most efficient in administration, because he was the treasurer of the band, although one might imagine that Matthew-Levi, the tax-collector, might have served equally well. The Gospels refer to him as a liar and a cheat, stealing from the common purse. Thus one can conclude that he was ambitious and anxious to see Jesus rise to military power, so that he might be swept upward with Jesus!

Judas left before the consecration of the Lord's Body and Blood and before the words, "Do this in memory of me," which were the words of the apostles' priestly ordination. Hence he was neither ordained nor did he receive Holy Communion (but he was the first to leave Mass early!). He appears not to have repented but to have committed suicide, so it seems he lost his soul, although no Church official would presume to assign him a place in hell!

The Gospels of Holy Week are part of the Last Supper narrative, but only the final part of John's Gospel is used for the Supper of the Lord on Holy Thursday. With the stage set for his betrayal, the passion of Christ is beginning. Mary, too, enters her own mournful passion. Both chapter 8 of Vatican II's *Lumen Gentium* and Pope John Paul II's encyclical about our Lady, *Mother of the Redeemer*, mention that Mary had to say another "Yes," as at the Annunciation, to the death of Jesus on the cross. She was required to relinquish her maternal rights over Jesus to become the mother of us all. Incidentally, she probably was present at the Last Supper, because during the Passover the entire family was assembled to share in the meal. As Mother of the High Priest, she offered the sacrifice of her Son. In her "priesthood" she did not say, "This is my Body...my Blood," because she cooperated in his original Incarnation in her womb. The Council of Trent proclaimed that the flesh we adore and receive in the Eucharist is the same flesh born of the Virgin Mary! Therefore, she is a part of every Holy Mass. We call her "blessed among women" even when we pray the sorrowful mysteries of the Rosary, because she understood her key role in the necessary drama of redemption. It was Mary's faith and obedience that enabled her to find meaning in her suffering.

It is by illness that we appreciate health, so it is in suffering that we best understand happiness, especially eternal happiness. Nothing better prepares us for heaven than sorrow. Why? Because we are emptied of ourselves by every wound to our hearts —to make room for God—and that is the essential concept of heaven:

becoming empty of the "self" of sin and being filled with God, the Beatific Vision. Pray for this kind of faith and obedience today. As St. Paul wrote, "I consider the sufferings of this present time not worthy to be compared with the glory which shall be revealed in us."

EASTER TRIDUUM

Holy Thursday, Mass of the Lord's Supper, A, B, C

Ex 12:1-8,11-14;
1 Cor 11:23-26;
Jn 13:1-15

The liturgy of Holy Thursday carries many powerful messages to believers. The washing of the feet by the celebrant (as Jesus did) leads us to understand that we are to serve each other. Particularly those in authority, such as bosses, bishops and parents, are to interpret their authority as service, but without surrendering the right and duty to command!

The procession indicates, as on Palm Sunday, that we are on the move. But today adds another dimension. Like the Jews on the Exodus, who carried the Ark of the Covenant with them and daily set up the Holy of Holies in the tent of the Lord, in today's procession we take our God—or rather he takes us—to establish his eternal covenant, his eternal kingdom. We demonstrate our trust by following....

We first close our ranks, that is, defend truth against the alien world, a hostile world—not claiming our superiority just because we alone have the fullness of truth, but rather showing the world symbolically that you cannot be part of the march "when the saints go marchin' in" without loyalty to Christ. Our vision and goal is resurrection—otherwise we would be foolish and deluded, as St. Paul warns us. What is the link between the Eucharist and the resurrection? In the Eucharist we discover the real live Jesus Christ, gloriously seated at the right hand of the Father. The Eucharist is not the Baby Jesus, not the suffering Jesus, but Jesus as he is now, reigning on high. Our adoration through the night testifies to our belief!

With the promise of our own glory, all meanings of life are changed: there is a future life; hope has eternal fulfillment! Jesus has set our world into the final trajectory of its history; we may be entering the final orbits around the sun as we know it. Jesus is LORD to the glory of God the Father, and we are proud to join the procession behind him. All human endeavors and achievements should be penetrated by that one factor and theme: Jesus died for us to share his divine life with us by our own resurrection! Yet how little he is known, loved and adored!

God's purpose will not be thwarted. The kingdom is coming upon us, and we cannot reverse its direction. The Church may be locally destroyed, as it occurred in past centuries, but the Church survives governments and persecutions. Jesus guaranteed, "I am with you all days." The Eucharist is the pledge not only of future glory, but also of his immediate presence. Non-believers may think us crazy to be carrying wafers of bread in golden cups, ringing bells, smoking up the church with incense, singing in a parade, but they do not understand that we are a stream of saints passing through salvation history!

Of course, we must remember that Jesus is present in many ways among us, even if his appearance is obscure. He is in the Christian who lives a moral life, in the words of the Bible, and wherever two or more are gathered in his name. When you look for the Jesus who dwells in those to whom you are ministering in some way, remember to be aware of the Jesus who dwells in you. In this passing world only you can bring a lasting meaning. This is the work not only of priests and religious, but also of the laity—to take the words of salvation into shopping malls, the workplace, businesses, the university and laboratories.

You must be eager to talk about your faith to others, to act justly, to defend the rights of the abused, to pay your debts, to respect the law. In countless ways you can carry Jesus into the world, just as surely as we carry him in the procession. You can interpret the spiritual meaning of the world, both its hardships and its beauties, as in marriage, business and technology. There is a mystery of holiness locked up inside the world, waiting to be released. As priests offer and consecrate, you must offer and consecrate the secular world's pursuits. Teach others that something is missing without God; that this world has no blueprint for eternal happiness.

Even the Sacred Host is transitory. It passes away when Christ is received or when the appearance of bread corrupts and ceases to be. The Eucharist does not even belong to the endtime; in heaven we shall see face-to-face him whom we see now only veiled in the Eucharist.

Good Friday,
The Passion of the Lord, A, B, C

Is 52:13—53:12; Heb 4:14-16; 5:7-9
The Passion of our Lord Jesus Christ
Jn 18:1—19:42

Punishments for capital crimes in the ancient Roman Empire were designed to terrify as well as punish and execute! Those who were condemned to the galleys were chained to their benches. There were frequent wars and shipwrecks, so the slaves had the incentive to obey and row with all their might, lest they go down with their ships in defeat. They were exposed to the elements and were mercilessly beaten to keep up the pace. Their life expectancy on board the galley was two years. Many Christians were condemned to the galleys and were martyred in this way for their faith.

The Roman Empire received much of its wealth from mining, primitive though it was by our standards—lead, tin, silver, copper and iron. Some prisoners never saw the light of day once they went underground. They were driven by cruel taskmasters, who knew there would always be other stronger men to replace the worn out slaves! It was back-breaking work with rotten food, poisonous gases and cave-ins to cause sickness, injury and death. Life underground was even shorter than on the galleys. To prevent even the attempt to escape, often the prisoners condemned to death in the mines—the sentence was "condemned to the metals"—were blinded in one eye and hamstrung behind the opposite knee, so that in that state of imbalance they would be helpless.

Being stoned to death was not a Roman mode of execution, but Jewish. Decapitation or beheading by the sword was reserved for Roman citizens, because it was swift and relatively painless. As a Roman citizen of Tarsus, St. Paul was beheaded in Rome outside the city walls at Tre Fontane. Nevertheless the worst execution was crucifixion. It was the most degrading and the most humiliating; the victim was totally naked and became the butt of the jokes and mockery of the passersby. It was likewise the most inhumane and could last several days, depending on the physical condition of the malefactor. In the case of Jesus he had already lost much blood and was weak from the torments by the Syrian cohort of the Roman army. After the Servile War against Rome—an uprising of slaves in Italy before the birth of Christ—the victorious Roman army crucified over 100,000 defeated slaves, lining the Appian way to the south.

Subsequently, when the Empire was Christianized, crucifixion was outlawed as a means of capital punishment. Over the centuries the horror of the cross was lost, until nowadays one sees the cross of Jesus worn as pendants, earrings and highly ornamented pieces of jewelry. It is correct, of course, to wear it as a symbol of faith and a protection against evil. But just as we would not walk into a funeral chapel and exclaim, "Oh what a beautiful corpse!" so the cross was never meant to be an adornment nor a pretty sight! That first Good Friday 2000 years ago was the funeral of Jesus, the dissolution of his human life.

It is actually a marvel and a spiritual wonder that we celebrate the death and funeral, even re-enact them, two millenia later with a Good Friday commemoration. This is the triumph of the cross by which we received our salvation from the law, sin and death. When there is little comfort for those who suffer anguish and physical pain, at least there is the ennobling aspect that they can somehow share in the redemptive suffering of Jesus. They must embed themselves into the passion of Jesus. In our dehumanized world it seems that everyone is an alien, a stranger, an anonymous outsider. So many are condemned to death in various ways—by drugs and alcohol, by sexual excesses, diseases, and natural disasters, by hunger, by poverty, homelessness. We do not celebrate their different kinds of death, nor do many of them know how to embed themselves into the suffering of Jesus. In fact, the very name of Jesus is not even known to at least half the population of the world!

Let us try to harness the love and forgiveness of Jesus towards those who bring death unnecessarily upon themselves and others. We in turn must look beyond this world and forgive it for not providing the healing of which it is incapable.

Easter Season

Easter Vigil,
The Resurrection
of the Lord,
Holy Saturday Evening,
A, B, C

Gn 1:1—2:2; Gn 22:1-18;
Ex 14:15—15:1; Is 54:5-14;
Is 55:1-11; Bar 3:9-15, 32—4:4;
Ez 36:16-28; Rom 6:3-11;
(A) Mt 28:1-10; (B) Mk 16:1-8;
(C) Lk 24:1-12

Holy Saturday is a quiet pool of rest between Friday and Sunday. It provides a bridge of meditation as the Lord sleeps in his tomb. The many readings that precede the resurrection Gospel of the Easter Vigil rehearse salvation history. God made the world good, and despite mankind's sins, he promises to cherish and preserve the covenant with his people. His Word is the guarantee of his everlasting mercy and love. The waters through which the Israelites passed on the Exodus are recalled by Ezechiel's mention of cleansing water and St. Paul's comparison of baptismal water to the tomb from which Christ rose. These readings form the final catechesis of those who have been preparing for Baptism on this sacred night.

St. Paul reminded us that Jesus was like us in all things but sin. The Letter to the Hebrews declares that in Jesus we have a high priest "who was tempted in every way we are, yet never sinned." Today's reading subtly shows us the link between Good Friday and Easter Sunday. The quiet beginning of the Jewish Testament texts suggests that we are keeping watch at the grave of Jesus while he "descended into hell" (the only available word for "limbo" at that time) to bring the news of his triumphant death to the patriarchs and prophets, who, denied entry into heaven, were awaiting their redemption with all the other good persons who died before the crucifixion. Can you imagine the holy conversations and exultation, the relief and hope and praise of God? Although his body was lifeless in the tomb, Jesus' created soul as well as his uncreated divinity, the two natures of Christ, were joined in this announcement in the netherworld.

The passion and rising of the Lord form a single mystery, the Paschal Mystery—and it goes beyond the resurrection; we are awaiting the return of the Master. The acclamations of the four Eucharistic Prayers are perfect summaries of this mystery: "Christ has died, Christ has risen, Christ will come again." "Dying, you destroyed our death; rising, you restored our life; Lord Jesus, come in glory." "When we eat this bread and drink this cup, we proclaim your death, Lord Jesus, until you come again." "Lord, by your cross and resurrection you have set us free; you are the Savior of the world." These phrases suggest that at the crack of doom, on the Day of the Lord, all things will be settled, and what we have perceived only in the signs of the Sacrament will be eternally achieved and understood!

Without the resurrection of Jesus and the sending of the Holy Spirit, the Paschal Mystery would have been lopsided, unfulfilled. We, the Mystical Body of Christ, are the continuation of that mystery. The Holy Spirit is the soul of that body; the body itself is Jesus' risen body—or rather his whole Person—extended through us who believe in him. Each person plays his or her proper role. In the human body, only the eye sees, but it watches out for the whole body. The kidneys eliminate wastes that would poison the whole body. The hand works to feed the stomach, but the whole body is nourished. So St. Paul clearly argued.

You must never say that you have no talents to use for the kingdom of Jesus. Every member who was born of the Paschal Mystery, rising from the waters of Baptism as Jesus from his tomb, can at least love and thus attract others to Jesus. The weeping women of Jerusalem on the Way of the Cross did not help Jesus actively by wiping his face, carrying the cross with him, nor lifting him when he fell. All they offered was compassion and their presence in his agony. But that was all they had, so they served him well. Love gives meaning to all the other activities of the Mystical Body.

Jesus died once for all on the cross, but the blood and water from his side still flow today. His blood signifies redemption, to which is subjoined all human suffering that is united to his, filling up what was wanting to the chalice of Christ. The water signifies life, which Jesus gives us through his Church and the sacraments, the means of encountering him in life-sustaining ways.

Jesus' humanity is no longer confined by space and time, although the Church-on-earth, the militant Mystical Body, is confined to a spatial and temporal ambience. Our own resurrection will allow us to escape this confinement. Scientists today are trying to find what they call a "gut feeling," that is, a Grand Unified Theory, which encompasses all the activities in the universe. They want a general formula that explains the whole cosmos, including gravity, atomic structure, curvature of space, light, and so on. The only formula possible (which they reject as being non-measurable) is God's eternal *now*: everything is concurrent, simultaneous in God's view. Heaven is the real world and measuring stick of created being. Eternity is the norm, but scientists cannot get that "gut feeling" until they themselves resurrect into glory with Christ!

Easter Sunday, A, B, C

Acts 10:34, 37-43; Col 3:1-4 or 1 Cor 5:6-8; Jn 20:1-9

We stress so much the fact that Jesus did not return to the same life he had had before the resurrection, that we may be tempted to think that his "new" body was a substitute for the one laid in the tomb after the crucifixion. No, it was the same body, but with a different kind of life. That may prompt the question, "Then how can we resurrect to glory if our bodies dissolve into the earth, or if our ashes are strewn over the earth and become part of other life organisms, or if we drown at sea and our bodies are eaten by sharks, and so forth?"

Perhaps this is more a subject for a philosophical lecture than a reflection on the Scriptures, but so many persons ask just such questions, that it may be helpful to provide some light, to the degree that we are able when we enter mystery!

All through our lives our faculties of intellect conceive ideas, based on the data received through our bodily senses. Therefore the soul develops a relationship to matter, particularly the material substance of the body. Even though the body is said to completely change as often as every two years and certainly within every five to seven years, ideas persist beyond any time restriction and stay "in" the soul's faculties for life. Our memory alerts us that we are the same persons we always have been. Hence it seems that we are not necessarily bound to a particular configuration of molecules of matter.

When you read all the resurrection stories, you will note that nowhere is the actual event of the resurrection described! This is the most important miracle, event and sign of Jesus' life, yet there is no eyewitness account. But we base our most profound faith on it, as well as our own hope for resurrection! We can turn only to the "encounters" of those who saw him in the flesh after his death. We do not use the words, "apparition" or "experience," of Jesus; these words bespeak a personal and subjective event, and possibly a figment of the imagination. We base our faith on the witness of those who spoke and ate with Christ during the forty days of Easter. Their testimony generates our certainty. Yet we cannot forget that St. Paul points out that Jesus could be seen only by those who believed in him. Although we depend on post-resurrection stories by eyewitnesses, it is faith in Jesus that is paramount! The grace to look for the resurrected Christ implies that he himself has already found us and graced us to have faith in him and await his return in glory.

Christ's demands upon us, consequent upon his own death for our sake, are so immense, that only the resurrection can seal our faith-commitment. St. Paul wrote that if Jesus has not risen, all our hope is in vain, and we are the most miserable, the most seduced of persons! Without the resurrection, in fact, there is no Christianity. Even if the soul were to remain immortal (as it is), without our bodies rejoining our separated souls, we would not be truly human, just ghosts or shades wandering the eternal shores.

The one reaction to the resurrection that is not spelled out, yet would have been very interesting, is that of the Temple guards who had been posted to watch the tomb. The wily Sanhedrin remembered that Jesus predicted he would rise from the dead and did not want his disciples to steal the body and make such a claim. It must have been a wearisome forty hours, when suddenly the stone rolled back in its trench and Jesus "blasted off" from his tomb. Actually his spiritualized body could have simply walked through the huge disk of stone. Yet because the guards ran away in terror, we know they had some unusual experience! They came the closest to being eyewitnesses, except because they were not believers, they could not have seen Jesus anyway!

One of the proofs that scholars adduce for the veracity of the Gospels is the seeming contradictions about even this most important of events in Jesus' life. It is helpful to read all the resurrection stories to discover the incongruities and variations—never of the basic truth, but of the details. (Probably most of these can be reconciled.) Just one example might suffice. Matthew has two Mary's come to the tomb as the day was dawning; only then an earthquake signals the descent of an angel to roll back the stone, while the guards are still present. Mark places two Mary's and Salome at the tomb right after sunrise, with the stone already rolled back and no mention of the guards. Luke simply mentions the women coming at dawn, with no guards and the stone rolled back. Matthew and Mark have a single angel present to tell the good news and instruct the women; Luke has two of them.

John, who wrote much later than the Synoptics, has Mary Magdalene come alone while it was still dark. The stone is rolled away, no one is in sight, not even the helpful angel, so she runs off to inform the apostles. The point is that the evangelists would have gotten just one story straight if they were contriving the resurrection to deceive the world, lest these discrepancies generate disbelief of the entire event later—as they actually did in this last century!

What is necessary to remember about Jesus' resurrection is not the scholarly details, although they are important for our knowledge. We need to remember rather what is important for our motivation. Our true life does not have to wait for our death to begin. Jesus told his contemporaries, "The kingdom of God is within you." Our genuine spiritual life begins with Baptism, even if we are unknowing infants. After that, as we mature, we continually ask the Lord to enter our lives to conquer sin and death. The resurrection of Jesus permits this conquest, first of death-dealing sin in this life and then the eternal death of hell in the next. In Matthew 22 Jesus says that the heavenly Father "is the God of the living, not of the dead."

OCTAVE OF EASTER

Monday of the
Octave of Easter

Acts 2:14, 22-32;
Mt 28:8-15

There can be no real "proof" of Jesus' resurrection in the sense that our contemporary world expects it. The rising of Jesus from the dead cannot be measured, calibrated or quantified. No one was standing next to the bier of Jesus inside the tomb when his body trembled, sat up, and was transformed into spiritualized matter. Nevertheless the eyewitness testimony of the Gospels remains true and relevant. As modern medical science has it, the "blood and water" flowing from his side after being pierced by the soldier's lance showed he was clinically dead. Three days later he was seen by small and large groups who had believed in him during his pre-resurrection life.

The apostles and women who claimed to have seen Jesus alive would have gained a temporary "justification," but they would obviously have imperiled their salvation eternally if they had lied. Nor would they subsequently have undergone harassment by Jewish and Roman officials, torture and even death for a lie—and we recall all the apostles except John were martyred!

So we look first for an empty tomb. Because of his spiritualized body, which later passed through the locked doors of the Upper Room, he did not need the stone rolled back. It was pushed aside not to permit Jesus' exit, but to facilitate the entry of the early morning visitors, so they could report that Jesus was gone. They did not realize the implication of the empty tomb, because the angel had to instruct them why the body of Jesus was absent. None of them apparently remembered or understood Jesus' own predictions about rising. He had told them that only the "sign of Jonah" would be given them, that is, that the Son of Man would be only three days in the grave, as Jonah had been in the belly of the fish. When Peter and John ran to check out the news, they, too, were ignorant as we read in John: "As yet they did not understand the scripture that Jesus had to rise from the dead." The same attitude was reflected by the disciples on the way to Emmaus.

We read in today's Gospel that Jesus' rising was challenged from the beginning by bribing the soldiers guarding the tomb to lie. This also implied their dereliction of duty, for having allowed the supposed theft of Jesus' body. Matthew's Gospel was written about the time when converts to Christianity from Judaism were being thrown out of the Palestinian synagogues as "heretics."

Later on, even up until our own time when Catholic "theologians" deny the resurrection of Christ, the Gospel record has been challenged. Early on, during the first and second centuries after Christ, the Gnostic Christians, the "lunatic fringe" of those days, denied that Jesus revitalized his earthly body, because, they held, the material world is evil; hence Jesus must have reappeared as a disembodied spirit or ghost. This heresy, which deprives us of the true meaning of the resurrection both of Jesus and of ourselves, recurs from time to time. We, however, echo St. Paul, "If Jesus didn't rise from the dead, then we are the biggest fools of all time; what we believe is rubbish, and we are the victims of a massive sting. But if Jesus has risen from the dead, then HALLELUJAH! We are on a roll, the luckiest people in the world!" That's not exactly a direct quotation, but it is a realistic translation of the meaning.

Tuesday of the Octave of Easter

Acts 2:36-41;
Jn 20:11-18

The Church reads from the Acts of the Apostles for all seven weeks of Eastertide. When St. Luke completed his narrative of the physical life of Christ, he turned his attention to the "spiritual" life of Christ or the Mystical Body of Christ, which is another name for the Church. As Jesus himself grew in wisdom and age and grace before God and men, so the Church multiplied its membership, reflected on itself, and developed along creative lines.

At first the Jerusalem community was the whole Church. The Master himself was sent primarily to the house of Israel and only thereafter to the Gentiles. The early believing community continued to worship on the Sabbath in the synagogues and to follow Jewish practices, such as circumcision, holidays, kosher foods and Temple worship, as we read in chapter two of Acts. About thirty-five years after the resurrection, considering the Christians as heretics to Judaism, the Jewish authorities banned them from the synagogues. The Gospels were written from that time onward with the idea of reassuring the converts that they were, indeed, the proper heirs of Judaism. Meanwhile the Gentiles were attracted to this new faith and religion. At first the misguided Jewish Christians, whether out of conviction or chauvinism, expected the Gentiles to conform to the precepts of Judaism. In this affair St. Paul was the primary advocate of the freedom of the Gentiles; it became a point of "bitter strife" among the apostles. Looking at all this historically, we probably cannot conceive the pain and alienation this altercation caused right at the inception of Christianity. We remember how the post-Vatican II Church was divided over much less significant issues!

In addition, Jesus was not concerned with establishing structures for his assembly of believers. He sent the Holy Spirit to instruct the community how to proceed. Jesus rather gave us the criteria by which we were to judge all structures: authority is for service, the greatest shall be least, do not lord it over one another, etc. In several texts of Acts the writer records the kerygma of the first community; this is the essential message about Jesus: He was a true human being, born of David's stock, and he died. As Messiah he was the Savior of all mankind. As the one who rose from the dead he was also God, the full revelation of God upon earth. He sent the Divine Spirit to teach us how to observe what he taught. This simple message required preachers, rather than administrators, although the latter are mentioned among many other charisms or gifts of the Spirit to the Church. Even though the early Church was grouped into parishes (Thessalonica, Corinth, Rome, Ephesus, etc.), the situation was fluid. The laity emerged according to their personal inspiration as teachers, catechists, pastors, deacons of service, presbyters or priests, deaconesses, preachers, administrators, ministers to the sick or imprisoned or poor, supporters of widows and orphans, caretakers of hospitality for travelers and visitors to the parish, lectors, acolytes, exorcists, and so forth.

In the twentieth-century Church we are trying to recover this concept. It was probably never absent from the Church throughout its history, just as radical commitment to "religious life" always existed from the beginning (virgins, monks, hermits, anchorites, stylites, penitents and widows as a special class, etc.). Early on, however, the hierarchy took over the organization of these works of charity and leadership. Now the laity are encouraged to discover for themselves their own inner inspiration, much as in the early days. Naturally, true believers would not wish to divorce themselves from the spiritual direction of the Church, yet the "Spirit blows where it wills."

Personal gifts or charisms are discovered in prayer and openness to the Holy Spirit who builds up the Body of Christ by these means. Here nature joins with grace, and self-analysis joins spiritual direction to clarify each person's possible contribution. I remember one genuinely pious, humble lady who thought she would not be of much use in "building up" the Church in any visible, much less spectacular way, but felt she was exceedingly competent to scrub floors. This she made her gift to elderly disabled men and women living in poverty and helplessness!

Wednesday of the Octave of Easter

Acts 3:1-10;
Lk 24:13-35

The Emmaus Gospel is one of the most beautiful and deeply theological passages of St. Luke's Gospel and an important post-resurrection story. This village is only about ten miles from Jerusalem, a good day's walk from the capital. (The text reads "seven miles" on foot, but the bus route is understandably longer.) The church, built on the site of Jesus' encounter with the two disciples, is flanked by an ancient Roman road where the meeting undoubtedly took place, and it is a spiritually rewarding experience to walk over the same paving blocks where the Master set foot on that Easter resurrection Sunday over 1900 years ago. The foundations of long-gone stone houses are likewise visible, but the town today is mostly Moslem, Palestinian Arabs of whom only a handful are Catholic.

Four villages have claimed to be the modern location of Emmaus, but El Qubeibeh today, as described above, seems to best fit the Gospel description and tradition. It was late afternoon, so the village could not have been too distant from Jerusalem. As the hour was growing late, the two disciples asked Jesus to tarry with them and take supper.

Clopas was a disciple of Jesus, and he was headed for his home in Emmaus. His home today, that is, its foundations, are enclosed within a Catholic church. The outline of his house forms the left aisle, and the probable area in which the three sat down to eat is marked by a small altar. It is a marvelous altar at which to celebrate or participate in Mass, where Jesus himself was *"made known to them in the breaking of the bread! "*

The record of the disbelief of Clopas and his partner, variously thought to be either Simeon or James or even John (although one suspects that John would have been with our Lady), is for our sake, too. Even after the report of the women who found the tomb empty, they could not figure things out, that the Lord had to suffer and so enter into his glory. Their doubt is recorded for our sake!

Thus Jesus gave a homily, which means he explained the Scriptures to them, from Moses through the prophets to his own life. Then he had a characteristic way of handling bread, blessing and breaking and giving it to others. So they recognized him in this action. Only then, when their faith was restored, were they able to recognize the Lord.

We, too, cannot fathom the resurrection, the miracle of Jesus' transformed life, without sufficient faith. We therefore look to Emmaus as a source for our belief. The

Lord ate food, which shows his continuity in the same body, yet he who died was alive again. His sudden appearance and disappearance testifies to his newly empowered humanity! We also recognize Jesus in the breaking of the bread—not only in this text from the Bible, but also whenever we encounter him in the Eucharist. This is the risen Lord who sits at the right hand of the Father. In the Holy Scriptures we likewise encounter him as the Word spoken eternally by the Father and repeated in his human nature as the full revelation of the Godhead. To the disciples Jesus was making a self-disclosure; to us he does no less!

We learn finally that we must walk with the Lord, invite him into our lives, ask him to linger with us, because at any given moment *"the day is almost over."* We must sup with him at his Eucharistic banquet, listen to his intimate self-revelations—that is, study his presence in salvation history through the Bible—and recount what has happened on the road of our lives!

Thursday of the Octave of Easter

Acts 3:11-26;
Lk 24:35-48

The readings this week from the Acts clearly feature St. Peter emerging as the spokesman for the Twelve. One cannot help but notice the transformation of the chief apostle after his post-resurrection encounters with the Master. He had first drawn his sword to defend Jesus in Gethsemane, perhaps confident that Jesus could once more effect an escape from his captors. But seeing that the Lord did not defend himself, he fled in panic and later that night even denied that he ever knew him! The Easter Gospel from St. John recorded that both Peter and John ran to see the empty tomb, but only John is mentioned as believing. On the shores of the Sea of Galilee

Jesus had to ask Peter three times, "Do you love me?" Peter's track record was fairly dismal!

But the Acts show him as a vigorous exponent of Christ and his messianic message. In the early chapters of Acts Peter preaches fearlessly, heals in the name of Jesus, scolds his fellow Jews for rejecting Jesus, and even confronts the spiritual leaders of the nation for being so obtuse. The Church militant reveals its strength and determination to become, indeed, militant!

In today's text, reflecting the first self-concept of the primitive believing community, St. Peter appeals to a "Jewish" God: *"The God of Abraham, [the God] of Isaac, and [the God] of Jacob, the God of our ancestors...."* As the Lord himself originally said, they were sent first to the house of Israel, hence Peter emphasizes the Lord as the Messiah. A final statement of Peter, *"...Jesus, whom heaven must receive until the times of universal restoration of which God spoke through the mouth of his holy prophet from of old,"* has led to a vague, but constant impression that the Chosen People will not permanently frustrate the designs of God, but convert to Jesus before the end of the world! *"You are the children of the prophets, and of the covenant...."* Over the centuries the Gentiles have ignored this passage and have not welcomed the Jewish people as their potential brothers and sisters, but have typically harassed them. The Gentiles have rather remembered the words spoken during Jesus' passion, "His blood be upon us and our children!" That is exactly the point: the blood of Jesus was shed for all peoples and surely for those who were the "apple of his eye" and the object of God's special providence through the ages. Can we forget that Jesus, his parents, apostles, disciples, and the first believing community were all Jewish? Clearly Christians should follow the lead of the popes in recent times and strive to heal the division and cement better relationships. One may, of course, disagree with

Israeli politics—many Israelis disagree with the policies of their own government, but anti-Semitism is immoral, sinful, reprehensible.

The personal lesson from viewing the transformed St. Peter is that we must be patient with ourselves and others whose transformation is still in progress. God is the most patient of all: he accepts us where we are as long as we have good will (there's the catch!), then invites us and directs us to where we ought to be. In the journey of life we all suffer from ambivalence and wavering commitment to the Lord. He continually pursues us to ask, "Do you love me?"

Jesus once said that God causes the rain to fall and the sun to shine on both the just and the wicked—and waits for everyone to become just. God, like the sun, always has time to do everything well. The sun consumes itself (of course, the comparison with God fails here!) as it provides light and warmth and holds the solar system in proper orbit around itself. Yet, as Galileo observed in a kind of holy wonder, the sun ripens every bunch of grapes in the world as if it had nothing else to do. Our transformation will be complete when we attend to the important events and values of our lives without underestimating the importance and value of the little things and persons in our lives.

Friday of the Octave of Easter

Acts 4:1-12;
Jn 21:1-14

If the disciples were slow to understand and interpret the prophecies concerning the Messiah, what can we say about the Jewish leaders? They imprisoned the apostles for doing good and preaching, then insulted them, *"By what power or by what name have you done this?"* One of the strongest statements concerning Jesus outside the Gospels themselves is *"There is no salvation through anyone else, nor is there any other name under heaven given to the human race by which we are to be saved."* We ought to be grateful that we are Catholics, because in the Church are found the full meaning of that sacred Name, the full self-disclosure of God in Christ, and the complete complex of truths to instruct us.

Let us turn to the Gospel for today. A literary device of playwrights is going a full circle and completing the drama where it began. For example, in "The Man Who Came to Dinner," the protagonist slips on the door stoop of the house to which he was invited to dinner, necessitating his remaining for several weeks until he is able to walk. During this time he makes himself utterly obnoxious to the household. As he is leaving, he slips again in the same place. Suggesting a repeat of the same hilarious events of the past several weeks, the writer brings his play to its end.

Analogously, Jesus' public ministry ends where it began, in Galilee, probably with no artifice intended by the evangelist. Jesus began in Nazareth, performed his first miracle in Cana of Galilee, and made Capernaum his northern base of operations. We can be sure, however, that the Holy Spirit, principal author of the Bible, did not intend to be theatrical! If you read the preceding chapter 20 of St. John, you will readily see that the Gospel concludes there; Chapter 21 is an "appendix" by an editor as an afterthought, compiled from recollections of the community. The very vocabulary betrays this fact. The opening line refers to the "Sea of Tiberias," the Roman name given to the Sea of Galilee, or Lake Gennesareth (*Kinnereth* today in Hebrew). Nowhere else in the Gospels is this title used, but it indicates the Latinizing influence after the conquest by Titus and Vespasian, and later Hadrian.

There was no cogent reason for the disciples to return to Galilee, inasmuch as the other appearances were all in Jerusalem, except for the command of the Lord who told the women at the tomb that his "brothers" (a new title) should go back north to Galilee. Saint Gregory the Great points out that it was not evil for them to return to the tasks they followed before being called by the Master. In any case, they had to support themselves, and fishing was their trade. When Jesus appeared on shore and told them to cast their nets off the starboard side, he may have been using no special divine power, because sometimes one can see a shoal of fish more easily from shore. The great catch is, of course, a subtle allusion to their future effectiveness as fishers of men and the abundance of the kingdom.

Even today a reef leads out of the water on to the shore, where a Catholic chapel is built to commemorate this event. The reef was a natural place to moor a boat, empty the catch, dry the nets, than walk dryshod to land. In one of the natural depressions, Jesus made a fire to cook the brunch. Hence the place is called *Mensa Domini*, "The Lord's Table"! The number of fish, 153, hides some obscure mystery about which commentators disagree. An ancient ichthyologist figured out that there are exactly 153 kinds of fish in that sea; he thought, therefore, that the totality of mankind is to be included in the kingdom: No one should be excluded from Peter's net.

We should study and cherish these appearances of Jesus; they are God's "special effects," to use a Hollywood term. They point out the powers of Jesus' divinized humanity and what we may expect when we rise to glory. All this is only the "frosting on the cake." Our essential glory will be the Beatific Vision and the community of the elect, to which may God lead us all!

Saturday of the Octave of Easter

Acts 4:13-21;
Mk 16:9-15

In the first reading from Acts today the Church continues the narrative of how the power of Jesus emanates from his apostles, and how they who were fearful and rebellious before the resurrection went forward courageously to proclaim the Lord. In retrospect one wonders why Jesus did not appear on the Temple Mount and show himself to the people, letting them see his wounded hands and feet and side, so that they might believe.

Yet the reason is clear. You first believe and accept Jesus and only then you understand. Once again: Faith leads to understanding; understanding something intellectually does not require faith, God's free gift, which is not given to all. Only if you believe that Jesus died, then rose, can you understand. As in Jesus' public ministry of three years, as you recall, he downplayed his miracles and often said: Do not broadcast my signs and wonders, but accept me; then my teachings and everything else will fall into place! So the nascent Church followed his lead. The apostles were explicitly witnesses to his death and resurrection—this is the essential concept of "apostle"—but they emphasized what the Master had taught them.

In today's Gospel the same theme appears: Jesus upbraids the Eleven (Judas, of course, was absent) for not believing his appearances to Mary Magdalene and the two disciples at Emmaus. They refused the testimony of eyewitnesses until they, too, saw with their own eyes and touched with their own hands. Jesus indulged their weakness (as God did with the Jews in the Jewish Testament) for the sake of their imminent ministry, to proclaim the Good News to the world.

The last Chapter of St. Mark is the scholar's baili-wick. The high point of his Gospel occurs on Calvary when the centurion cries out, "Truly this was the Son of God!" But no doubt Mark was pressed by the early Christians to add some material about the resurrection, or else subsequent editors added their own conclusions. In fact, Mark's Gospel actually has four separate endings in the New American Bible! (It is helpful to read the footnotes under the texts!)

Chapter 16 begins with a detailed account of the women who had looked for Jesus in his tomb with Mary Magdalene, but ends, "Because of their great fear, they said nothing to anyone." Then with an apparent change of heart the text repeats the story, but says Mary Magdalene *went and told his companions...*." Then the text continues with the ascension.

Next follows the so-called "shorter ending," just one verse of two sentences—which is a backward glance! The women tell St. Peter's enclave the whole story! Finally there is the "Freer Logion." (Logion simply means "the phrase" or "words"; freer derives from the fact that the original of this fourth-century text is conserved in the Freer Art Gallery, Washington, D.C.)

Each of these conclusions adds details to the skimpy text of Mark and reflects the beliefs and memories of early Christians. The point is that we need scholars and theologians and the authority of the Church to sort this all out. Other Christians have no authority to guide their thinking. But the bottom line is simply this: Believe the eyewitnesses and become "heartwitnesses" to the whole world that "Christ has died; Christ has risen; Christ will come again in glory to judge the world."

SECOND WEEK OF EASTER

Second Sunday
of Easter, A

Acts 2:42-47;
1 Pt 1:3-9; Jn 20:19-31

Today's Gospel is so important and so filled with theological implications that the Church reads St. John's text for all 3 cycles of A, B, and C. But the first and second readings change for each year. Acts 2 is a "classical" passage that describes the lifestyle of the Jerusalem community and allows us to stand in the wings to glimpse what might be termed the "radical response" of believers to the message of Jesus. Incidentally, this same passage describes the essence of religious institutes in the Church.

The community studied the apostolic teaching; lived a communal life; shared the Eucharist *("...the breaking of the bread...the prayers");* shared their property and goods according to every member's needs; participated in the Temple liturgy each day; and ate their meals in common. This is manifestly the life of a religious order without specific reference to any particular charism. It bespeaks a kind of ideal Christian existence, not only the foundation of religious life. It is the springtime of the Church!

This lyricism is developed in the second reading from the First Letter of Peter. One can readily see that the first half of the text is a poem, probably an early baptismal hymn. (This may indicate that a proper theologian must have the instincts of a poet, and good poetry is profoundly theological!) The neophyte receives a merciful birth unto hope from Jesus' resurrection, and this inheritance is imperishable! The writer says so beautifully, *"Although you have not seen him you love him,"* which may indicate that the Letter was composed after the time when there were living memories of the Lord.

Jesus also said that they are blessed who have not seen, yet believe—a great comfort to us who are separated by time and space from his earthly physical life and for whom so many biblical concepts are separated from our experience. It has not even entered our minds to consider what God has prepared for us in heaven. Yet we do try to speculate and satisfy our wonder. As it has been said, a mystery is not something about which we know nothing, but something about which we can never know everything. Yet we do know a lot about the Trinity, grace, the Mystical Body, the Eucharist, even heaven.

It is appropriate to think of our own coming resurrected glory during Eastertide, when Jesus' resurrection becomes the down payment on our future! The resurrection texts show the Lord free of suffering, moving with the speed of his thought, passing through solids, and so forth. Of course, the vision of God is the essential concept of heaven and mostly an impenetrable mystery. Often we imagine ourselves staring fixedly at God, our intellectual functions unproductive and passive. Yet Jesus enjoyed the Beatific Vision—this is the common teaching of theologians—as he grew up, worked at manual labor, preached and died. After his rising he returned to some of those functions to demonstrate his continuity with the body that had died; he ate food and discussed his kingdom with his followers. Thus he showed he was fully human, even if not enclosed within space and time capsules.

After the Day of the Lord and the General Judgment we shall not just sit on "Cloud 9" or on a crystal throne with sundry musical instruments, nor sing the "Halle-lujah Chorus" in multiple voices. "We look for a new heaven and a new earth according to his promise." Many other biblical texts suggest that the physical universe it-self will be somehow transformed at the crack of doom. In the same chapter of 2 Peter we read, "The heavens will pass away with violence. Earth and its works will be burned up." This may be simply a metaphor of the judgment itself.

As the Infancy Narratives of Matthew and Luke are in themselves a summary of Jesus' life, so the post-resurrection stories are similarly an encapsulation of Jesus' life and message. The kerygma is his fulfillment of all the prophecies of death and resurrection, repen-tance leading to glory, the apostolic commission to preach this Good News to the whole world and to for-give sins (as in today's Gospel), and everlasting life for those who believe in him. John closes this passage by commenting that these events "...*are written that you may [come to] believe that Jesus is the Messiah, the Son of God, and that through this belief you may have life in his name.*"

No doubt we have had our difficulties like St. Tho-mas and have wanted to put our fingers to the nail holes and to the wound in Jesus' side and hear his comforting words directly. Each of us has stumbled in our faith and commitment. We all have failed to pray with full trust and confidence, and have been negligent in sharing our faith with others. God is more aware than we are of our failures, yet he desires our salvation more than we desire it for ourselves—and this is our title to confidence: "No one who comes to me will I ever reject."

Second Sunday
of Easter, B

*Acts 4:32-35; 1 Jn
5:1-6; Jn 20:19-31*

St. John the Evangelist is surely a frustrating author. At the very end of his Gospel (not quoted today) he wrote, "Many other things Jesus said and did, which, if they were recorded, I think not all the books of the world could contain." He tantalizes us but doesn't add a single fact, not even in the one long and two short letters attributed to him. Today's text says, *"Now Jesus did many other signs in the presence of [his] disciples that are not written in this book."* How we hunger to know more about the Lord! How our hearts would burn within us if we had just a few more facts, precious details about the Master. The Gospels, however, are not full biographies, but they narrate exactly what God intended and what we need for our salvation.

The point is that it was time for Jesus to disappear physically from this earth, so only a few post-resurrection encounters are recorded on paper, those burned into the memory of the closest disciples. We can be sure that Jesus had many such encounters with that person closest to him, the one who had been the perfect disciple for thirty-four years, his mother Mary. Jesus, her spiritual director, prepared her to be the Mistress of the Apostles, as he had been their Master, and the Mother of the Mystical Body, or "Mother of the Church" in the words of Vatican Council II. In meditation one can fantasize what their dialogue may have been!

But the disciples had to let go of him, no longer clinging to his physical presence, but relying on his mystical presence, as he suggested to Mary Magdalene on the day of resurrection, when she came to the tomb seeking his physical person. Now that person had to "decrease" and his Mystical Body increase throughout the world through faith. The task of the primitive believing community was to evangelize, as the Acts of the Apostles narrates. The Spirit of Truth testified through them that Jesus came through "water and blood," as in the second reading. The water refers to Baptism, by which believers are "added" to Christ; the blood refers to his passion and death, by which our sins have been washed away.

Today's Gospel brings us back to Easter Sunday; in fact, this day is the octave of Easter, which is itself a week long celebration of the resurrection. Several appearances of Jesus are recorded on this day: to Mary Magdalene, to the disciples on the way to Emmaus, to the apostles in the upper room behind locked doors, as we read today. The opening of today's Gospel says, *"On the evening of that first day of the week...."* The passage is distinguished by two events. Absent was Thomas the Doubter, who wanted living proof that the wounded Christ was alive. The second event is Jesus' establishment of the Sacrament of Penance, or Reconciliation. I have had many discussions with Protestants about this text. They readily admit that the apostles had the power and the authority from Jesus to forgive and bind sins, but, they claim, there is no evidence that Jesus intended that power to be passed on through the centuries.

The Church replies that what the Lord said and did applies to all times; the Bible was written for our instruction. Jesus obviously intended his own activities and the apostles' activities to be the wellspring for us today, the model of the past and future Church. Above all, if there was need to forgive sins in the first century of Christianity, when the memory of Jesus was clearest and most compelling, how much more would such forgiveness be necessary in subsequent times, when fervor would cool and the living memory of Jesus would fade!

So Jesus tells us as he told them, *"As the Father has sent me, so I send you."* We, too, have received the commission to be ambassadors of Christ, as St. Paul says, and vehicles of the Good News about Christ. It is the task of every age to revive the memory of the Lord, to increase fervor, and to keep returning to the springtime of the Church!

It was the resurrection of Jesus, coupled with the descent of the Holy Spirit, that made the disciples "hustle" for the Lord and work against the currents and values of the world. Someone has compared our spiritual lives (in a kind of modern parable) to taking one's automobile to a carwash, symbol of the world's antireligious activity. Your car is chained in place and drawn into the vortex of the "world." You put your motor (life) into neutral and sit there, locked in and totally passive (not resisting the world), while your vehicle is being flooded (like your spiritual life) with the tides of this age. You can't see anything (being spiritually blinded) through the windows. The moral lesson is to refuse to be hooked on this world and dragged into a situation where everything is whitewashed, so it looks clean and attractive. Don't let your motor idle in neutral passivity, so that you lose control, and can't see through the windows of your soul! In other words, this world seduces us by the disguise of beauty and goodness and desirable pleasure.

But it is possible to resist this whitewash. In the second reading St. John writes, *"...whoever is begotten by God conquers the world. And the victory that conquers the world is our faith."*

Second Sunday
of Easter, C

Acts 5:12-16;
Rev 1:9-11, 12-13,
17-19; Jn 20:19-31

The doctrine of the Holy Trinity is the central dogma of Christianity, but the fact of the resurrection is the most personally relevant of Christian mysteries. The resurrection concerns the nature of our humanity forever, life after death, our hope of future glory. One way of explaining the central service of the Church, its principal mission, is to keep the world aware of God's plan to share his divine life with us who are his heirs through the resurrected power of Jesus. This requires of us a high level of morality and activity to show that faith has indeed changed us into different persons. We see the apostles in today's reading from Acts attending to that mission by teaching and healing in the manner and power of the Master.

"They were all together in Solomon's portico," reads the Acts today. This was the pillared arcade that ran around the large plaza in front and to the side of Herod's Temple. Herod had enlarged the space available to worshipers, and the "porch" named in honor of the builder of the First Temple, Solomon, protected the pedestrians from rain and the rays of the hot Judean sun.

The Book of Revelation, which we used to call the Apocalypse, which means "uncovering," provides the second reading. The resurrected Jesus identifies himself and promises to give the writer a series of visions, which were to refer to that century and to the endtime of the world. *"I am the first and the last, the one who lives. Once I was dead, but now I am alive forever and ever."* This impressive statement in the final book of the Christian Testament reinforces the centrality of resurrection.

The Sundays of Easter provide the eyewitness accounts of the Lord's appearances. Once more the theme emerges: believe so you will understand. This was a medieval slogan, popularized by St. Anselm of Canterbury: *Credo ut intellegam*, "I believe in order to understand." So Jesus told Thomas (about us), *"Blessed are those who have not seen and have believed."* John himself, you remember, was the first of the apostles to believe; he alone of the Eleven did not flee from the cross on Calvary. Perhaps his love of Jesus, which marks his discipleship, gave him the edge of faith over the others.

Why did Jesus consider faith more important than some objectively reached "proof"? A proof could be contrived; after all, the Sanhedrin accused the disciples of that very thing! A "proof" could have been called a trick of mass hysteria, a "ghost" or an impersonator! Other religions contain stories of resurrection, too. But Christianity is different: First of all, Jesus did not rise to the same life, which would end in the same ultimate death anyway. He rose to a new kind of life, as these appearances indicate. Secondly, the Master promises that we shall share in his transformed life. This second difference, unlike the first, can be based only on faith, for the endtime has not arrived!

After the resurrection, to the titles of Son of Man and Messiah, the Christians added, "Lord," which was attributed only to God in the Jewish Bible. This was not clear until Pentecost and the descent of the Spirit. Saint Paul points out in the First Letter to the Church at Corinth, "No one can say 'Jesus is Lord' except by the Holy Spirit." In Philippians 2 we read, "At Jesus' name every tongue must proclaim, to the glory of God the Father: Jesus Christ is Lord." This is faith from the divine standpoint: Belief is God's free gift, initiated by the Divine Spirit.

A remarkable passage from the Second Letter to the Church at Corinth reads, "For our sakes God made him who did not know sin to be sin, so that in him we might become the very holiness of God." Jesus did not "take on" our sins, but our sinfulness; he was penetrated by all sins from Adam to the last moment of the world. That is why he had to be crushed, beaten down, completely destroyed in death. Our sin is "emptied out" in his kenosis in order for us to become God's holiness. That is why his resurrected body had to also be transformed and glorified—in contradistinction to his total infirmity. How God will effect this change in us poor mortals is God's business; what we do during our transitory life to be worthy of this gift of eternal life is our business. When the Book of Genesis states at the beginning that men and women are made in the "image and likeness" of God, the immediate conclusion is that this text refers to our spiritual soul and its faculties. Yet another insight is that this text refers prophetically to our godly status at the end of time, when we shall become in the flesh the very holiness of God! Mankind will then truly be "supermen"! The victory over death and sin will be complete. Even though Jesus released us from bondage to the Old Law with its complex regulations, he left us with the harder mandate to have love, mercy and forgiveness. Meanwhile, when we are asked the reasons for our faith, we should have our answers ready.

Monday of the Second Week of Easter

Acts 4:23-31;
Jn 3:1-8

The first reading from Acts is obviously the continuation of the Pentecost event. They were gathered together in prayer, as on Pentecost, and the room shook and trembled, which was a very charismatic manifestation! We, too, must join in prayer with others of like mind, or "in the same boat," to receive the help of

God—pro-life groups, families in trouble, a parish trying to pay off a huge debt, an institution with a special need.

The disciples who met after the release of Sts. Peter and John from jail prayed in the classical biblical way: praise of God for his wonderful works in the past and a plea to continue his benefactions. The "raging Gentiles" to their mind included not only the foreigners, such as Pilate the Roman and Herod the Idumean, but also the Jews who crucified Jesus and harassed the apostles due to their (Jewish) "alien" mind and "pagan" mentality of resisting the message. Then the group asked for reassurance of their mission by healings, signs and wonders in the name of Jesus!

The text shows that from the very beginning the Church needed rejuvenation regularly, so the leaders could speak God's word with confidence. The Church must continually update its activities, guided by sure tradition and authenticated inspiration of the Holy Spirit.

The Gospel makes the same concept explicit. When Jesus speaks to and requires rebirth of Nicodemus, he does not mean a return to his mother's womb, as Nicodemus objected. Here we enter a theological mystery. The Sacraments of Initiation which the Church confers at Eastertime are Baptism and Confirmation. This is the probable meaning of "water and the Holy Spirit." Catholic theology, moreover, clearly asserts that the Holy Spirit is given to us in every sacrament. At Holy Saturday's Vigil Service candidates are both baptized and confirmed by the celebrant.

We can also read into Jesus' dialogue with Nicodemus a subtle reference to our Lady! Whereas we do not re-enter our mother's womb for rebirth in Baptism, nevertheless Baptism likens us to Jesus by the power of the Holy Spirit, our principal spiritual director, who acts through his spouse, Mary Immaculate! She, as the Mediatrix of all graces (not that it had to be so, but God willed it so), does "bear" us mystically as she bore Jesus physically. Adequate catechesis of baptismal candidates must include the awareness of Mary's role in their spiritual lives!

Jesus compares the Holy Spirit in today's Gospel with the wind. You cannot see the wind, but you can see the effects and evidence of the passage of the wind in the movement of clouds, the bending of trees, the rippling of ponds, and the massive waves of the sea. In the same way we "test the Spirit" to discern whether divine effects exist in the life of those who claim some special ministry from the Spirit. Is such a person charitable, generous, zealous, helpful, prayerful, faithful to authority? "By their fruits," Jesus remarked, "you will know them." St. Paul enumerates these "fruits of the Holy Spirit" in the Epistle to the Galatians, and the Master underscored the principal motive, "By this shall all know that you are my disciples, that you have love for one another."

Tuesday of the Second Week of Easter

Acts 4:32-37;
Jn 3:7-15

Most of the readings of this week run on parallel tracks. The first readings all derive from the Acts of the Apostles, which is the life of the primitive believing community and the missionary journeys of St. Paul. St. Luke, author of the third Gospel, wrote the Acts and views his small "history book" as the continuation of the life and ministry of Jesus. The Holy Spirit is at work in the Mystical Body, the Church, just as he was active during the physical life of Jesus. Now we see how the disciples use those divine powers to heal and teach.

The Church today is the inheritor of those powers, duties and rights.

The Acts are not history in our contemporary sense of research and scholarship. It is more like a long "term paper" about St. Peter leading the "mother church of Jerusalem," and about St. Paul, whom St. Luke accompanied over the eastern Mediterranean countries. Acts does not report the activities of the rest of the apostles. St. James reached Spain, then the western outpost of the Roman Empire (until Britannia was subdued shortly afterward). There is no report in Acts of St. Thomas reaching India and leaving a Christian heritage that endures to this day. So this book is rather the spiritual history of only part of the Church as the vehicle of divine grace in the ancient world with its attendant problems, victories, strengths and weaknesses.

The Gospels of this week are cut from the same cloth, all of one piece—a dialogue between Jesus and Nicodemus early in the former's ministry. Like the Acts, this dialogue concerns the life of Jesus in us human beings through the enlivening action of the Spirit. We remember that Jesus was conceived by the power of the Holy Spirit in Mary's womb; that the Spirit appeared at his Baptism; that he was the Force of Pentecost; that Transubstantiation takes place by his power.

Yesterday's closing lines are repeated today, so the two readings should be read as one.

Nicodemus was a wealthy and influential voice of moderation in the supreme Jewish council of the Sanhedrin. Jesus had to set him straight regarding his literal interpretation of rebirth, because it takes the Spirit to beget spiritual offspring. "Water" signifies not just purification, but life. For a nation that considered the Exodus into the Sinai the most significant event of its history, life-giving water is an important symbol.

St. Paul wrote elsewhere, "We were buried with Christ in baptism and rose to a new life!" The work of the Spirit is as mysterious as the wind; you don't know how or where it arose nor where and why it finally dies down somewhere else! (This was long before "isobars" and "convection currents.")

Thus the work of the Spirit is subtle and gradual. We receive the Holy Spirit first in Baptism. It is fallacious that we do not receive the Spirit without some "conversion experience" as adults. No doubt such an experience does intensify the presence and power of the Spirit, but that is true of all the sacraments. The movement of charismatic prayer among Christians has been praised by the recent popes, yet theologians warn of two fallacies: 1) that no one receives the Spirit without some charismatic, extraordinary experience (yet even unknowing infants receive the Spirit and his gifts at Baptism); and 2) that charismatics have the "inside track" with God and are somehow holier. Such elitism is an echo of the ancient heresy of Gnosticism—which means "special knowledge."

Jesus may have used the metaphor of the wind because *ruah* in Hebrew means both "spirit" and "wind" and similar ideas, as whirlwind, tornado, gale, zephyr and soul! The inference we draw is that just as we are helpless in the face of the wind, so we must be passive and subject to the movements of grace—and like a vessel on the high seas, often led whither we do not wish to go!

Wednesday of the Second Week of Easter

Acts 5:17-26;
Jn 3:16-21

I heard an advertisement on the radio recently. The ad was for a clothing store downtown. The announcer surprised me when he said, "Our three stores are in three inconvenient locations. We provide no parking. The garments are often poorly displayed and you have to ask the clerks for help to see the merchandise!"

This was an obvious ploy: to use humor and "reverse psychology" as it is sometimes called. The closing shot, however, was, "the clothes nevertheless are of the best quality!"

This could be a parable of Christianity. The kingdom of God is located inconveniently at the end of a long, bumpy, slippery, winding road. There is no place to park or just sit or dawdle along the way. You have to keep moving for Jesus—even leave your comfortable vehicle, heated in winter and air-conditioned in summer, to get to your destination on foot. You have to trust in the guidance of Christ, who went ahead of us to "prepare a place for us in his kingdom."

Of course, you have to ask for help, because the merchandise is often poorly displayed, not only because it is a "treasure hidden in a field," but also because other Christians are not always very good salespersons! Yet the clothing you are seeking is the wedding garment of grace and the crown of eternal glory. Jesus told Nicodemus in today's Gospel, *For God so loved the world that he gave his only Son*," not to condemn us or hinder us with flat tires and misleading road signs, but to give us enough light to find our way through the darkness of sin. In fact, *For everyone who does wicked things hates the light.... But whoever lives the truth comes to the light...."*

To "live the truth" is a continuation of Jesus' comments on the action of the Holy Spirit in our lives. At the Last Supper Jesus promised to send the Paraclete, the Spirit of Truth, to teach us all things and to obey whatever Jesus has commanded us. This is a continuing process and lifelong development. Mary herself, the

guiding star of Church membership, grew under the tu-
telage of the Spirit. He took her as his spouse, possessed
her completely, and made her the pattern of how all of
us become like Jesus. It is itself a theological mystery
that she who formed the Child Jesus in her womb in turn
had to be formed into the likeness of her own Son to
reach her ultimate destiny and perfection. In his encyclical on the Mother of God, Pope John Paul II pointed out
that Mary was made queen of the universe in order to be
fully conformed to her Son, the king!

As married people become "two in one flesh," Mary
and the Spirit of God become "two in one spirit." We
may think that all her privileges and graces were consummated before she became the Mother of God and
that was her final status. With Jesus as her spiritual director, and prompted by her Divine Spouse, she learned
more and more about his messiahship, the redemption
and his glorification. The enlivening action of the Spirit
continued for the rest of her life. In fact, the principal
place where the Church was being perfected was in her,
its most perfect member. Thus she has already attained
what we are striving for, hoping for, working for.

Jesus' remark to Nicodemus about the indefinable
pattern of the Divine Wind, the Holy Spirit, makes us
aware that we must listen more than talk during prayer.
That Spirit, so often forgotten or neglected in our spiritual lives, provides us with our good resolutions, insights into Church teaching, the meaning of puzzling
biblical texts, sensitivity in our human relationships
with family and friends, the direction and purpose of
our lives, increase in sanctifying grace, and our charisms
to build up the Church.

When everyone's charism is in place and effective,
then the living portrait of Jesus emerges in the world,
like pieces of a giant mosaic in which each of us plays a
special role!

Thursday of the Second Week of Easter

Acts 5:27-33;
Jn 3:31-36

Both readings today emphasize that we must rise above our merely earthly perceptions and put on the mind of Christ in no uncertain terms! The texts are quite confronting; Peter told the Sanhedrin, *"We must obey God rather than men."* He boldly accused them of crucifying Jesus, yet the Lord still offered them "forgiveness of sins." The leaders of the people *"...became infuriated and wanted to put them to death."* Jesus made it equally clear to Nicodemus, *"Whoever disobeys the Son will not see life, but the wrath of God remains upon him."* Nicodemus' fellow members of the Sanhedrin responded by plotting to kill Jesus. The early Church was replicating the life and death of Jesus.

We sometimes think that the first generation after Christ was swept along by the Holy Spirit without ostensible problems—which was not so! The apostles were criticized for neglecting the poor, yet they were deeply committed to preaching, so deacons had to be ordained for service. There were false prophets, even "wonder-workers," who tried to make capital of the Gospel, so the concept of excommunication developed. Back-sliders were living immorally, even incestuously, which led to "shunning," which meant avoidance by other believers. Gentile believers resented being made subject to Jewish customs and religious practices, which led to a Christianity divested of Jewish ways to become worldwide in its appeal. Thus from the beginning the Church was beset with human problems. It is evident that we need the same Holy Spirit to preserve the Church of today, when so many ignore the guidance of the Church and walk in the darkness of sin.

In light of the confrontations that we described in both readings today, sometimes we are puzzled that

Church authority does not speak out more forcefully. But the Church looks to the pattern of Jesus, the Suffering Servant of Isaiah's prophecy—the One who did not smother the barely-smouldering flax, but tried to fan the flame of ardor; who did not simply break off the bruised reed, but tried to nurse it back to health. Thus the Church tries to be patient, heal and nourish, generally preferring to reason with and pray for her erring children. There will always be problems and "problem children." Each century brings its own stumbling blocks. The ancient world did not have to contend with birth control, nuclear disarmament, pollution of the environment, and so forth! Each century must figure out how it is "better for us to obey God than men!"

We read an interesting phrase in today's Gospel, *"For the one whom God sent...does not ration his gift of the Spirit."* The New English Bible translates, "So measureless is God's gift of the Spirit." In other words, it takes the Divine Spirit to adequately express the full meaning of the "words of God."

The Church had to develop, in fact, a whole new vocabulary for such common Christian concepts as faith, hope, charity, grace, fellowship, Eucharist, but especially love. St. Paul described this process, "The whole world is in the agony of child-bearing labor," and the baby was the Church! The summary of the nature of the believing community, as found in St. Peter's first Letter, is an echo of the Jewish Bible with a new interpretation: "You are a chosen race, a royal priesthood, a holy nation, a people he claims for his own, to proclaim the glorious works of the One who called you from the darkness into his marvelous light."

Yet we should become neither smug because we have the fullness of truth, nor presumptuous that salvation is automatically guaranteed for us. In fact,

St. Augustine, probably the single greatest theologian of the Church, wrote long ago, "Many whom God has, the Church does not have; and many whom the Church has, God does not have." This sad truth obviates both arrogance and presumption! We are a "chosen race" if we accept our election as a commitment; a "priesthood" if we offer and consecrate our world to God; a "holy nation" if we make our citizenship in heaven; and "claimed by God" if we proclaim his glorious works in the light!

Friday of the Second Week of Easter

Acts 5:34-42;
Jn 6:1-15

The "certain member of the Sanhedrin" who spoke in today's first reading is said to be Gamaliel, the teacher of Saul, later St. Paul. This famed teacher spoke thus: *"For if this endeavor or this activity is of human origin, it will destroy itself. But if it comes from God, you will not be able to destroy them."*

When St. Francis of Assisi appeared on the world scene, his movement had its detractors, too. The College of Cardinals lined up on both sides of the issue: Can a person or group really follow the Gospel and live as poorly as the Lord in his public life? Francis countered, "Do we dare say that Jesus commanded the impossible? Did the Lord trick us?" The response of one cardinal parallel's today's text from Acts: If the Franciscan movement is of human origin, it will fail by itself; if God is behind it, then nothing will stop it. The "watch and wait" attitude has prevailed from the beginning of the Church.

The Sanhedrin had the apostles scourged and dismissed. This was not the inhumane Roman scourging, as Jesus received, but the Jewish "forty less one" lashing that St. Paul mentions about himself, as one of the sufferings he endured for Christ.

There were thirteen leather thongs which were laid on the bare back three times, constituting thirty-nine strokes, "forty less one." This was relatively merciful, but painful nevertheless. Yet the apostles were *"...rejoicing that they had been found worthy to suffer dishonor for the sake of the name."* But this was only the "down payment"; all but St. John were to lose their lives in martyrdom of various kinds.

Jesus set the pattern. As he died, he prayed for his Father to forgive his captors. St. Stephen, the first martyr, as he was being stoned to death, similarly cried out, "Don't hold this sin against them." Jesus told us to pray for those who persecute and calumniate us. St. Maximilian Kolbe told his brothers to try to love and pray for the Nazis, as he himself did, even though he would be put to death by them. He never allowed his brothers to speak disparagingly of them either!

About thirty years ago a Polish boy, named George, entered the seminary and was ordained. His family was harassed and he himself imprisoned for a time. He took St. Maximilian as his model. Other priests were warned by the government, even the hierarchy, to avoid involvement with the Polish union, Solidarity, but Fr. George realized that the cause was just and needed spiritual direction. He celebrated Masses all over the country "for the fatherland" and, as the rallying point, was instrumental in conversions.

After he evaded several attempts at his murder, Moscow decreed his elimination. He was brutally beaten, tortured in an indescribable way, and thrown into a river half alive. Yet he never preached hatred. On the day of his funeral thousands of workers marched past the Communist headquarters carrying placards which read: Forgive, forgive! Fr. George, whose name in Polish is Jerzy Popieluszko, lived and died for his favorite quotation from St. Maximilian, a distillation from the Gospel: "Hatred destroys; love alone creates!"

Saturday of the
Second Week of Easter

Acts 6:1-7;
Jn 6:16-21

Today's Gospel is the conclusion of yesterday's text and is best understood in its light. All four Gospels recount the miraculous multiplication of the few loaves and fishes. This event foreshadowed the institution of the Eucharist. The multiplication suggests the multiplied presence of Jesus in the Eucharist in thousands of tabernacles throughout the world. Jesus' care in gathering even the fragments indicates how careful we must be with every recognizable crumb or drop of wine that has been consecrated into the Body and Blood of the Lord.

A popular antiphon in the liturgy is, "O Sacred Banquet...at which a pledge of future glory is given us." Holy Communion, therefore, is a pledge of future resurrection. Jesus himself had said, "Whoever eats my flesh and drinks my blood will have life, and I will raise him up on the last day." At the Eucharist we prepare our minds and hearts for the entry of the Lord, but also our bodies; we are destined to be temples of the Holy Spirit during this life and eternal tabernacles of the Most High, enjoying the Beatific Vision somehow even corporeally.

The events of John 6 took place along the north shore of the Sea of Galilee. Jesus crossed over to Tiberius, a city that is thriving even today because of the thermal baths and because of the tourist center it has become, especially for winter sports. Followed by his disciples and a huge crowd of adherents, Jesus went along the coastline to the location identified today as Tabgha, from the Greek *Heptapegon*, meaning "seven springs" from the rivulets which seeped up from the earth and flowed into the sea. In the isolated chapel built in recent times over the spot of the miracle, there is a floor mosaic of the five barley loaves and the two fishes.

After the miracle, fearing they would "carry him away to make him king," Jesus climbed the mountain alone. There is no mountain that reaches the shore here, but the whole north end of the Sea of Galilee is ringed with mountains. Towards evening, however, when the disciples had already embarked for Capernaum, not knowing where the Lord had gone, but knowing Capernaum was the center of Jesus' Galilean ministry—Jesus appeared near the boat, "walking on the water." Because the passage of the disciples was along the littoral, "on the sea" may indicate that Jesus was walking along the shore, especially because the disciple's boat went aground on the shore. Due to the wind and adverse waves, a person could certainly walk at least as fast as a boat was being rowed.

This does not mean that the Lord was unable to walk on the surface of the water, because another text relates that he actually did and then calmed the sea as well. The lesson comes from the words of the Lord, *"It is I. Do not be afraid."* Whenever we are beset with habitual sin, strong waves of temptation, and a sense of powerlessness, we must rely on the presence of Jesus in our lives. Storms abate, waves subside, and we find a respite from our depression and feelings of helplessness. But during the crisis we can turn to the Lord and see him coming along the shore of our lives. At times, he appears distant or disinterested in our struggle, but his words ring clear across the raging water, *"It is I. Do not be afraid."*

THIRD WEEK OF EASTER

Third Sunday of Easter, A

Acts 2:14, 22-28;
1 Pt 1:17-21; Lk 24:13-35

The kerygma, or "preached proclamation," about Jesus continually focuses on two historical events, the crucifixion and resurrection, death and life, humanity and divinity. Peter, the spokesman of the Eleven, quoted King David the psalmist, *"My flesh, too, will dwell in hope...nor will you suffer your holy one to see corruption."* This allusion to immortality in the Jewish Bible indicates the natural longing of us all to live forever. The same Prince of the Apostles in today's second reading emphasizes the same kerygma. You were delivered *"...with the precious blood of Christ."* And God *"...raised him from the dead and gave him glory."* Thus crucifixion and resurrection have always remained the chief perceptions of the Christ preached by the Church. Once you accept them, you implicitly acknowledge Jesus as your Savior, and everything else soon falls into place.

On the way to Emmaus, the scene of today's Gospel, Jesus sounded impatient. *"Oh, how foolish you are! "* So long had they been with the Master, yet they did not even begin to understand. Jesus provided the homily that afternoon, yet they still did not recognize him until the *"...breaking of the bread."* The Eucharist as sacrifice, meal and worship is the characteristically Catholic doctrine, and we, too, recognize the Eucharistic Lord in the breaking of the bread at Mass. When anti-Catholic groups or individuals attack the Church, the thrust of their attack is usually against the Eucharist, our Lady and the pope. All three doctrines are connected. In the Eucharist we receive and adore the flesh born of the Virgin Mary; papal authority conserves these truths by its teaching and tradition. It is interesting to note that historically those Christian non-Catholic churches which have preserved veneration of Mary have also remained faithful to the Holy Eucharist.

We can be certain that our Lady was deeply involved with her Son after his resurrection and concerned about the first believing community. If Jesus appeared to his disciples, assuredly he appeared to his first and best disciple, his own mother. Jesus and Mary "go together" in God's plan of salvation; God is never fully your Father, nor Jesus your brother, until Mary is your mother. It's all "in the family." Our Lady encouraged the post-resurrection community; she was their link to the physical person of Jesus and the source of information about his childhood, growing up, and possibly some aspects of his ministry unknown to many others. It is not as if God needed Mary to effect our salvation, but he chose to have her at the side of Jesus.

When we say that we recognize Jesus in the breaking of the bread, it means that we take our strength, our meaning and model from the Eucharist. In his Real Presence we find the pattern of virtues we are to reproduce on this earth. See how available and accessible he is in the Sacrament. Anyone, anytime, with any kind of problem, voicing any kind of prayer, is received by the King. Look how forgiving he is: those who approach him with unconfessed sin, with blasphemies in their past, with arrogant hearts—all are drawn into his divine life to be changed. He gradually chips away at our obstinacy and hardness of heart.

See how charitable he is. He does not condemn, but asks us to judge ourselves. He desires not the death of sinners, but that they be converted and saved. He could have destroyed his enemies, but he wants us to live forever in glory, not punishment. See how generous he is. He holds back nothing of himself: Body, Blood, Soul, Divinity. We receive his entire Person.

Are you sad, depressed, put down? Bring your tears into his Real Presence. Are you joyful, upbeat, singing? Share your happiness in the Eucharist, which means "giving thanks." Are you worried, uncertain, confused? Bring your problems to the Table of the Lord. Are you lonely, alienated, rejected even by those who profess to love you? Bring your emptiness to his Sacred Banquet so he can fill you with his affection. Let your heart beat in unison with his Sacred Heart. His Body was bruised, and his Blood poured out for us; do not be afraid to follow in his bloody footsteps; he has gone before us to prepare a place for each of us in his kingdom. It is easy to learn from him because he is meek and humble of heart, and therefore approachable.

Manifest Jesus to the world. He has chosen to work through his Mystical Body. Be his head to find the means of alleviating suffering and ignorance. Be his hands to work for the disadvantaged and underprivileged. Be his heart to love the unlovable, forgive the unforgivable, and cherish what this world rejects. Don Luigi Guanella, a religious founder of the last century, remarked, "Every new person who enters our lives is an act of providence, inviting us to prove our love of God."

It is a sobering thought that everyone you meet every day of your lives will one day become, after the Final Judgment, one of two classes of beings. If one of the

damned souls suddenly comes down the center aisle of
the church, you would recoil, shudder and run away
from such a hideous pile of human refuse! But if one of
the saints came into your presence, you would want to
fall down and actually worship what appears to be a divine being, so perfect, beautiful and shining. Everyone
whose life we touch is affected, either for shame or
glory!

Third Sunday
of Easter, B

Acts 3:13-15, 17-19;
1 Jn 2:1-5; Lk 24:35-48

Although this is the Third Sunday of Easter, the
events described in today's Gospel still belong to Easter
Sunday—and it seems the Lord was mighty busy! After
his death and "descent into hell," he rolled back the
stone, scared the soldiers away, sent his angels to tell
Mary Magdalene that he had risen. He appeared to
Mary Magdalene later in the morning, then ran off to
Emmaus where he lectured to the two disciples and was
recognized in the breaking of the bread. Next, in today's
Gospel, he appears back in the Upper Room. And we
can be sure that he spent time with his own dear mother,
who was his first and best disciple, and who had shared
his life, ministry and death.

Jesus' resurrection was the "down payment" on our
own; what he did in his post-resurrection appearances
indicates our own future glorified bodies' movement
with the speed of our thoughts (Where do you want to
go?); our spiritualized bodies' passing through solids,
just as Jesus passed through the locked doors of the
Upper Room (Where do you want to be?); our freedom
from suffering (no more angina, lower back pain, arthri-

tis). Yet this is the least part of resurrected glory. There is the eternal vision of God; the company of the angels and saints and our loved ones who made it to heaven; our fullness of knowledge to satisfy all curiosity; the tranquillity of our will, so that we no longer crave to possess the world.

Jesus taught his disciples something through each appearance. In today's Gospel he shows the continuity of his body with the body that died on the cross. He tells them to observe the scars in his hands and feet, and to touch him, because ghosts don't have flesh and bones. Then he eats a piece of cooked fish to show he still has the biological abilities he possessed before, although he does not need the nourishment or sleep. Jesus also once said, "In heaven they neither give nor take in marriage"—which may be a disappointment to some! Finally Jesus gives them a homily, which by definition is an explanation of Scriptures with a relevant application to the listeners. "He opened their minds to understand the scriptures." With that he commissions them to preach to all nations. But this does not occur until St. Paul enters the picture. It is a sad commentary on our Christianity that after 2,000 years, more than half of the world's population has not even heard the names of Jesus and Mary, much less believed in them!

We will not need food in heaven, because our bodies will not deteriorate. Although we shall remain men and women—not become angels—and therefore sexual beings for all eternity, we will not be driven to express our sexuality in an erotic way! Sharing as we shall in God's nature—and God is love—we will be able to love everyone unequivocally and altruistically. Our bitterest enemy, those who cheated us during our lives, even our in-laws, we will accept as God has accepted them, as God has accepted us all into his kingdom. Grace is defined as our share in the life of God, who is the Great

Lover. St. John wrote, "He who abides in love, abides in God and God in him."

Now the wise and Christian response to love is to begin on earth as perfectly as we can. When people are young, perhaps under thirty-five, they tend to love to discover whether they themselves are lovable and will be loved in return. As love matures, we learn to love because it is the right thing to do, even without hope of return. God loved us even when we were in our sins and sent his Son to be our Savior. He gave us the example : when he was dying, he forgave those who crucified him—and in this we are the guilty ones!

Why is purgatory a theological necessity? Because we have not loved enough, not forgiven completely. We suffer an agony of self-accusations and could not even bear to look upon God until we have loved and forgiven like Jesus. We are driven by an inner necessity in purgatory to forgive other people, to forgive God (!) for not answering our prayers as we wanted him to, and especially to forgive ourselves for not having become what we should have been! Only then will we be fit to face God eternally and enjoy his loving embrace!

One Franciscan saint, Maximilian Kolbe, who gave his life for another in Auschwitz concentration camp, wrote, "Hatred destroys; love alone creates." Of the early Christians it was said, "Behold how these Christians love one another." The Christian response is always to love, to tolerate, to forgive. In family life love is expressed by compromise. If you try to love others particularly when they are not so lovable, perhaps you will give them something to live up to. Perhaps your love will stimulate some self-respect and good will.

When I was a young priest, I thought I had all the answers. My seminary education was wonderful; I thought there was a footnote in one of my textbooks to cover every human contingency. In my "old age" I realize the answers are not nearly as important as the questions: What does it profit a person to gain the whole world, yet suffer the loss of his own soul? What can I return to the Lord for what he has given me? Do I pray for those who persecute and calumniate me? What is my commitment to Jesus? How do I learn to forgive the unforgivable and cherish those I have despised? And, as St. Francis used to say with every passing birthday, "When will I begin to serve the Lord?"

Third Sunday of Easter, C

Acts 5:27-32, 40-41;
Rv 5:11-14; Jn 21:1-19

St. Peter is the central figure in the first reading and today's Gospel. In Acts, Peter preaches Jesus "...*as leader and savior to grant Israel repentance and forgiveness of sins.*" In the Gospel Peter himself is shown repenting and seeking forgiveness of his sins. This scene took place only a few days after the chief apostle denied the accusation of a barmaid that he was a follower of the Galilean. No doubt he wept bitter tears and longed to fall at the feet of Jesus and beg his pardon. But Jesus appeared the other times to the whole group of apostles. This time, however, Jesus must have taken Peter aside.

The fact that the disciple had wished to be with Jesus is illustrated by his response to the excited exclamation, "*It is the Lord.*" Peter threw on his clothes and swam or waded to shore. Once again the Master showed that his body was real and ate a grilled fish. Because he had made the fire and distributed the bread and fish, the chapel built on the site today is called *Mensa Domini,* "The Table of the Lord."

St. Matthew, in chapter 28, records that the women were told earlier to explain to the apostles, "He has been raised from the dead and now goes ahead of you to Galilee, where you will see him." But Matthew does not record that encounter in Galilee. St. Mark records the angel at the tomb, who has the women deliver the same message in his chapter 16, but he too fails to tell his readers about the Galilee appearance. Luke and John do not mention that the disciples are to return to Galilee to meet Jesus, but St. John does record this scene in today's Gospel. Yet scholars unanimously attribute this section to another hand, a later addition or epilogue, as it is titled in the New American Bible. Yet this passage reveals so much about Jesus, that we are glad it was inserted.

Near the chapel one finds a moving and magnificent statue, cast in bronze and depicting Jesus' dialogue with Peter. One might expect to find a fisherman's net, trident or anchor in the statuary group, because this is where the Lord is giving Peter his commission, right on the shore of the Sea of Galilee. But the dialogue of Peter's repentance and Jesus' mandate to him is as pastor, which means "shepherd," rather than the Big Fisherman.

The bronze statue stands outlined against the clear Galilean sky, close to the waters of the sea. Jesus holds a shepherd's crook and hands it to Peter, who kneels in contrition and wonder. Three times Jesus asks him, "...do you love me?" which must have evoked Peter's guilt for having denied the Master three times! Peter was hurt and responded, "Yes, Lord, you know that I love you." A triple question, a triple affirmation of love, then a triple mandate: "Feed my lambs.... Tend my sheep.... Feed my sheep."

Thus St. Peter was made the surrogate of Christ, his vicar on earth, the first pope. Some commentators think that the "lambs" refer to the laity at large, and the "sheep" which need tending and feeding refer to the other apostles and leaders of the Church. Jesus often used pastoral metaphors and even called himself the "Good Shepherd." Lambs are frisky and easily led astray, but readily follow the sheep in and out of the fold and around the pastures. Jesus seems to give responsibility, therefore, to the sheep. We cannot be certain of this explanation, but we can speculate about it. If the more mature sheep fall into the culvert of error or get caught up in the thorn bushes of this world's values, then the lambs will be scattered and lost as well. The sheep must model for the lambs and teach them acceptable behavior—especially to listen to the shepherd's voice. It is simple to translate these figures of sheep into the Church of today!

When St. Peter is told to feed the lambs and guide the sheep, Jesus obviously did not speak for that time only, because the need of guidance and nourishment continues to exist, probably more so today in our complex world. The Lord is setting a pattern for the Church to provide the vehicle to continue his earthly acts and intentions throughout the ages. Jesus provided the inspiration; the Church under the guidance of the Spirit provides the structures. As Jesus healed, taught, consecrated at the Supper, forgave sin, and confirmed with his Spirit, so the leadership and sacraments of the Church provide continual encounters with the Head of the Mystical Body. This is how we live the life of grace, which is already the life of the resurrected Christ. We do not suddenly get "plugged" into God and begin to "glow" when we reach heaven. We are already incandescent on this earth. "The kingdom of God is within you," he said.

Monday of the
Third Week of Easter

Acts 6:8-15;
Jn 6:22-29

The crowd chased Jesus around and across the Sea of Galilee after the miraculous multiplication of loaves and fish at Heptapegon (Tabgha). Jesus returned to his familiar theme: you should not be anxious for perishable food of which you have had your fill. He called them rather to faith: *"Do not work for food that perishes but for the food that endures for eternal life."* He always asked his listeners to accept him above all: *"...believe in the one he [God] sent."*

Essentially we are to hold loosely in our hands whatever is not of eternal value. It is not the goods of this world that are evil, because God has given them to us for our use and sustenance. It is the anxiety and craving and fixation on the goods of this world that leads to evil. Nevertheless we are not to conclude that we should be indifferent to those who are without the necessities of life and who barely survive under minimum standards in their quality of life. The rich should be rich for the sake of the poor, and the poor exist for the sake of the rich, so that the rich may attain eternal life by their benefactions. On one hand, what is taken from the rich by violence and revolution is wrong; the wealthy are, on the other hand, directed by the Lord to contribute generously to alleviate the lot of the needy. This is the one great social program of the Church, but it is not very effective, given the worldwide exploitation of the indigent and deprived.

It is ironic: the very objectives that nations legitimately seek for their people could be readily attained by ending the arms race and threats to other governments, the lust for more territory and spheres of influence. The money spent on arms could easily feed the starving world. Indebtedness paralyzes industry and reinforces more deficits.

One person in three in the world is illiterate; one out of five barely subsists due to extreme poverty. Torture and terrorism are the stock-in-trade of most military regimes. Many Third World nations are deeply involved in drug traffic, much of which is directed at the U.S. This causes a dollar drain in the billions every year. Does our own government tolerate this situation in order to keep such governments anti-Communist? There seems to be only a token attempt to counteract these forces of evil that destroy individuals and their families and lead to most of the crime in our nation! Meanwhile health care, education and research into the resolution of worldwide problems goes begging for support.

There is, of course, a spiritual message in all of this. God is running the world; his will ultimately prevails. He has committed to us those works which will reverse the world situation. Peace and plenty do not come automatically; they are the result of prayer, social striving, and political activism. For this enterprise the clergy and religious are the motivators and spiritual directors; the laity are the troops. Statistics are dead numbers; people are living entities, our brothers and sisters. It is precisely because we are Christians—resurrection people who look for a new heaven and new earth—that our activity must reflect that all human beings are vessels of grace on earth and potential vessels of glory in heaven. Our social and political actions must bring us all to God, to a recognition of his fatherly care.

Therefore, work for political change; write letters; make a substantial donation; vote for those who support our ideals. Above all, pray, because in the final analysis that accomplishes the miracles which change the heart and mind of the world!

Tuesday of the
Third Week of Easter

Acts 7:51—8:1;
Jn 6:30-35

The stoning of St. Stephen, the first martyr, is the subject of today's first reading. This was the signal for a full-blown persecution of the Church. Stephen was a deacon, engaged in the care of the poor and hence very visible. His name means "crown," or perhaps "one who is crowned," which is the translation from the Greek. Yesterday's pericope shows him debating with "Roman freedmen," who were Hellenized Jews from other parts of the Empire. This means they accepted the dress and customs of the Graeco-Roman world and were probably natives of those cities whose citizens were accorded Roman citizenship after their conquest by Roman legions.

When he was hauled before the Jewish Sanhedrin, Stephen did not merely defend Christianity, but attacked the Jewish leaders and the whole nation for their long history of opposing the prophets sent by God. Stephen himself replicates in his life what had happened to the Lord Jesus, just as the Acts is a continuation of the life of Christ in his body, the Church. Stephen sees Jesus at the right hand of the Father in heaven, a relationship the Lord often mentions. Jesus on the cross said, "Father, forgive them, because they do not know what they are doing"; Stephen cries out, *"Lord, do not hold this sin against them."* The last words of Jesus were, "Father, I commend my spirit into your hands"; Stephen echoes, *"Lord Jesus, receive my spirit."* Like the Master, Stephen was executed at the insistence of the "elders and scribes." When Stephen asked them, *"Which of the prophets did your ancestors not persecute?"*, he reminded his hearers that Jesus had accused them of killing the prophets, then of building pretentious tombs in their memory. Jesus cried over Jerusalem with the words,

"Jerusalem, you who stone the prophets and kill those who are sent to you, how many times I would have gathered you as a hen does her chicks under her wing, but you would not!"

Preaching painful truths never makes one popular. The preacher is suspect by right-wingers; the left-siders try to win him to their side by cajolery and the seduction of popularity. Usually the centrist position is where the truth lies and what the magisterium has taught. Stephen called Jesus "the Son of Man," a title the Lord used of himself many times in the Bible. The "pious" Jews covered their ears at this, others tore their cloaks in pharisaic scandal. Preaching truth is a dangerous profession; they stoned him to death for his honesty!

Stephen's criticism of the Sanhedrin became the definitive break with Judaism, and his death was the seal that confirmed that break, just as Jesus' death had spelled the end of the Old Law, symbolized by the splitting of the Temple veil in two! From henceforth Christianity would spread from Jerusalem into the rest of Palestine (reinforced by two Roman conquests), and thereafter to the whole Mediterranean world. Stephen's was only one death, but it was the sparkplug to ignite change in the Church. And we cannot forget the aftermath: the conversion of Saul, persecutor of the primitive Church, into St. Paul, Apostle of Nations. We never know the consequences of our actions. Paul must have been "holy," at least according to his lights, even at that time, yet he "...*was consenting to his [Stephen's] execution.*" The dynamic of his psyche is uncertain, but later on the way to Damascus the Lord said, "It is hard for you to kick against the goad." This suggests that Saul resented the new sect, which was threatening to eclipse the Jewish religion which he had studied and propagated, and from which he took his meaning. In other words, his chagrin may not have derived from his defense of his existing faith, but rather from the fear that it was possibly false—and he had to eradicate this possibility from his mind. So he agreed with the execution of Stephen. No greater self-satisfaction grows out of anything than what is performed for religious motives, even if it is evil!

Wednesday of the Third Week of Easter

Acts 8:1-8; Jn 6:35-40

Chapter 6 of St. John's Gospel is a classical text about the Holy Eucharist. After the miracle of the loaves and fish, the populace wanted to crown Jesus their king, so their pantries would always be full! Whenever we read John's Gospel, we must be prepared to follow his line of thought from our inmost soul to the very courts of heaven! This chapter 6 is very long and the Eucharistic texts proceed from the miracle of loaves and fish to the application to Jesus himself, *"I am the bread of life."* Jesus' resurrection and our own and the Eucharist are closely bound. Before the resurrection Jesus was able to relate on the human level to only the number of persons within earshot (like everyone today, unless you have amplification or use the video camera). But when his body was divinized and spiritualized, he was able to relate to everyone in the world who communicated with him, for all time. *"...this is the will of my Father, that everyone who sees the Son and believes in him may have eternal life, and I shall raise him [on] the last day."* Those specifically divine powers that the Lord possessed as the Second Person were conferred also on his human nature. We will share in those powers (and not be confined to the limitations of human language and spoken words), but to the degree that our preparation on earth has merited.

John's Gospel is subtle, expressive of a more mature Christianity than the simpler theology of the Synoptics. Having been written around 100 A.D., it is the last in order of time and hence the result of the longest reflection of the believing community on the message and meaning of Christ. In today's first reading from the Acts we read, *"On that day, there broke out a severe persecution of the church in Jerusalem."* A few years earlier in 90 A.D., the Jewish Council of Jamnia excommunicated the converts to Jesus, so they were forbidden entry to the synagogues. The battle lines were clearly drawn and were heartrending: you have to accept the laws of Moses with all its Judaic implications, or accept Jesus; you could not have them both, although the converts had for two generations worshiped in both assemblies.

It is difficult for a Christian to understand what the choice implied. Judaism is a whole way of life, a culture with its proper rituals, feasts, foods and a family feeling. All the Jewish archetypes came into focus: solidarity with the group, tradition, the prophecies, being the "apple of God's eye," dancing with the Torah, and "marrying the Bible" on Succoth. St. Matthew's Gospel was directed at the Jewish-Christians to show the continuity between the two Testaments. St. John's message similarly is meant to fortify the existing members: not that they were choosing a good Christianity over a bad Judaism, but passing from a good Judaism to a better Christianity. Hence all the Gospels are at pains to show that Jewish leaders were concerned with their clout and position rather than the promise of a Savior. Jesus did not come to destroy the Law, but to fulfill it.

To believe in Jesus requires a frame of mind, a mental set of openness to new truth, and a pure heart— which means "single" or "undivided"—that accepts the reality and relevance of Jesus' words. The distance of Jesus from us in time and space sometimes generates a sense of unreality and an impression that the words of Jesus are merely "pious platitudes" better suited to the past than the present. But Jesus spoke to all persons for all times. Human nature remains the same, fallen but redeemed. And God's fidelity to his promises remains unchanged for all those to whom he gave the power to become the children of God.

Thursday of the Third Week of Easter

Acts 8:26-40; Jn 6:44-51

During his Last Supper discourse (which appears in John 14—17), Jesus told his disciples, "I no longer call you slaves, but friends." Many of his statements were aimed at fostering just such a divine friendship with his followers. In today's text he promises the gift of himself: *"...the bread that I will give is my flesh for the life of the world."* As a friend will do, he introduces his faithful followers to his Father and will raise them up on the last day and bring them home! It is the nature of friendship to give gifts and make sacrifices; thus Jesus shares himself completely with us by his very sacrifice.

Jesus in his humanity cries out for our acceptance and belief, for understanding and love, for friendship. How do our own friendships begin? C. S. Lewis once wrote that we discover we have something in common with another—a hobby, a vacation experience, a career, or other interests. So Jesus asks in the Gospel, "Who do you say I am?" That is, what is our relationship and what do we have in common? Essentially the Lord wishes to know: do you care about the same values and truths that I do?

Examine your friendships. What do you have in common with your friends? What do you truly share? It may only be bird-watching or pumping iron. In the case of the early Church, the common denominator was a profound belief in the Gospel. Therefore the members of the early Church presented a united front of loving friendship. They were faithful to and preserved the same morality and lifestyle. Like all friends they were able to resist outside pressures, even persecution and death, by mutual support and affirmation.

Basing ourselves on communication and association we choose our friends not for profit and gain—although false friendships may be based on such a motive—but to enhance our lives, make our lives more joyful, and add value to our daily existence. Friendship should not be a "mutual admiration" society; on the other hand, without mutual admiration and respect there can be no friendship. So the Lord respects our freedom of will, and we cherish his self-giving humanity.

Between two believers friendship becomes a holy relationship, leading both persons to God. Those who merely use or manipulate us, who distract us from our spiritual goals, are not our friends, but enemies who are occasions of sin for us. In fact, friendship of the proper kind is the flavoring in our social virtues of compassion, social justice and generosity. We all need someone as a confidant to share happiness and bear grief. Best of all, when you talk with a friend, you don't have to guard your words, for you can be forthright and candid. You don't have to watch your step, because you can trust a friend not to trip you up. You can be yourself and do not have to wear a mask nor put up a smokescreen.

That insightful author, C. S. Lewis, wrote that physical love needs naked bodies, but spiritual love, as friendship, requires naked personalities: you can reveal your inner self, recount your triumphs without being accused of pride, and speak of your failures without embarrassment. A person who has had half a dozen genuine friends in his whole life can count himself blessed by the Lord. And whoever makes the Lord himself his or her intimate friend on this earth will make an easy passage to the intimacy of everlasting life.

In a sense, you never choose a friend; friendship simply grows. And you recognize it in retrospect, when it has borne spiritual fruits. Be especially anxious to pursue friendships with fellow believers, as in the first community of Jerusalem. Of them it was written, "They were of one mind and heart," and "Behold, how these Christians love one another!"

Friday of the Third Week of Easter

Acts 9:1-20;
Jn 6:52-59

The Church has been building up to today's Gospel text for three weeks of Eastertide. Although chapter 6 does not conclude until tomorrow, today's text is the theological climax which is linked with Easter. In summary the Master said: if you eat my flesh and drink my blood, you will have eternal life, and I will raise you up on the last day; we will remain in one another and share my life, just as the Father and I share the same life.

This is the setting for a profound theological digression. *"For my flesh is true food, and my blood is true drink."* In other words, all that we eat and drink on this earth symbolizes and leads us to the real, ultimate, eternal food and drink, the Holy Eucharist. This earth's nourishment is impermanent and transitory, whereas the Body and Blood of Christ is timeless.

We should not say, therefore, that receiving Holy Communion is similar to eating dinner at the family table, but rather that the family dinner is like receiving the Eucharist at God's family table. The real food and drink—once again—is the Body and Blood of the Savior.

The effect of your morning toast and coffee quickly passes as it is metabolized by your body, but the Eucharistic effect is that we are changed into God! The consecrated Host is the true "Wonder Bread." The spirit is greater than the flesh, it outlasts the flesh, it can transform the flesh. In St. John's Gospel this idea is repeated with the themes of water and light and wind.

St. Paul moreover gives us another point of reference that illustrates this idea. He wrote, "All fatherhood (or paternity or family structure) on earth is named after (or patterned after or modeled upon) the fatherhood of God in heaven." In other words, this earth is but a shadow of the real and everlasting world of heaven. Obviously God does not observe earthly fathers to see how he can be an effective heavenly Father, but we observe him in action in the Bible to learn about our own physical and spiritual fathering on earth. Once more, like the Eucharist, the primary reality is the heavenly and divine; the copy and surrogate is of the earth!

As we look at our universe, we see that it is transitory; it will pass away—at least as we know it now—at the end of time. Even the Eucharist, although it is the Divine Presence of Jesus in an earthly form, will pass away in the sense that it will not be necessary in heaven. We will possess the vision of God and his presence without a mediating process. The model of all that exists is primarily in the mind of God because he is the Creator of all. (This is called the exemplarism of the Greek philosopher, Plato, whose writings were very influential on the subsequent theology of the Church.)

Therefore this earth is a shadow of the great reality of the spiritual world, not only with regard to bread and wine and fatherhood, but also with regard to everything else we perceive. The deeply religious person is always on the lookout for the fingerprints of God on his creation and his footprints all over the universe. No wonder the Bible tells us to beware of this world, which is fast passing away, because we get off track in chasing the handiworks of humanity.

Saturday of the Third Week of Easter

Acts 9:31-42;
Jn 6:60-69

Today's Gospel records the touching dialogue between Jesus and Peter. Saddened by the people who would not accept his teaching about the importance of the spirit over the flesh and his difficult teaching about eating his Body and drinking his Blood, the Master asked his close followers, *"Do you also want to leave?"* In a human way the Lord was putting forth a cry for help and understanding. Speaking for the rest, Peter responded, *"Master, to whom shall we go? You have the words of eternal life."*

In the reading from Acts we see St. Peter, the natural and appointed leader of the apostles, continuing the life of Jesus and his ministry. In fact, the first part of Acts centers on Peter, as the second part focuses on Paul. So the Word of the Lord continued to spread and make progress in the hearts of many. Nothing can stand in the way of the Gospel; God's will is not to be contravened. Luke's Gospel included many stories about the Gentiles' contact with Jesus; the Acts will gradually include all the nations, starting with the conversion of the eunuch of Ethiopia, probably the first black to accept Christ as his Savior. Yet the first generations of converts from Judaism probably went to their graves thinking that the Mosaic Law was necessary for salvation!

After Peter's cure of Aeneas in Lydda the talk went forth about this healer who acted in the name of Jesus. So he was called to Joppa, a seaport town nearby, today called Jaffa. A sweet and gentle lady, Tabitha, renowned for her benefactions, was being mourned by the local citizenry. No doubt her kindness had led to many conversions. Her being raised from the dead *"...became known all over Joppa, and many came to believe in the Lord."*

The very last line of St. James' Letter reads, "He should know that whoever brings back a sinner from the error of his way will save his soul from death and will cover a multitude of sins." Actually no one can save another's soul, that is the gift of Jesus, the application of the merits of his death on the cross. Probably the most effective way of helping convert another from sin is example rather than instruction and sermonizing, particularly the example of struggling despite the problems in one's life. Like every soldier, the Christian is essentially a struggler, not always a winner, but one who accepts defeat like the Lord, with nobility, with courage.

Often St. John's Gospel records the words of Jesus about walking in the light and avoiding the works of darkness. How startling the light of grace in one's own soul can be and how useful to illuminate others' souls! I am put in mind of the stories consequent upon the Rural Electrification Act of 1935 by Franklin Roosevelt. Light in the lives of the farmers was a sensation! Women wept to see the agitator run in a washing machine. Men got choked up to hear the news on the radio. Kids made up games, running through the house and turning lights on and off. School children couldn't concentrate on their studies, because they were so distracted, just staring up at the lights overhead.

Perhaps this should be our attitude towards our inner lights and graces of illumination. If human beings thrill at the sight of electric power and other marvels of our technological world, how much more should we be delighted to be switched on by God!

FOURTH WEEK OF EASTER

Fourth Sunday of Easter, A

Acts 2:14, 36-41; 1 Pt 2:20-25; Jn 10:1-10

The power of the Holy Spirit surfaces in today's passage from the Acts. When Jesus ascended into heaven, two men dressed in white—probably angels, the apostles were used to them by now—asked them why they were hanging around, looking up into the clouds. They told them to get busy. So they took care of some administrative matters and elected Matthias to replace Judas. Then the event they were all waiting for took place: the descent of the Holy Spirit. The same day Saint Peter preached in Jerusalem, and 3,000 persons were baptized that day! Peter's stirring words which run for 35 verses give us an example of the first homily preached in the Church, the first evangelization, the first catechesis. Peter also promised the Holy Spirit to all who would accept Baptism. It was abundantly clear that success in the Church's work came from the action of the Divine Spirit.

The rest of the readings turn our gaze upon pastoral scenes familiar to the ancient peoples and Jesus' favorite metaphors. Today's second reading ends, *"For you had gone astray like sheep, but you have now returned to the shepherd and guardian of your souls."* The whole passage reflects the four Suffering Servant Songs of Isaiah, chapters 42 to 53, where the central theme is that the Messiah was to be led like a lamb to the slaughter. The responsorial psalm is a favorite for many, Psalm 23, "The Lord is my shepherd; there is nothing I shall want."

Whereas we are all familiar with the self-disclosure of Jesus, "I am the Good Shepherd," the Lord switches gears a little and within the context of the same figure of speech, calls himself the "sheepgate." We are to enter the fold, the kingdom of God, through him. Like being grafted onto him, the vine, we are joined to him by passing through him. Those who enter by climbing over the fence are thieves and marauders, who are up to no good. These have been false prophets, phony theologians, and wayward leaders. No doubt Jesus was referring to the leaders of the Jewish people who opposed his ministry, but the words are applicable to all times.

One hears that some believers resent being referred to as sheep (granted that sheep are somewhat smelly and dumb!). They consider themselves independent agents, fully capable of caring for themselves, even spiritually. But in the Lord's mind, I suspect the quality of "sheepness" is analogous with the qualities of childlikeness: teachable, enthusiastic, easily able to believe and follow. Jesus said, *"...[they] will come in and go out and find pasture."* We do not simply enter once, but go in and out. That is, we find safety and refuge in the darkness, but feed in the pastures of spiritual life every day, form a community with the other members of the flock, and serve as an attraction to others who are not of this fold! No wonder that this text ends with one of the most widely quoted expressions of Jesus, *"I came so that they might have life and have it more abundantly."*

Jesus is referring to a common pastoral usage of shepherds even today in the Near East. All the individual owners of flocks herd their sheep into a common pen for the night. In the morning each shepherd calls to his own sheep (many of which have a pet name), and they come to him at once. As Jesus himself said, *"They hear his voice"* and recognize me. This is partly explained by the phenomenon of "imprinting," which takes place when the shepherd assists at the birth of a lamb, which finds in the shepherd a surrogate parent.

If one of the chief qualities of "sheepness" is recognizing the Master's voice and following him, then we might well ask how to recognize the voice and presence of Jesus. We recognize him in his own Word, the Bible, when we receive insights into the meaning of the texts and try to answer the questions of the Lord: "Who do you say that I am?" "Who by worrying about it can add one inch to his height?" "What shall a person give in exchange for his soul?"

We also hear the voice of Jesus in the affirmation by others who are significant in our lives: parents, spouse, child, colleague, close friend. Someone whom we love, admire or respect has the capability of uplifting us and helping us find self-worth. Sometimes even honest criticism is the voice of the Lord, helping us to discover our failings and hangups. Do not ask whether the criticism comes from a friend or enemy; ask only whether it is true.

Finally, we hear the voice of Jesus in prayer when we receive the inspiration to make peace and reconcile ourselves with others whom we dislike, to begin some worthy project, to follow a good resolution or to turn away from habitual sin.

Psalm 23, when analyzed, provides a beautiful meditation. *"In verdant pastures he gives me repose"*: He nourishes me with his Word and Eucharist. *"Beside restful waters he leads me"*: Sheep will not drink from rushing or troubled waters, so we cannot be refreshed when we are distracted and troubled by our surroundings. *"Even though I walk in the dark valley I fear no evil":* We survive times of despair and temptation with our trust in the Shepherd. *"You are at my side with your rod and your staff that give me courage":* The Lord defends us as a shepherd drives away predators with his rod; with his crook he lifts the wandering sheep out of a ravine and disentangles it from the briars. *"You anoint my head with oil; my cup overflows":* At the end of the day the shepherd applies oil to the scratched faces of the sheep, as the Lord heals our wounds; the sheep drink deeply from a pail of cold water so that it overflows, just as Jesus brings cool refreshment to our souls. *"I shall dwell in the house of the Lord for years to come":* Everlasting life is the final reward of the faithful follower of Christ.

Fourth Sunday of Easter, B

Acts 4:8-12; 1 Jn 3:1-2; Jn 10:11-18

Jesus, our High Priest, was actually, in his own culture, a layperson. As an itinerant rabbi, he seems to have done everything wrong. He called king Herod a "fox," and the Jewish leaders "whited sepulchers"—fancy on the outside, but filled on the inside with death and corruption. He called his number-two man, Peter, a "satan" or tempter. Jesus had no public-relations department, no slick Madison Avenue techniques, just truth, painful, unvarnished truth; he knew how to express his negative feelings! But he paid the price of honesty. He ended up a seeming failure: his closest followers deserted him, one betrayed him with a kiss, another denied him three times. He suffered the most humiliating and agonizing execution of the ancient world, attended by a couple of women and one disciple, John. Yet he triumphed because he persevered until the end.

It is therefore easy to see that the essential Christian is not necessarily a winner, but a struggler. Even if you are a spiritual success—I do not speak of trivial worldly success—what is important is to have been committed to the struggle for holiness. God does not ask success of you like your boss, spouse, children and colleagues, because his Son set the pattern for handling failure, not success! (I sometimes wish Jesus had written the Christian Testament himself, so that everything would be clearer, but all that he ever wrote, as far as we know, is some doodling in the dust of the street, when he saved the adulteress from stoning.) He communicated with his hearers as he does with us, in dialogue. Its other name is prayer: we talk, then we listen while God talks. His message is typically simple: turn away from sin.

In the Bible sin has several definitions. First, it is some kind of idolatry or worship of a phony god, such as money, power, clout, sex, fame—these are the "idols of the marketplace," when you make pride, ambition or getting your way your priority in life, your "golden calf." Second, it is defiance of God, trying to manipulate him into your will and reverse the decisions of his providence—as we often try to do when we pray and "make deals" with God. Thirdly, sin is also opposing the good by favoring the opposite, as with abortion, premarital sex or refusing reconciliation with enemies. Lastly, perhaps the best insight into the nature of sin comes from the Greek word in the Bible for sin: *hamartia*, which means "missing the mark" or "missing the bull's eye." This comes from archery contests, like the Olympics, which St. Paul liked to compare with the Christian struggle. He used analogies with sports: run the good race and win the imperishable crown of glory. Thus the archer may have hit the target, more or less, but missed the bull's eye and won no prize. Those who do not turn away from sin miss the point of living, which is struggle.

They miss the boat, which is the Church that brings you safely home to port.

In the second reading, St. John wrote, *"We are God's children now."* This is not a figure of speech nor just a pious platitude. A child shares the life of a parent, so we share the very life of God, which is another definition of grace: God's life in a person. Even adoptive parents share their lives with their children, perhaps even more so, because of the element of choice. This is the greatest affirmation we can experience: God has loved us first, even when we were in our sins. When Jesus tells us in the Gospel to be childlike, it is not a theological put down. It means to accept the fatherhood of God and the brotherhood of Christ, and allow ourselves to be led, formed, taught and affirmed by God himself.

Some persons don't like to be called a "child," others dislike the title of "sheep." But Jesus called himself the Good Shepherd in today's text, and we don't have the right to tell him to change his figure of speech! The "good shepherd" is one who knows his business—which transports us back to the Near East, where shepherds, especially Bedouins, take their flocks across national frontiers as they choose. The various flocks are mixed at night in the pens, but in the morning each shepherd calls out to his own sheep and they know his voice, possibly because of the "imprinting" that takes place when the shepherd assists at the birthing of lambs. When wild beasts or robbers approach, the shepherd stands on a mound of earth and calls his sheep to gather around him. The application to Jesus, the Good Shepherd, is obvious. He "imprints" us, he calls us, he defends us.

If the Lord is our model, then we have to shepherd one another, call out to others, help them turn away from sin, especially help them to reach maturity. Perhaps the greatest sign of both spiritual and emotional maturity, which Jesus showed in his public life, is the ability to honestly express negative feelings in a socially acceptable way. This is the ability to criticize, to disagree, to express distress at another's behavior. Jesus was a master at this kind of honesty, yet his assertiveness was abrasive to the leaders of his people. The scribes and Pharisees "missed the mark" not because they were irreligious—in fact, they were scrupulous in keeping the laws of Judaism. Their sin was in trying to be the master minds of their own salvation: to put a lien on God, as if he "owed" them for their religiosity.

I have for a long time thought that the fundamental Christian virtue required in the struggle is honesty, which is truthfulness about oneself and one's perception of the world. As for humility, we never really know who is humbler, because the nature of humility precludes self-scrutiny. As for charity, the queen of virtues, it may be a facade, because I have known so many visibly charitable persons who are internally and invisibly judging others' motives and actions. What spares us these failures is honesty about our sinfulness; about our having been saved by the power of Jesus, not by our own actions; about our reliance on God for his mercy. Honesty is not arrogant, it is not self-serving, it does not seek its own glory or justification. Honesty is never sure that it possesses all the truth. In the end it will include also humility and charity and trust.

Fourth Sunday
of Easter, C

Acts 13:14, 43-52;
Rv 7:9, 14-17; Jn 10:27-30

In the first reading we see that Paul and Barnabas were successful in their tour of duty in Asia Minor, which was the first area of evangelization after the Judaeo-Christians left Palestine, due both to their proscription by the Jewish leaders and to the conquest of the Holy Land under Titus and Vespasian. They reached Antioch, where the city turned out to listen to them. The Gentiles were overjoyed that Jesus' message was available to them as well, that he was the "light of the Gentiles" (which is also the title of the Vatican II document on the Church).

When the two apostles were harassed by the Jewish leaders of the town, who got the wealthy matriarchs on their side, they "...*shook the dust from their feet in protest...*" not wanting even a remnant of memory to carry with them, and left. St. Luke, the author of Acts, always tries to illustrate that the fortunes of the members of the Mystical Body are similar to what the Lord suffered in his physical person, that is, harassment and persecution. Paul's history, which begins with today's chapter 13, shows how the nature of Christianity was changed forever—from a narrow Jewish sect to an international assembly "...*from every nation, race, people, and tongue,*" as the second reading from Revelation puts it. Chapters 10 to 12 of Acts is the bridge between St. Peter's Jewish viewpoint and St. Paul's universalist viewpoint.

Thus the infant Church escapes Jewish law and ritual and customs, but it is a battle all the way! The other apostles were conservatives in their orientation, but Paul was the liberal, broadening the scope of evangelization and dropping what was no longer useful to the nascent Church. He even argued with Peter, the first pope, and, as it is recorded elsewhere, stood up to him to his face, and a "bitter contention arose between them"! We can see why the official Church is slow to condemn and excommunicate, but ponders before it acts, to see whether a new idea can be reconciled with the deposit of faith. We remember that scholastic philosophy and theology were roundly condemned by St. Bernard. Other ideas were slow to gain acceptance. Also the geographic centers of Christianity changed over the centuries. North Africa was once totally Christian, now it is mostly Moslem. Europe and North America became centers of our faith, yet now those continents are divided in their theological perspectives. It seems that the areas of greatest growth today are in the Third World.

It is salutary to remember that all baptized believers are one with Christ. When Paul was struck on the way to Damascus, the Lord asked, "Saul, why do you persecute me?" Jesus is united with all his flock, his body, the branches grafted onto the vine. No wonder that Paul is rhapsodic when he writes about the body of Christ in his Letters. These Letters reveal more about the passion and emotion, anger and loving tenderness of Paul than Luke's descriptions in the Acts. We see Paul's own growth. In the beginning he identifies himself as a strict Pharisee, a student of Gamaliel, a son of Abraham, a Jew, a Hebrew, as he himself put it, who converted to Christ. Then the free-born citizen of the Hellenized city of Tarsus, a Roman citizen, emerged. He was fluent in Greek and sensitive to Greek rhetoric, so he could appeal to the Mediterranean world. He was finally decapitated in Rome for the crime of being a Christian in the reign of Nero, about 66 or 67 A.D., near the time when Peter was crucified, also in Rome. I suspect that during his incarceration in Rome, Paul was aching to get a chance to preach to Nero himself!

Sometimes St. Paul was not above a little sarcasm against his critics, and his golden, oratorical tongue was often barbed. When he impatiently argued against those who wanted to impose circumcision on the Gentiles, he told them to go all the way and castrate themselves! But we remember that he preached without compromise, as Jesus himself, no matter how painful the truth. Nevertheless, the lesson of his life is to be patient with those who do not share our viewpoints.

We also learn from Paul's experiences in Acts that "when you come to the service of God, prepare for battle!" The victorious throng in today's reading from Revelation is precisely those who survived the period of trial and washed their robes white in the blood of the Lamb, Jesus. In the Gospel today we have the strength of Jesus on which to rely. He says, *"I give them eternal life, and they shall never perish. No one can take them out of my hand."* We can do all things in Christ, who strengthens us.

Sometimes our suffering is the result of sin, our own or someone else's. It may just be nature taking its course or the just God punishing us—although typically we punish ourselves for our own foolishness. At times good people suffer because they oppose the values of this world, for which the world resents them. Jesus said, "Blessed are those who suffer persecution for the sake of justice." "Justice" is the term that describes our being "right" with God. Of course, the most impressive and beneficial kind of suffering we find in the Bible is "substitute" suffering, like the vicarious suffering of Jesus and those who follow him, as we see in the Acts. Jesus did not merely assume our sin; he became sin to redeem us.

Even this last form of suffering is not withheld from us. We can embed our trials and agonies into Jesus'; he foresaw not only those who would reject him, but also those who would imitate him. Paul himself wrote, "I complete in my own body what is lacking in the sufferings of Christ." This is quite overwhelming as if Jesus' full cup needed our few drops of suffering to make it overflow. Thus we are mediators with Jesus himself!

Monday of the
Fourth Week of Easter

Acts 11:1-18;
Jn 10:1-10 or 10:11-18

Chapter 11 of Acts is part of the bridge between part one, the role of Peter, and part two, the role of St. Paul. The other apostles take Peter to task for "consorting" with Gentiles. By eating their foods and even entering their homes a person could become ritually impure, unable to participate in Jewish rituals. Calling the Gentile's "uncircumcised" was tantamount to an insult, just as the Gentiles made jokes about the Jews in reverse! Two points emerge: It was important to have the Church think with Peter, the leader that Jesus left behind him; hence the apostles and Paul later always went to consult him. Secondly, Jesus left us inspiration and motivation, but not structures; he left that to the budding Church, allowing it to flower according to changing needs. (This is an important biblical argument supporting the need for a papacy.) Actually it took stern words from God to shake Peter into compliance. Somewhat pharisaically he answered God in the vision, *"Certainly not, sir, because nothing profane or unclean has ever entered my mouth!"* God had to tell him not to call unclean what God had purified and found acceptable.

The lesson is that we ought not "second guess" God. We are all guilty of bias and prejudice and of forcing our opinions on others. We can never be sure that in the pursuit of the truth we have all the truth, much less God's truth. By reflecting on the scriptures it helps to discover God's purpose and intentions, and how he enters human history and chooses the events that bring us into the kingdom.

In the Gospel today we see the process of bonding that takes place between the shepherd and his sheep, who know his voice from their birth. This is another application by Jesus of his figure of branches grafted into himself, the vine, and of Paul's body of Christ. Jesus said, *"This is why the Father loves me, because I lay down my life in order to take it up again."* We all die to some extent in small ways, and our small deaths have value if they are inserted into the death of Christ. When we suffer the loss of a dear one—family or friend—something of us dies as well. There will be someone missing who knew us in a special way. When we lose our job or income or home, we again suffer a small death, particularly if we see our family or dependents experience some privation. This comes from our sense of having somehow failed or "died." When we see our family divided by divorce or arguments, or having to move to another city for work, or living an immoral lifestyle, we feel that life has gone out of our lives. Finally, when someone would be happy to die because he or she is so miserable or terminally ill or lonely and abandoned, to go on living and continuing to struggle is a kind of living death!

It is always a pity and loss for such a person not to be embedded into the death of Jesus, for only then is ones human suffering of value for the kingdom of God and even redemptive. Just as Jesus conquered death and rose to glory, he empowers us to rise above our many small deaths through faith in him who is our Savior. A friend of mine was at home at night when she heard a rock against her window. She went outside to investigate, and a man stepped out of the shadows, choked her into unconsciousness, and raped her. Her aged mother came out of the house and found her. When I phoned to comfort my friend, it was I who received strength. As a convert, she had always worried whether she could survive a real test of faith—yet what good actually came from this senseless act of violence? The family was never so close; neighbors rallied to her side. God even provided that she be choked unconscious, because she remembered nothing of the sexual violence. So she passed the test and forgave her attacker.

The tests that God allows are never the ones we would have chosen; yet this woman's symbolic dying led to the resurrection of her faith!

Tuesday of the Fourth Week of Easter

Acts 11:19-26;
Jn 10-22-30

The passage from Acts continues the narration of the successes of the first believing community in spreading itself. Behind them all stood the figure of Jesus, the Good Shepherd, who was calling to the evangelized to hear his voice. The tenth chapter of St. John provided last Sunday's readings and continues on Monday and Tuesday. I think the liturgists have chosen to read this chapter in the wake of Easter because in the post-resurrection appearance of Jesus at the shore of Galilee he told St. Peter to feed and tend his lambs and sheep.

Some of us do not feel comfortable with the analogy of being sheep, especially because they are among the most mindless of God's creatures. The point behind Jesus' metaphor, however, is the relationship between sheep and shepherd: confidence, bonding, the provision of food, especially the sense of security the flock felt during the terrors of the night, when wild animals lurked nearby to tear the unwary sheep to pieces if they were caught outside the safety and security of the sheepfold.

When the pen was closed and barred against intruders, the shepherds made a fire and prepared their supper around it. They played their haunting Oriental melodies on reed flutes (which the Arab entrepeneurs still try to sell to tourists in the Holy Land), told tall tales and made up stories about the constellations of stars.

Then they took turns at the watch while the rest slept. We read in the Christmas story that the shepherds took turns in watching their flocks by night. The Lord always took his similes from homespun and familiar experiences of ordinary folk: the woman who lost a coin, the bridesmaids who fell asleep, the enemy who sowed weeds among the farmer's wheat, the flowers of the field, and the birds of the air. I suppose that contemporary preachers should find parallels with the Master's figures of speech and apply spiritual meanings to football games and skyscrapers, moon shots and laser beams, assembly lines and birthday parties.

The qualities of sheep, therefore, include trust and confidence in the shepherd. We are to step out in faith, invite the Lord into our lives, and allow him to be our Savior. We need to allow healing to take place, not living in the past and erupting old wounds and "worrying" about old scars. We often paralyze ourselves by rehearsing past sins and spiritual failures. The same Jesus who told us to forgive not seven times, but seventy times seven, will surely practice what he preaches. He is more anxious to forgive and save us than we ourselves long for salvation! In the same chapter 10, Jesus said that he gives his life for his sheep—and that was no metaphor!

All the Jewish Testament prophecies that centered on pastoral themes were a preparation for fulfillment in Jesus. He is the full meaning of the covenant with Abraham; he is the guarantor of the promise. The old covenant passed away, but Jesus abides forever. Meanwhile the flock is diverse; there are even some "black" sheep. The Mystical Body keeps its doctrinal consistency, but with considerable diversity about non-essentials. Unity does not mean uniformity. There are many liturgical rites and customs. Yet teachings cannot vary in essentials, because God cannot endorse opposing concepts of doctrine or morality. If our nation requires a Supreme Court, how much more do the subtle and gray areas of theology require an arbiter! Once you accept Jesus, everything else falls into place; he left us his Church as the arbiter of Tradition.

Wednesday of the Fourth Week of Easter

Acts 12:24-13:5;
Jn 12:44-50

In today's Gospel Jesus says, *"I came into this world as light, so that everyone who believes in me might not remain in darkness."* St. John's Gospel is often referred to as the "Gospel of Light," because so often the Johannine theme is light vs. darkness. In the opening chapter of John, in fact, we find this theme loud and clear: "Whatever came to be in him, found life, life for the light of men. The light shines on in darkness, a darkness that did not overcome it." John the Baptist came only to testify to the light, for he was not the light itself.

As suffering is considered the second nature of our humanity, so living in darkness is our connatural environment, due to the original sin. The spiritual life—to apply the text from today's Gospel—is a gravitation towards the light, step by step. We are all impressed by the dramatic events in the lives of the saints, but we generally read about the times when they seem already confirmed in their sanctity. For example, we see St. Francis confronting the emperor and the pope and the sultan in North Africa; we remember his stigmata and the marvelous growth of his Order. But we may forget the years of confusion, distress and darkness in the search for the light of holiness, which gives his life a realistic meaning.

One typically grasps more theology from an hour of attentive prayer than many hours of theological study. Study is the act of the mind, but knowing God is an act of the heart. St. Bonaventure, the Franciscan doctor, when he was already the minister general of the Order, a papal legate and renowned writer, chanced upon an old woman weeping, and he inquired what might be the cause of her grief. She sadly told him that she could never love God as much as he with all his knowledge and education. He gently reassured her that knowledge has very little to do—unfortunately—with the love of God. In fact, when knowledge is not coupled with humility, it is generally a detriment. Of course, we would say that we should omit neither study nor prayer.

During the Easter season, when we see the Paschal Candle lit for all the liturgies, it symbolizes the constancy of Jesus in our lives as the light which overcomes darkness, especially the blackness of sin and death. But too often we let the light remain in isolation from the rest of our world. As witnesses of that light in our own lives, we need to let it shine for other people outside the church building. We need to raise the roof and push out the walls. The stone of Jesus' tomb did not have to be rolled back in order for him to walk out, because he could pass through solids. The opening of the tomb was to let us inside to be aware that Jesus lives! Similarly we ought to open the treasure of the Church to everybody, so they can escape the darkness outside. What we proclaim in the liturgy, which is the community of prayer, must be asserted by the community at work in the world: feeding the hungry, liberating the prisoner, comforting the sick, teaching the ignorant. Of course, the worst hunger, imprisonment, illness and ignorance are spiritual. This is the primary liberation that the Church gives to the world. When these needs are met, the physical alleviation will quickly follow, because every believer is obliged to give witness to the light by the works of charity and social justice.

Thursday of the Fourth Week of Easter

Acts 13:13-25;
Jn 13:16-20

The words Jesus speaks to us in today's Gospel come from his Last Supper discourse, right after the washing of the disciple's feet—a text that appears only in Saint John's Gospel. The Lord gives us several points to ponder: 1) Because no slave is greater than his master, we will have to pass through sufferings similar to his own. 2) Once we learn his message well, we are supposed to put it into practice, lest it remain only cerebral and sterile—which will persuade no one to our way of life. 3) If we accept Jesus, then we will have to accept anyone whom he sends us in the future. 4) By referring to himself as "I AM," Jesus is clearly placing himself on a par with God our Father; hence, his authority and power come from his Trinitarian existence.

When Jesus speaks of the power he shares with us, we are not to think of the analogy of the electric company—a kind of natural mystery that somehow works, but which we cannot understand. Nor may we think that Christianity requires a "slave-like" mentality, patterned after Christ who allowed himself to be crucified without opening his mouth, silent as a sheep before its shearers. Nor are we to think of the Lord as a kindly gentleman who keeps forgiving us when we fall into the same old deliberate sins without trying to reform ourselves. (Yet each of these errors have a grain of truth, if we examine them carefully!)

Then there are the screen versions and television ministries that try to portray Jesus: generally blond, blue-eyed, innocuous, never confronting, never completely human either! Yet he was crucified precisely because he did challenge people and make demands that his listeners change their behavior! The Jewish leaders thought he was truly dangerous. He did not spare the feelings of his own closest associates and friends; he reprimanded them for their dull wits and failure to understand his message, even though he took pains to explain his parables only to them. The very priests of Judaism, whose endorsement would have won him an even greater following, he rebuked and criticized for laying heavy burdens on the people which they did nothing to alleviate; he termed them a "brood of vipers," venemous snakes! I think that even today Jesus is the hardest on priests and religious, whom he has called to service and expects to work hard, pray consistently, discipline themselves and be totally honest.

The litmus test of us all is whether we look at the cross and the One nailed there and say, "I want to be like you!" Even during this Easter season we must remember to live in the shadow of the cross; we remember that the Risen Lord kept the marks of his wounds. As I quoted from the Gospel and now repeat, Jesus says that we will suffer like him, if we are committed to discipleship; that we cannot allow his teachings, once understood, to lie fallow; that we must accept the prophets whom he sends us, that is, his spokespersons. They are not always in the Church (yet), not necessarily friendly towards us, not always proclaiming something agreeable to us nor something with which we always agree. They tell us the truth about politics, racism, phony religious values, war and peace. Most of all, Jesus sends us his part-time prophets to tell us the truth about ourselves. *"Whoever receives the one I send receives me, and whoever receives me receives the one who sent me."*

Friday of the Fourth Week of Easter

Acts 13:26-33;
Jn 14:1-6

Today's Gospel derives also from the Last Supper teaching by Jesus; this text is also one that is used very often for funerals. The Lord's words of comfort were directed to his disciples to prepare them for his coming immolation the very next day. Yet still they did not understand!

In the preceding section St. Peter told the Master he was willing to die for him, but Jesus countered with the prediction of his triple denial. This startled them all, so Jesus continued, *"You have faith in God; have faith also in me."* The *"...many dwelling places..."* in heaven is probably an oblique reference that Peter will make it after all, and that we will all come to glory in different ways, as long as we have that required faith. So Jesus had to be off to his destiny to prepare a place for them all and bring them home.

St. Thomas the Doubter always needed concrete evidence of Jesus' claims. *"We do not know where you are going; how can we know the way?"* The answer was, *"I am the way and the truth and the life."* The very sequence of the three terms suggests the work of the Holy Trinity, because all Three were involved in the ministry and redemption by Jesus. In faith we come to him first, attracted by his teaching and the movement he founded that became the Church. Thus he is the way, the model and pattern of all human life, the road we follow to reach the kingdom. Therefore he says immediately, *"No one comes to the Father except through me."* Earlier he had said, "No one knows the Father but the Son, and those to whom the Son reveals him."

When we come to the Father we arrive at the truth. Truth is not what we discover about this universe, but rather how God views the universe. In him is all truth. But he speaks truth by his Word, who is the Son, Jesus Christ. Because he said that the Father and he are one, the Lord assures us that he is also the truth, possessing the same nature as his Father. In his discourse at the Last Supper, Jesus went on to say that he would send the Holy Spirit who would teach—he is also identified with Trinitarian Truth—and also confer life upon them, particularly at Pentecost. The Spirit is the soul, hence the life of the Mystical Body of Christ.

We read these references to the Spirit as Truth in John: "I will ask the Father and he will give you another Paraclete. The Holy Spirit whom the Father will send in my name will instruct you in everything, and remind you of all that I told you. When the Paraclete comes, the Spirit of truth who comes from the Father—and whom I will send myself from the Father—he will bear witness on my behalf. When he comes, he will prove the world wrong about sin, about justice, about condemnation. When he comes, however, being the Spirit of truth he will guide you to all truth."

Jesus calls himself "truth," yet he refers to the Third Person likewise as the Spirit of truth. We know that he is also the "life," because of Jesus instructing Nicodemus that he had to be born of water and the Holy Spirit—birth signifies life. On the most profound and accurate theological level, all three Persons are way, truth, and life, because the actions we appropriate to One apply to the Three—as at the Incarnation and baptism of Jesus, when all three Persons are named. Of course, one can take these three terms and apply them to each Divine Person after careful analysis of the divine actions upon humanity. Eminently in our thinking, however, we apply these words to Jesus: the way to the Father, the truth he speaks as the Word of God, and the life, because he is the vine and we are the branches!

Saturday of the Fourth Week of Easter

Acts 13:44-52;
Jn 14:7-14

Jesus' dialogue with Philip, his apostle, in today's Gospel also comes from the Last Supper discourse, as the texts of the past few days. The Lord's response to him describes his relationship with his Father: *"Do you not believe that I am in the Father and the Father is in me? The words that I speak to you I do not speak on my own. The Father who dwells in me is doing his works."*

Even though we have the same Father by our life of grace, Jesus always carefully distinguished between his and our filial relationship. He said, "My Father and your Father; my God and your God." When the disciples asked Jesus to teach them to pray, he answered, "This is how you are to pray: Our Father...." He was careful not to say, "This is how we pray." He made this distinction because he is the natural Son of God; we are raised above our nature, which is inferior to his, to be adoptive supernatural children of God. Yet because of our adoption into the divine family, Jesus told Philip, "Amen, amen, I say to you, whoever believes in me will do the works that I do, and will do greater ones than these." When we recall the healing, the raising from the dead, the exorcisms and miracles of the Master, his promise is extraordinary. Our powers as God's adopted children are effective because: *"If you ask anything of me in my name, I will do it."*

We recite the Lord's Prayer so casually, so often, that we do not always see that the very title hides the mystery concealed for ages, but revealed in Jesus Christ: that we can share in the nature and power of God himself. This is what St. Paul calls "God's secret plan." The original Mass, celebrated in catacombs and private homes in the days of the persecution, was separated into the Mass of the Catechumens and the Mass of the Faithful or Baptized. Basically this first half of the Mass was our liturgy of the Word, during which the neophytes were instructed and exhorted. Then they left the assembly; they were not allowed, of course, to participate in the Eucharist, not even "from the sidelines." And here is the point: They were not even taught the "Our Father" until just before Baptism. The concept was that they had no right to call God "Father" before Baptism, because they did not share in his nature yet by adoption.

Elsewhere St. Paul wrote, "No one can say, 'Father,' except in the Holy Spirit." In those days the sacrament of confirmation was conferred with Baptism.

These two sacraments initiated life in the newly baptized. This is the love life of the Blessed Trinity; this is the life in which we share that makes us adoptive children of our heavenly Father.

FIFTH WEEK OF EASTER

Fifth Sunday
of Easter, A

Acts 6:1 7; 1 Pt 2:4 9;
Jn 14:1-12

"Lord, let your mercy be upon us, as we place our trust in you." This is the response to the psalm and, as it often happens in the liturgy, a good summary of all the readings. "Trust" and "faith" are interchangeable words for the most part, and the latter recurs in all three readings. Among the seven deacons chosen to do the charitable works to which the apostles could not attend, was Stephen, "a man filled with faith." In the second reading St. Peter refers to Jesus as the cornerstone of our faith: *"'Whoever believes in it shall not be put to shame.' Therefore, its value is for you who have faith, but for those without faith: 'The stone which the builders rejected has become the cornerstone.'"* Finally, in the Gospel, Jesus strengthens his disciples right after he warns Peter that he will deny Jesus three times: *"You have faith in God; have faith also in me."* At the end of the text Jesus concludes, *"Amen, amen, I say to you, whoever believes in me will do the works that I do, and will do greater ones than these."*

From these texts we learn that faith has degrees. The implication is that if Stephen is filled with faith, then some persons must be less full of that virtue. We learn that faith is a personal relationship with Christ; we "put our faith" in him. We learn that following Jesus means to accept as our leader one who was not successful, and in many senses a failure; the Lord was a stone which was rejected by humanity. We learn that despite our sins and failures (as Peter) our faith will make us whole and healed. We learn that faith will empower us to replicate his actions with an effect equal to the Lord's.

Jesus speaks his memorable words in today's text: *"I am the way and the truth and the life."* Although these terms can be applied to all three members of the Holy Trinity, we appropriate them primarily to Jesus. The way of love in Jesus' message translates as mercy, forgiveness, acceptance and tolerance, especially that great tool of interpersonal relationships, compromise. Traveling the way of faith leads to the truth of faith. We believe in order to understand truth—here, the truth of what Jesus said and did while on earth and what he committed to the Tradition of the Church. He taught us about true riches: the pearl of great price, the treasure hidden in the field. We are not to worry: no one by worrying about it can add one inch to his or her height—nor subtract one inch from the waistline. Finally we grow in the life of Jesus within us, which we call grace. Other persons see the face of Christ in our faces as we turn to them with compassion and social service, the corporal and spiritual works of mercy. When we all do our Christian duty, then Christ comes alive in the world's perception.

We learn to walk his way, know his truth and live his life by conversing with the Lord in prayer. So many persons easily get bored in prayer because they try to do and say too much. They think they are not praying unless they multiply words, keep talking, make resolutions and promises, pour out feelings. As in any realistic conversation, the word traffic is not one-way; we listen to what the Master has to say. I suspect each of us has that nagging feeling that we have not prayed enough: that we have not answered the call of God to place ourselves in his presence, that we have sidestepped that mandate Jesus gave his disciples, "Come aside with me to pray a while," and that guilt from Gethsemane, "Could you not watch one hour with me?"

We do not learn much about the way, the truth and the life of faith by imagining that we have to receive deep insights during prayer, effusions of emotions, or profound revelations as we gaze heavenward with a sigh—right out of a Renaissance painting! Prayer (communication) is simply the right thing to do, the next task to be done. The distractions of our fast-paced urban (and even rural) lives drown out the call of Jesus to converse with him privately, all alone. Actually most busy fathers and mothers making a living and making a home would give anything to have time for private prayer—or private anything. Even many retired persons are forever on the run, when it should be their golden age when there is enough time for the leisurely things, shopping, babysitting, preparing meals, socializing and praying.

Ask yourself what your hangups are that prevent time for prayers. You say, "I don't get anything out of it." That sounds more like the complaint of a teenager who tries to rationalize not attending Mass on Sundays. We do not pray for a feeling of euphoria and exultation and well-being. We pray so that we can in turn listen to what God has to say about his world. Our decision to pray, at least when we are novices at prayer, is first of all an act of the will, a determination, not a feeling. The attraction and drive and longing to pray comes with time! Subsequent feelings of satisfaction are terrific, but not essential to the nature of prayer.

Often we fail to know Christ in prayer because we do not use a helpful environment to avoid distraction. Or

we delay until the end of the day, when we are crowd-
ing the last chores of the day into our schedules. The
earlier in the day, the better, before problems and anxieties impinge upon our consciousness. Some persons
find it helpful to sit in a comfortable chair facing a wall
with a crucifix or devotional picture in order to fix their
gaze on heavenly things and persons. It may be necessary to rise early before other members of the household, unless you are going to a church anyway for Mass
or meditation.

A misconception is that we have to pray for extended periods to be successful at prayer. Whereas it is
likely that longer periods immerse us more deeply into
God, yet it is the quality of prayer that is more significant. Fifteen minutes of intense engagement of mind
and heart every day for a year would attune us most effectively to God's thinking.

A subtle difficulty some find in prayer, especially at
the beginning, is that there surfaces in prayer a clarifica-
tion of aspects of life that may be painful: a sin that must
be dismissed from our lives, a virtue we had better try
to acquire, a resolution God expects us to keep, a calling
we should exercise, a reconciliation we must undertake.
In short, perseverance in prayer could make us saints!

Fifth Sunday
of Easter, B

Acts 9:26-31;
1 Jn 3:18-24; Jn 15:1-8

In the first reading from Acts we see the effectiveness of St. Paul in preaching Jesus; he was a man with
a speech to give and a story to tell. Yet even words are
only the beginning, as St. John warns us in the second
reading: *"Let us love not in word or speech but in deed and
truth."* In the gospel metaphor of the vine and the

branches Jesus focuses on his message: *"If you remain in me and my words remain in you, ask for whatever you want and it will be done for you."* Once more there is the power of the word.

In the ancient Near East, where all the Bible was written, people were more sensitized to the word than we, to the memorization of texts, verbalized genealogies and so forth. In the creation story in Genesis God simply says: Let there be light, let the earth separate from the water, let every living creature come forth—and it happens by the effectiveness of his word. Once spoken, a blessing, curse, oath or contract could not be revoked. Remember Jacob and Esau, the twin sons of Isaac. Esau the elder was the rugged outdoor Marlboro type, who should have been the chief heir; the younger twin, Jacob, was a dreamer, a mama's boy. As Isaac lay dying, he wished to bless Esau to prevent civil strife over the inheritance. But Jacob, with the connivance of his mother, tricked the half-blind old man and got the blessing of a first-born. Esau was miffed, but the blessing could not be revoked! Similarly at the Consecration, when the right words are pronounced over the right species with the right intention, the presence of Jesus, Body, Blood, Soul and Divinity, remains as long as the appearance of bread and wine.

Our age has the same preoccupation with words. We recall President Nixon's Watergate tapes and the diaries of Colonel Oliver North: words can control our lives and destinies. The three network anchormen have incredible power to manipulate news facts according to their own biases. Before elections the public-relations power brokers can change the course of history! Then we all have our school and work records that irrevocably mark down our achievements and behavior. Promotions in the workplace and military depend on such records, reviewed by persons who never met you! And we cannot omit the effect of our tax returns, social security, credit rating and health records in somebody's computer: We are controlled!

We are flooded with idle chatter all day long, the blaring car radio, newscasts, talk shows. Over five hundred books are published every day in the U.S. alone. Magazines compete for our subscriptions. There is junk mail, and who can read the whole Sunday newspaper? "Talk is cheap," and "Actions do speak louder than words." That is why we need quiet time to sort out all the words in our lives and reflect on our priorities and escape the experts, who tell us more than we really want or need to know!

In the end the only word that lasts—even into eternity—is the Word of God, who is a Person, and also a book, the Bible, for they are the same. The Bible always makes the annual best seller list, but the point is not the sales, but the reading and practice. Nevertheless the Bible says of itself that it is keener than a two-edged sword, cutting through to the bone and the marrow—that is, cutting us to the quick and shaking us up. Salvation is complete in Jesus, but not until we invite him into our lives and he claims us for himself and changes us.

A favorite musical form is the Negro Spiritual. One is "De Gospel Train Am Comin'" and the chorus tells us, "Git on board, li'l chillun, git on board." When the Lord wanted to get us on track with his heavenly Father, he saw all the deviations, washed-out tracks, and rusted locomotives. Ancient religion was largely bankrupt. He tried to remain within the existing railroad system of Judaism, a beautiful religion, but its board of directors refused. He could have repaired the tracks, greased the engines, fixed the couplings and updated the passenger cars, but instead he decided to build a whole new railroad! The New Testament became the new train schedule, new prices, the qualifications of travel and arrival times. The spiritual meaning is obvious. Jesus did not tell us every detail; hence, there is a need for the Holy Spirit as the engineer on the Gospel Train to direct the Church in issues such as disarmament, abortion, narcotics, nuclear war, because Jesus couldn't say everything—and no one would have understood the hydrogen bomb anyway!

We read the Bible to discover what Jesus' words meant to his own time and culture, then try to apply them to today. What does it mean to be a city set on a hill, the salt of the earth, and the light placed on the lampstand. We must be people of the Word, but God is a gentleman and does not force his Word down our throats. But if you do accept him into your life, it must be complete. He is easily pleased, but he is never satisfied! He wants everything from you: your family, career, bankbook, future. Than he returns it all to you, only purified, as part of his kingdom.

With your Bible in your left hand and your rosary in your right hand you can develop the faith that conquers the world and brings peace, as Our Lady of Fatima has promised. As the Gospel says, the Lord will prune you and trim you to make you more fruitful. Apart from him you can produce nothing of lasting value. The Father's commandment is this (second reading): *"We should believe in the name of his Son, Jesus Christ, and love one another just as he commanded us."*

Fifth Sunday of Easter, C

Acts 14:21-27;
Rv 21:1-5;
Jn 13:31-33, 34-35

Eastertide always coincides with spring. The new and changed life of the resurrected Jesus and the new life of the Church after Pentecost herald the season of flowering and greening. Of course, there remain the same old problems of the crabgrass of sin and the dandelions of those attractive vices which bloom and blow their seeds all over the yard of our lives. Yet the newness goes on. In the second reading from Revelation John records: *"I saw a new heaven and a new earth.... I also saw the holy city, a new Jerusalem, coming down out of heaven from God, prepared as a bride adorned for her husband.... The one who sat on the throne said, 'Behold, I make all things new.'"* Finally the Lord speaks in the Gospel, *"I give you a new commandment: love one another.... This is how all will know that you are my disciples, if you have love for one another."*

When the Gospels were first composed along with other writings, the primitive believing community had a sense of the newness of what they were experiencing. Novelty always commands attention. That is why we are so addicted as a nation to newscasts and newspapers. Our typical greeting is "What's new?" We have new fashions, new hair styles, the New Deal, and new frontiers of technology. With the planned obsolescence of so many of our products, however, newness assumes the nature of the transitory and perishable. The truths of the Gospel nevertheless are not passing, but permanent.

The text from Revelation hinges on the newness that will be finalized at the end of time, when the heavens and earth pass away, but the word of the Lord, as Jesus once proclaimed, will not pass away. The kingdom of God, which is called the new Jerusalem, is the newlywed, the bride of Christ, the Church, ever ancient, yet ever new, without spot or wrinkle or anything of that sort (St. Paul). God will remain in his dwelling among men and women. Absent forever will be weeping and mourning, tears and wailing. This is the best news of all; we will have achieved the status of the risen Christ!

With this in mind we can better assess the novelties of this world. When America was first discovered and explored, it was called the New World, the place where new prosperity would reign, new forms of government would flourish, and new freedoms would be granted. This actually happened, yet in time the shine of newness wore off, like a new car's. There were nicks and bumps and accidents never anticipated, which left the once shiny automobile rusted and dented. In the United States, Democrats and Republicans both promise a revival of the springtime of our democracy, but nothing ever seems to change, except new bills before the Congress, new descriptions of poverty and new wars to subsidize. Evidently new freeways, skyscrapers and moonshots could not deliver us from aging.

Only one thing has retained its freshness, the Gospel, which promises new and eternal life in Christ and the power to resurrect. That is the Good News, which is the translation of "gospel" from the German source of that word! All our tired old world can offer us is a repair job. Those who hear and accept the Good News, however, must be committed to struggle. Paul and Barnabas told their converts in the first reading, *"It is necessary for us to undergo many hardships to enter the kingdom of God."* Whereas conflict is destructive in this world of the flesh, conflict renews those who abide in the realm of the spirit. Jesus reminded us often that only love will make the struggle possible and the conflict positive in its results. *"As I have loved you, so you also should love one another. This is how all will know that you are my disciples, if you have love for one another."*

Often we realize too late that love is the only answer. That is why Jesus' words are always motivational. His inspiration gives us the tool by which we can judge all human structures, all human struggles, all human aspirations. If he had outlined all these in detail, the Gospel would read like the Code of Canon Law, rather than Good News. He did not tell us so much how to live as why we have lived at all. Because everything passes into obsolescence, don't take your meaning from what you produce or how you function, but from how well you have loved. We were made for happiness, hence it is better to be happy—that is, without frustrations—than sad or suffering. Yet it is more important to be content with what we have and what we have become, because such an attitude eliminates frustration. Happiness is elusive and of this world, unless it is eternal happiness or what leads to it. Perhaps the great fascination of heaven's happiness, when every tear will be wiped away, is that it will always remain new, not geared to time and space, which is the environment of obsolescence. Nothing less than our loving God and one another, and God's loving us, could sustain an eternity of satisfaction. That is why it is not simply that we should love one another, because it could be only on the natural level or for natural motives. Jesus clarifies the mode of loving: *"As I have loved you, so you also should love one another."*

Monday of the Fifth Week of Easter

*Acts 14:5-18;
Jn 14:21-26*

Today's Gospel is again an extract from Jesus' final words to his disciples at the Last Supper. Only St. John records this wonderful farewell discourse. Jesus promises to come with his Father and dwell in whoever loves him. He also promises to send the Holy Spirit. *"The Advocate, the holy Spirit that the Father will send in my name—he will teach you everything...."* Thus all three Persons are mentioned (another proof of the reality of the Holy Trinity, the central doctrine of Christianity) as being present to us, to sanctify us by the Divine Indwelling, a very ancient spiritual doctrine.

Jesus once remarked, "The kingdom of God is within you," and "The kingdom of God is at hand" (recorded by Matthew), when at the beginning of his public life he made contact with John the Baptist. Nevertheless on the Friday of his death he told Pilate, "My kingdom is not of this world."

We must conclude not that Jesus was ambivalent about the establishment of his kingdom, but that he was communicating two different ideas about the same reality. His kingdom is both here and now among us and within those who love God and remain in the state of grace; and the kingdom is also in the process of happening. Nevertheless that future kingdom will not be consummated until the Day of the Lord, that is, judgment day.

An analogy with the altars of most churches' sanctuaries is helpful. During the Mass Jesus is in the process of coming to us on the altar; in the tabernacle on the altar of reposition he remains. It is the same Jesus, coming and staying; it is the same kingdom, both in process and consummation. The Lord in the tabernacle suggests that hidden, transcendent God. As theologians put it: the God who is far beyond our grasp, surpassing our grasp and exceeding our speculation and understanding. When he is brought to the sacrificial altar we recognize the God who approaches us in intimacy and comes into our bodies, yet as we digest the Bread of Angels, Jesus transforms us into himself spiritually and even, in a sense, corporally, because he makes not only our souls but also our bodies holy, temples of God, and ready for a glorious resurrection.

We cannot leave these truths without trying to understand a little better the "coming" and the "abiding" Christ. Jesus is a composite of the Word, or Second Person, and the human Jesus—one Person with two natures or modes of activity. Thus we are drawn always to look to heaven and our eternal union with God. But we must also work to make Jesus "happen" in our space and time. In the Eucharist this depends on the power of the ordained priest, but the Lord is also present in the ministering community which is gathered in his name. We are to think out solutions to social and political and moral problems in the Christian tradition. We are to carry out the corporal and spiritual works of mercy, knowing that when we benefit the least of Jesus' brothers and sisters, we also benefit him. Lest we think that the kingdom of God is only cerebral, or just social action without reference to religion, we must do everything in the name of Jesus and for love of him, holding him high in our hearts, because "the kingdom of God is within you."

Tuesday of the Fifth Week of Easter

Acts 14:19-28;
Jn 14:27-31

The Book of Genesis points out the goodness of creation. After each day we read that "God saw it was good." Nevertheless in the gospel text of Jesus' farewell today we hear the Lord call Satan *"...the ruler of the world."* The fact is that the world is good until we creatures with a free will give entry to the dark prince of hell. When the devil thought he had won his greatest victory—when Jesus was killed on Calvary—he actually suffered his greatest defeat by his divine adversary. This is the paradox of the cross. Jesus said, "The kingdom of God suffers violence, and only the violent take it by storm."

Yes, Jesus the peacemaker told us that the violent can storm heaven effectively. This is, first of all, a commitment to battle, but more a promise to do violence to oneself: to prejudices, hangups, rigidity and unforgiving attitudes. What Jesus apparently meant is for us to "mortify our flesh and its desires," as we read elsewhere; that is, avoid the occasions of sin and pull a shade down on our fantasies, which is the application of Jesus' dictum, "if your eye scandalizes you, then pluck it out!"

Because of our all-too-human proneness to sin, wanting to become "as gods, knowing good and evil" (as Satan tempted Eve), the Church has typically backed away from too much contact with this passing world and its prince. The world is not evil; it is fallen. People are not depraved, but deprived of the good that was their natural and supernatural heritage. Right from the beginning Christians ran from the world into deserts and onto mountaintops (in imitation of the Lord and John the Baptist); they shunned the entertainments of the theater and dance, avoided politics and the army, in which regular sacrifices were offered to pagan gods. This is not so different today, when one finds so much immorality and corruption in politics, the theater, and dance.

After the Protestant Reformation the Church entered a "siege mentality"—that Catholics should shun Protestants and all non-Catholics and avoid the secularizing influence of the "Protestant ethic"—even though subsequently the Church itself was often seduced by that same ethic, power ploys, and the accumulation of wealth. (And it is true today that the greatest "leakage" from the Church derives from inter-faith marriages.)

Scientific discoveries and technology have proved a great asset to evangelization, yet remain of dubious value overall. The quality of human life, poverty and especially the exploitation in the Third World and immorality have gotten worse and deteriorated the moral fabric of society. No wonder the Church proscribes the techniques that seek to make us like God in the manipulation of human life—not to mention the evil of abortion and euthanasia.

I doubt whether we shall ever achieve a peaceful balance between the world of the spirit and the world of the flesh—which St. Paul refers to as earthbound thinking and transitory values. Nevertheless since Vatican Council II the Church encourages us to be engaged in the world and enter it very cautiously and claim it for Christ. (Actually we are always "in" the world, but not necessarily a part of its thinking.) The prince of this world need not catch us in his death-dealing grasp; we can belong to the kingdom of Jesus. The world can discover that we love the Father and do what he has commanded us through Jesus Christ: change the City of Men into the City and Kingdom of God.

Wednesday of the
Fifth Week of Easter

Acts 15:1-6;
Jn 15:1-8

"I am the vine, you are the branches. Whoever remains in me and I in him will bear much fruit, because without me you can do nothing." The Lord proposes a symbiosis, which is different from leadership as we know it on this earth in the business and military fields. His "leadership" and our "followership" derive from the sameness of life and identity of values. Generally a leader separates himself or herself from underlings, employees and followers. The secular sphere is not the same as the spiritual realm.

The vine to which we are engrafted, Jesus, gives us his divine life through grace, and gifts us with his Holy Spirit. In the world of politics or business, the lifestyle and motives differ between leaders and followers. For example, a leader may enter politics for a variety of reasons: fame, remembrance in history, power over the lives of others, prestige and privilege, and so forth. But those who follow in the same political party or coterie may have entirely different ideas than the leader. Yet we, the disciples of Jesus, should try to maintain the same life-style of Christ—poverty, service, compassion—and the same motivation—glory to God in the highest and peace on earth to people of good will.

Leaders in the Church are obliged to share in that lifestyle and motivation, otherwise they lose credibility and are unworthy of leadership in Christ. For example, if a religious superior in a convent or friary does every-thing right—follows canon law, pays the utility bills on time, and makes a satisfactory schedule—that is fine, and he or she is likely to please the followers or "sub-jects." Such a person is said to be a good "manager," but these functions do not make the superior worthy of leadership in Christ.

Supervisors, bosses and public officials are sup-posed to do things right. But the true leader looks first to Jesus, then does the right things. Now Jesus was not a very good manager, because he didn't do the right, the acceptable things. He alienated the leaders of his people, he censured his disciples often, he was finally executed as a criminal. He pleased very few persons. But Jesus did the right things as our model. He challenged and drew the best out of his disciples. He brought them up short for their failings. He corrected their lack of understand-ing. On the positive side, he motivated and inspired them. Most of all throughout his public life he forgave them and always loved them—which a secular authority doesn't have to do; he simply fires the inefficient and culpable. Thus a good manager can be a poor leader, and vice versa. Those subordinates are fortunate who have a composite of manager and leader.

Some research indicates that unsuccessful leaders are all alike in their incompetence, but successful lead-ers are all successes in their own ways. Jesus became successful in his own way: by dying for his followers, and even for those who would later refuse to follow him! When he rose from the dead, he was able to pass on the power of his own success. Those who have a voice in the selection of their superiors have to decide whether they want a manager or a leader, that is, a manager who pleases them by administration or a leader who tells them the truth!

Thursday of the Fifth Week of Easter

Acts 15:7-21;
Jn 15:9-11

The Last Supper farewell speech of Jesus is recorded only in St. John's Gospel. It is so long that one wonders how the disciple, or several disciples, remembered it verbatim. This chapter 15 begins by telling us that we must be joined to the Lord as branches are grafted on to a vine—like varietal grapes are created in the Napa Valley of California—in order to share the identical life of Jesus. God is the owner of the vineyard, and the "abundant produce" is a rich and plentiful wine. Jesus said we must drink his blood to have life in us, so we can be raised up on the last day. What seems to be a disjointed speech hangs together as a unified appeal to all of us to love one another as he has loved us, by keeping the commands of our heavenly Father.

What is that life that flows through us "branches"? St. Paul explains this metaphor as the body of Christ and the life-giving Spirit who is the soul of that body. This is the mystery of grace, that is, God's love life in a person. We call this life "sanctifying grace." To "sanctify" us is to make us holy, other Christs, inheritors of heaven, the family of God—not just "God's people," but "God's family." One of the most dramatic and challenging statements of the Bible is, "Be holy as I am holy."

What a magnificent destiny is ours! The Father, Son and Spirit are a community of love. The Father expresses himself totally in his single Word, the Son. In this communication is conceived by their mutual love a Person, the Holy Spirit. As the Second Person is the Word, so the Third Person is the Whisper of God. The very notion of whispering suggests a zephyr of wind and an intimacy. (St. Maximilian Kolbe wrote that this Person is an Uncreated Conception, just as Mary is the created Conception, the Immaculate Conception!)

To be "in the state of grace" means not so much that God dwells in us—although that is also the truth!—but rather that we dwell in God: enveloped in, absorbed by, lifted up into the bosom of the Blessed Trinity. One can imagine that all of us who share in that divine life are centered within the Holy Triad, and their inter-Personal relationships shoot through us and transform us into their own holiness. "Be holy as I am holy." In verse 9 today the gospel text reads, *"Remain in my love,"* which seems to encapsulate the same idea. To gain access to the interior life of God, as Jesus says today, *"If you keep my commandments, you will remain in my love."*

What is both the effect and the sign that this is really happening to us? *"I have told you this so that my joy might be in you and your joy might be complete."* The best verifiable sign of God's love is joy. The unsmiling saint is a fraud; the sour mystic is only a mistake. Truculent, uncommunicative holiness actually betrays God with a subtle hypocrisy that shuts off everyone. Such a Christian is only a time-server and a hireling—possibly with the correct intellectual perception of what is right and availing to salvation, but without heart. The true believer may even have to suffer, yet because he is in Christ, his joy is complete. And we had better not trust anyone else!

Friday of the
Fifth Week of Easter

Acts 15:22-31;
Jn 15:12-17

We return once again to the issue of Jesus' leadership over us. *"You are my friends if you do what I command you,"* and, *"I have called you friends, because I have told you everything I have heard from my Father."* In the secular realm of mankind the leader does not have to befriend his underlings or subordinates, but Jesus calls us his "friends." In fact, in his resurrected state when he could completely share his divine life with the whole world, he, in the proper sense of the word, called his disciples his "brothers" when he told Mary Magdalene to tell his "brothers" to await him in Galilee. In the spiritual realm the leader and followers both have the same lifestyle, values and goals. *"I have called you friends [no longer slaves], because I have told you everything I have heard from my Father."* What Jesus, as divine, heard from his Father is essentially his own name and identity: the Word of the Father spoken eternally and in time as Jesus, the earthly self-disclosure of the Father.

Researchers who have investigated the qualities of leadership discovered that the best leader is the one who knows the group task the best. Our group task is clearly stated by Jesus: *"This I command you: love one another."* He added in the opening of this text, *"...as I love you."* The Great Lover of mankind and our Leader in Love is Jesus himself, who set the pattern. He clarified this even further: *"No one has greater love than this, to lay down one's life for one's friends."* He did this himself, in fact even for those who would refuse his friendship; he expects us to spend ourselves and sometimes even "kill" ourselves as living sacrifices. This is the "spiritual suicide" Jesus calls for: to die to oneself and one's desires, to one's prejudices and rigidities.

This self-sacrifice is expected of all leaders: superiors and bishops, teachers and parents, and, hopefully, politicians and business people. Even when one cannot perhaps achieve true spiritual greatness, one is nevertheless bound by the natural ethics which God has placed within our human nature. When we take a look at the leadership of the Lord—we can view it only from our human standpoint—we readily accept that he knew the group task the best: to love altruistically, without the necessary hope of return, because it is the right thing to do. His farewell address returns to this theme again and again, as in today's Gospel. Note that Jesus did not possess earthly power and authority, but he did have influence over the people. It is influence that counts, not authority. Parents have authority over their children, but sometimes very little influence! Besides knowing the group task or "common enterprise" best, leadership is marked by other qualities which Jesus inspires.

Jesus showed persistent honesty about the requirements of following him. "Take up your cross daily and come, follow me," and "The Son of man had to suffer and die." He showed practical judgment, which is the virtue of prudence. "Who by worrying about it can add one inch to his height? Not a hair falls from your head without your heavenly Father knowing it." Jesus was a specialist in his field of loving and had a clear vision of what needed to be done. "Blessed are those who hear the word of God and keep it." Jesus relied on his Father in the absence of human understanding and support. "No one knows the Father but the Son and those to whom the Son reveals him." Jesus was a great communicator. He expressed himself succinctly and clearly, yet with eloquence by asking questions: "What profit does he show who gains the whole world and loses his own life?" He did not mince words: "Go and sin no more."

To parents and educators, to bishops and bosses, Jesus would say, "Go and do likewise!"

Saturday of the Fifth Week of Easter

Acts 16:1-10;
Jn 15:18-21

Everyone's perception of Jesus is quite personal. Throughout the centuries, mystics and writers and theologians have attempted to express their concepts and experiences. An interesting twofold description comes to us from the early Middle Ages from the pen of Saint Julian of Norwich, a woman mystic who claimed visionary revelations from the Lord himself. Whereas we are never obliged to believe private visions and revelations, her words about the Lord have a perpetual relevance. She found in Jesus two special qualities. The first is homeliness, which means he was down-to-earth. We express similar ideas in our English expressions of "homey" and "down-home." Jesus felt "at home" with us human beings. The Bible says he was like us "in all things but sin." Jesus' practicality and realism are expressed in his words today: *"If the world hates you, realize that it hated me first."*

The second quality of Jesus described by Julian is courtesy. This does not mean mere politeness, but suggests the medieval ideal of knightly respect for others, gentleness and defense of the helpless. Many essays and poems have come down from that period of history about knightly "courtesy," especially in France. The importance of respecting others is suggested by Jesus' words today: *"If they kept my word, they will also keep yours."*

Of all the self-descriptions that Jesus provides, the most familiar is, "I am the way and the truth and the life." These terms correspond with the general views and expectations of Christians over the ages. We find three such perceptions of Jesus in theological writings: the Jesus of history, the humanitarian healer of mankind, and the Lord of the universe. Let us examine all these with the understanding that all three contain truth.

The first evangelists wrote for the Jews and Gentile converts of the middle of the first century. Each put his special slant on the ministry of Jesus. Nevertheless they shared the importance of showing how God entered human history in sharing our humanity in order to become the Messiah who was to save both Jews and Gentiles. He is the way by giving us the path to return to our heavenly Father and giving us the values and lifestyle to make that journey of faith realistic and effective as the One who went before us. This is the Jesus of history.

The humanitarian who called himself the Son of Man is the Christ who sometimes appears as an idealist who inspired us without having a concern for establishing structures. He was the spiritual healer of the physical and emotional misery of his fellow humans. Being, as they, a Son of Man, he remedied their miseries, healed, forgave, taught tolerance. This derives from his own statement, "I came that they might have life, and have it more abundantly"—on every level, including the physical, emotional, social and spiritual.

The historical Jesus did not take his followers from the world, but declares in today's Gospel, "...*because you do not belong to the world...the world hates you.*" Jesus the Healer offers the medication of his eternal truth, which may be a bitter pill to swallow. When Jesus warns us in today's Gospel of the harassment we will experience in adhering to this truth, he says, "*And they will do all these things to you on account of my name, because they do not know the one who sent me.*" "His own received him not."

The cosmic Christ and Lord of the universe is our Life, the Son of God who became our brother in order to share the divine life with us. He revealed God's mysteries and is, indeed, the summary of them all. In his resurrected humanity he is no longer limited, but can relate to and dominate all creatures. He said, "My kingdom is not of this world," and today, *"I have chosen you out of the world."* This is summarized in particular in Philippians: "At Jesus' name every knee must bend and every tongue proclaim to the glory of God the Father: Jesus Christ is Lord!"

Faith must keep leapfrogging from one idea to the other, but the whole vision is necessary to understand the mission of Jesus to our world. He is the historical way to heaven, the truth that medicates the earth, the cosmic life that is shared with both heaven and earth.

SIXTH WEEK OF EASTER

Sixth Sunday
of Easter, A

Acts 8:5-8, 14-17; 1 Pt 3:15-18;
Jn 14:15-21

As the Church approaches the Solemnity of Pentecost, the Sunday texts allude to the sending of the Holy Spirit and his effect on the believing community. Philip had gone up to Samaria, where the citizens were considered foreigners, or Gentiles, because of their mixed ancestry. Peter and John teamed up and visited there later and prayed for the Holy Spirit to descend upon them. They remembered what Jesus told them at the Last Supper (today's Gospel), that he would not leave them orphaned, but would send another Advocate, the Spirit of Truth, whom the world does not see nor recognize, but they would recognize him because he would remain with them and even in them.

The second reading from St. Peter's first Letter is an admonition for us. If anyone were to ask the Christians the reason for their hope in Christ, they should have their answers ready, but not with aggression and incivility, rather with gentleness and respect for others who do not share their faith. At the same time the believers are to expect defamation, but can overcome any accusations because of their integrity of conscience. *"For it is better to suffer for doing good, if that be the will of God, than for doing evil."* This is what happened to the Master, and we can expect no less if we are the branches on his vine.

St. Paul wrote to the Colossians about human suffering. "In my flesh I complete what is lacking in Christ's affliction for the sake of his body, that is, the Church." Not only from the spiritual viewpoint is suffering part of the Christian discipline, but it seems that suffering is practically a "second nature" to man. This statement appears in the moving encyclical of Pope John Paul II, *Salvifici Doloris* (literally, "Salutary Suffering"). The Pope wrote that suffering seems "essential to the nature of man," indeed, even belongs to the transcendence of our being, placing us into a profound mystery.

Because the Church itself was born from the suffering of Jesus on the cross, Church people must accompany suffering persons on their path of pain with compassion and respect, even though suffering, whether only witnessed or endured, can be intimidating. Yet the Lord himself towards the end of his earthly life found joy in his proximate suffering: "Now I rejoice in my suffering for your sake." Therefore, it is human salvation that imparts meaning to pain. Our history reveals a succession of wars and exploitation, persecution for reasons of conscience, loneliness and ingratitude, and most of all, that the just suffer and the wicked seem to prosper.

In this encyclical, issued in February, 1984, the Pope goes on to point out that evil is a distortion of what is good: personality, sex, property, pleasure, achievement, truth and so forth. Natural evils include epidemics, natural disasters, famine, the possibility of nuclear death. The order and beauty of creation reveal the existence of God and his power, but these various kinds of evil obscure God's hand in the world and the sending of his

Son into our history. Intrinsic to the idea of God the Creator is God the Remunerator—the One who has expectations of us, who rewards and punishes. Not all suffering is a punishment, of course; God permits it for the sake of purifying us and leading us to greater spiritual heights, especially to embed us into the mystery of Jesus' suffering. We know that suffering, particularly illness, often leads to conversion.

The most important liberation is from sin and its consequent eternal death. Nevertheless the family of God follows the lead of Jesus in trying to eliminate suffering in the world. If there were less evil, such as the excessive stockpiling of arms, exploitation of the masses, unbridled profit-taking, corruption in government, etc., then many of the evils to which we are prey would disappear: hunger, homelessness, displacement of families, ignorance, disease and so on. It is the personal sins of mankind that create suffering. That is why God gave his Son to us: he loved the world so that "man might not perish, but have eternal life." No matter what happens to us during our earthly journey, the bottom line of our existence is whether we make it into the kingdom of heaven. For the fortunate sometimes the only suffering is death itself, that final blow to our personal integrity. Yet it becomes the gateway to eternal life, as death was for Jesus, too.

Despite his good works Jesus was continually beset by pain and isolation and misunderstanding. No wonder he praised the various kinds of suffering he names in the beatitudes, yet he added, "Theirs is the kingdom of heaven." He was able to endure all this because he and the Father were one in love for each other. As the expression of his Father's will, he laid aside his human feelings and fears of suffering in Gethsemane to substitute for us, because mankind was still in its sins. Not even angels, but only human beings can suffer, yet it took God to survive such an accumulation of suffering in one human life of thirty-three years. Even though Jesus was sustained by his knowledge of his Father's love, he still felt "estranged" and abandoned by him, absolutely helpless on the cross. He was vindicated by his resurrection; he is able to transfer that victory to us to give our suffering a salvific effect and permanent meaning.

Nowhere more than in suffering and death can the dignity and nobility of human life be more manifest; there is glory hidden in suffering, wrote the Pope. Suffering is creative: Jesus did not bring redemption to a close at his resurrection; it goes on through his body, the Church. Hence our suffering brings hope to a hopeless world, even when suffering is unknown and hidden. Of all persons, Mary, the Mother of the Lord, completed in her flesh the afflictions of her Son. He tells all of us to come, follow him, yet does not explain suffering, but allows each of us to discover this mystery for ourselves as with each sorrow and pain the power of Jesus is unleashed again and again.

Sixth Sunday of Easter, B

Acts 10:25-26, 34-35, 44-48;
1 Jn 4:7-10;
Jn 15:9-17

The word, "love" appears in various forms seventeen times in the second reading and Gospel today. Jesus told his disciples at the Last Supper, *"As the Father loves me, so I also love you. Remain in my love. If you keep my commandments, you will remain in my love.... This is my commandment: love one another as I love you. No one has greater love than this, to lay down one's life for one's friends."* Love is the hallmark of a believer in Jesus. The main reason for conversions to his way is the exam-

ple of life. Jesus said the mark of his followers is to have
love for one another.

In chapter 3 of St. John's first Letter—today's second
reading is from chapter 4—we read this insightful
phrase, "We know that we have passed from death to life
because we love our brothers. Whoever does not love
remains in death," a zombie.

On the whole, Jesus was very laid back during his
earthly life. He could not very well keep a low profile,
however, because he had to be visible as God's represen-
tative and self-disclosure on earth. He was disinterested
in power and authority of the earthly kind; he wanted
only to have influence and persuasion over people's
minds and hearts. Jesus was an assertive person and totally honest—a necessary attribute in the One who came
to tell mankind the truth and meaning of life. Because he
was "like us in all things but sin," he had to learn in a
human way. We read, in fact, that "Jesus, for his part,
progressed steadily in wisdom and age and grace before
God and men." This is an astounding statement: the divine Son of God grew and developed not only in his
human nature, but also in grace, which is the divine life
of God in a person. "Wisdom" refers not to mere knowledge, but to the application of facts and experiences to
the kingdom of God.

A question asked when Jesus began to preach publicly was, "Where did he get this knowledge? Is he not
the son of the carpenter and is he not only a carpenter
himself?" There is no doubt in my mind that he, who
was like us in all things but sin, became the kind of person he was through the influence of his parents, Joseph
and Mary. Why did Jesus speak so easily and without
embarrassment about love, love, love, if he had not
learned its importance from his parents? In the Gospel
Jesus related well to rich and poor, young and old,
men and women. One time the disciples wondered

that he was even speaking to a Samaritan woman at the well of Jacob, both because Jews had nothing to do with Samaritans, and because in their culture men would never speak to a strange woman. Jesus was self-assured, had a clear identity, and was comfortable with himself.

Joseph taught Jesus his duties of the Law before Jesus' *bar mitzvah*; taught him his trade as carpenter; taught him to stand in the synagogue to pray with dignity alongside him; probably taught him how to throw a ball and how to fish in the nearby Sea of Galilee. Joseph taught Jesus how to be tough when there was a need: Jesus later had to outwit those who were trying to kill him; he had to stand up to the powerful leaders of his nation; he had to have nerves of steel against his enemies.

On the other hand, Jesus never appeared as a phony Marlboro man, but was compassionate, merciful, gentle, prudent rather than over-reactive. Surely he learned these qualities from his mother Mary. She taught him his prayers, as does every good mother; she told him stories from the Jewish Bible, of which he was both the prophecy and the fulfillment. She taught him how to relate to women, as we read many times in the Gospels. Jesus was also able to cry without shame when this was appropriate human behavior. This ability was no doubt a lesson from his mother!

Parents are models for their children. Teachers can often tell you what kind of home you maintain and what kind of relationship exists between husband and wife by the kind of child the teacher sees at school.

As Joseph was the head of the Holy Family, so Mary was, like every mother, the heart of the Holy Family. When the mother dies, as many of us know, then the heart goes out of the family. So it is important for us to tell our mothers often while they are alive that we love them. (As a footnote to this, I have typically seen that those who cannot relate easily to Mary, the mother of their God, are those who could not relate well to their own biological mothers!)

Jesus, as the Son of God, was the only one who existed before his own mother. How would you have made your mother if you had had the chance? Your mother would have been intelligent, sweet-tempered, "full of grace," no doubt even physically beautiful. Believe me, there is no saint ever recorded in the annals of Church history who did not have a tender devotion to the Mother of God. Those who downplay Mary insult her Son. Wouldn't you be insulted if someone ignored your mother? Nobody ever has God fully as Father nor Jesus fully as Brother who does not have Mary as Mother. Just read the last chapter of the document "On the Church," *Lumen Gentium*, which is entirely about our Lady, and discover that Vatican Council II was the most Marian of all general councils of the Church in the sheer weight of material about the Blessed Virgin! Those who use Vatican II to ignore Mary haven't read its documents!

Marian devotion is not an "extra added attraction" in our reverence for Jesus. The recent popes have called it an "essential" in Catholic religiosity, and whoever ignores her is "out of step" with the traditions of the Church. It is only a misbegotten theologian, a misguided priest, or a misinformed layperson who sets aside the Mother of God and expects to please her Son!

Sixth Sunday of Easter, C

Acts 15:1-2, 22-29;
Rv 21:10-14, 22-23;
Jn 14:23-29

All three readings today have particular interest. The first, from the Acts of the Apostles, records the rapid spread of the movement of Jesus from Jerusalem, throughout Palestine, then into Asia Minor (Turkey) and the Mediterranean area. Those were not the only places to which our religion spread, but these are the places recorded in Acts. As the Gentiles entered the fold of Christ, the Jewish Christians, especially because they considered themselves a development of Judaism, expected the Gentile converts to observe the prescriptions of the Mosaic Law. Today's reading is the compromise the two groups reached about what the Gentiles were to observe. Circumcision was not even mentioned, but the following were to be enjoined on the newcomers: *"...abstain from meat sacrificed to idols, from blood, from meats of strangled animals, and from unlawful marriage."*

Circumcision was the sign of the Jewish covenant with God; it was the Judaic equivalent of Christian Baptism and may have originated in hygiene more than religion, for it was common to several ancient peoples.

Jewish as well as pagan priests were supported by the sale of meat from animals offered in sacrifice. The Jewish Christians considered such meat tainted if it had been offered to pagan gods, yet it was the only source of protein for city dwellers! Using blood, as for soups and gravies, was likewise prohibited because of the ancient bias that blood was the seat or vehicle of the human soul: "Dead men don't bleed!" Illicit sexual union referred to marrying within close ties of kinship, even incest, as when a man might wish to marry his own stepdaughter. The letter to the Gentiles closes, *"If you keep free of these, you will be doing what is right."*

The Book of Revelation, which is the source of the second reading, is always an intriguing bible text. Revelation or, in its Greek name, Apocalypse, means "unveiling" or "opening the curtains," as one does at a play. This reveals the drama of the Lord's close of history and that he is behind it all. Revelation has vocabulary and imagery all its own, not found in the rest of the Christian Testament, so scholars question the authorship by John the apostle. The writer records he wrote from the island of Patmos in the eastern Mediterranean, a grim place, the "Devil's Island" of its day for exiles.

On the other hand, John's Gospel has some similar themes, particularly that Jesus is himself the Festival of God, the Feast of Lights, and the Day of Atonement. In addition, he said he would raise the temple of his body three days after its destruction. This corresponds with today's text, that the Eternal City of heaven has no temple and no illumination. God is the temple and his glory lights heaven.

The radiant description of heaven is archetypal and sums up what every religion presents as the eternal reward. Here the metaphor takes its beginning from the earthly Jerusalem, favored by Jewish kings and prophets, the abode of God where his glory dwells. The number 12 is considered to be perfect or sacred because it is divisible by 2, 3, 4 and 6, and corresponds to the 12 tribes of Israel and the 12 Apostles. Perhaps the author is describing the liturgy of heaven. The absence of the familiar Temple of Herod shows that the earthly is transitory, even the Eucharist, because in heaven we shall possess and see the reality of Jesus' resurrected presence.

In the Gospel Jesus speaks of "peace" as his gift and farewell. We are familiar with *shalom* of Jews and *salaam* of Arabs. According to the circumstances, it can mean: "hello," "good-bye," "bottoms up," "get well soon," "happy hunting," "have a wonderful honeymoon," etc. Jesus must have used the expression a thousand times in his life, just as the Italians say *ciao*. Nevertheless, Jesus' farewell carries a spiritual meaning: *"Not as the world gives [peace] do I give it to you."* He links peace to his going back to his Father, while yet remaining among his disciples. They could not grasp this possibility, because Jesus had not yet risen from the dead, when this multiple location became possible. All he could say at the time was, *"Do not let your hearts be troubled."*

We who live with the constant threat of nuclear annihilation, reports of bombing and terrorism, guerilla warfare, assassinations and televised scenes of violence—we who pray continually for peace without any evidence of peace coming to pass—need the peace Jesus offers. This means that one can be surrounded by mayhem and destruction, yet retain inner calm, which is confidence in God. Jesus said: "my Father will love him, and we will come to him and make our dwelling with him."

Monday of the Sixth Week of Easter

Acts 16:11-15; Jn 15:26—16:4

The Gospels for many days have come from Jesus' Last Supper remarks to his apostles. He says good-bye, prepares them for his absence (the Ascension), and the coming of the Holy Spirit—the two solemnities for which the Church is preparing us through the liturgies. Although this farewell discourse was immediately followed by his absence due to his shameful death, the readings must be interpreted after Easter in this light of his absence in glory, the ascent into heaven. Jesus tells us that we must bear witness along with the principal witness, the Holy Spirit. *"He will testify to me. And you also testify."* The disciples are not to be afraid, even when being excommunicated from the synagogues.

The first Christians, who had been Jews before, were so anxious to have their fellow nationals share the Gospel, yet the words of Jesus were directed to prepare them to take the Gospel away from Judaism to the Gentiles and throughout the Mediterranean. Today's first reading shows this happening. Philippi in Macedonia is in northern Greece—an important city named for Philip the Great, the father of Alexander the Great, who conquered most of the known world at his time. But the young conquerer's thrust had been to the east and India, whereas the road of the Christians led to Rome where Christianity would become the Roman Catholic Church, the theological unity of which was not to be threatened for centuries.

The Gospel records what we might call the graduation of the first seminary class of the Church, and Acts records their internship in preaching and suffering. Again and again the disciples of Jesus must reiterate the question, "Rabbi, where are you staying?" Then they tell others, "We have found the Messiah." From "Rabbi" to "Messiah," the disciples have begun their spiritual journey. Later in two other statements Peter reflects the sentiments of us all: "Depart from me, for I am a sinful man," and subsequently, "To whom shall we go? You alone have the words of eternal life." Trustfully we are to seek the Lord where he abides: in the Bible, the Eucharist, each other. We identify the true disciple by his likeness to the Master: Does he build others up? Is he compassionate? Does he wound or heal? Do we recognize Jesus in his breaking of the bread?

When you begin to follow Jesus, the first years seem so full of promise and many victories. But the glamour is followed by bitterness, failure, defeats. Yet this latter time is when our likeness to Jesus is most apparent: crucifixion! Within one's conscience only God and the disciple have total communion; no other may enter. When the disciple cries, it is always lonely. When he is lonely, it is because he is human. When he is human, he can make a mistake, even sin. The disciple must try to project the face of kindness and joy, even though he may be miserable inside. But Jesus is taking him by the hand as he trudges under his cross, stumbles and falls. He is denied support and affirmation and must live without it, because if he is pleasing everyone, then he is probably displeasing God.

The lot of a disciple is, therefore, bittersweet, a combination of pain and ecstasy. *"In fact, the hour is coming when everyone who kills you will think he is offering worship to God."* But the faithful disciple nevertheless carries the message forward. He is not always believed. But with believers he needs no defense; with unbelievers no defense will be enough!

Tuesday of the Sixth Week of Easter

Acts 16:22-34;
Jn 16:5-11

The most remarkable thing about the first reading is not the fortuitous, *deus ex machina* earthquake that loosed Paul and Silas from their chains—because God can arrange any combination of events—but the sudden impulse of the jailer and his household to accept the Lord in the middle of the night and be baptized. This was followed by a brunch early the next day, celebrating his *"...having come to faith in God."*

Paul and Silas had been stripped and flogged and imprisoned. Their singing the praises of the Lord literally "brought down the house." Despite the jailer's conversion, he did not appear to be very alert; the text says he woke up to find the cell empty, having slept through the earthquake, the singing, and the banging of the doors! The sermon or catechesis was not very long—just the essentials of the God-Man who died and rose from the dead, the core teaching about Jesus—which was similar to the conversion process of the eunuch of Candace, queen of Ethiopia, whom Philip catechized during a ride through the Gaza strip! He asked for Baptism and

Philip obliged. Because the first Christians thought the return of Jesus to claim his earthly kingdom was imminent, no one filled out questionnaires, gave long instructions, nor consulted chancery officials.

Today we must scrutinize, test, possibly convalidate marriages, prepare for the first confession, communion and confirmation. Today a convert receives instruction in the accumulated theology of centuries to be certain he or she is fully aware of the Church's teaching about every aspect of human life! The Holy Spirit, whom Jesus promises in the Gospel, was given to us to "fill out," as it were, the initial revelation of Jesus. The point is somehow to balance the development of a complex theology and organization with the simple faith in Jesus and the catechesis of the primitive community. Like Paul and Silas sometimes we can expect miracles, whether an earthquake to shake us up or an equal marvel....

In the Gospel Jesus says he has to go so that we can learn to live by faith in what the Advocate will impart to us. The Spirit will enliven the Church. The Gospel for today reads: *"He will convict the world in regard to sin and righteousness and condemnation."* It is obvious that there is condemnation about the world's sin, but righteousness refers to that attitude by which we live alone, *"...because I am going to the Father and you will no longer see me."* Thus in the physical absence of Jesus we carry on in faith against the violence shown us by this world, which is hostile to Christ.

"Advocate" literally means, from the Greek, "someone alongside you upon whom you lean or depend." Therefore he is a counselor, an advocate to speak for us, a lawyer to advise us. The most literal metaphor is "crutch," which does not sound too appealing, but the fact that we need a crutch is an admission that we are handicapped, even crippled, and need all the help we can get! Remember, the Advocate is with us every day, all day. Jesus' promise is fulfilled. Now it is up to us to convict the world about its sins, remind it that it labors under a condemnation, and proclaim its lack of justice, that righteousness that lives by faith.

Wednesday of the Sixth Week of Easter

Acts 17:15, 22—18:1; Jn 16:12-15

We have followed the fortunes of St. Paul in Acts as avidly as an earlier generation of moviegoers followed the serial "Perils of Pauline." At first a zealous "hound" of Christians, Paul was struck blind; then he had to fight even to be recognized as a Christian by the community. He carried the Gospel to the Gentiles of Asia Minor (Turkey), and then to Europe, to the city of Philippi. He was scourged and imprisoned several times, ship-wrecked a few times, delivered miraculously from jail and once was worshiped as the Greek god, Hermes.

You would think that would be enough for one life-time. But today's text finds Paul in Athens, the intellectual center of the ancient world, even when Rome predominated politically. Bringing a new idea to Athens was like getting your play on Broadway. The Athenians considered themselves the arbiters of all new ideas and the rest of the world as their intellectual inferiors, even barbarians! But Paul "bombed on Broadway." His act didn't play well there as it had in the "small" towns he visited.

He stood on the Areopagus, which means the "field of Ares," the god of war. In Athens the Areopagus was simply an outcropping of rock which provided an elevation whereon orators could be more visible when they spoke. This was equivalent to the rostra in the Roman forum.

Why did Paul fail after so many successes? He tried to speak the language of the sophisticated Athenians; he tried to "dress up" the Gospel with philosophy and play up to the superstitions of his hearers. He even quoted some Greek poet to win their approval. He had noticed that they had set up an altar to the "unknown god," because they did not want to take a chance to forget some god and thus merit that god's wrath. Paul said that he would tell them who that unknown god was, the real God, Jesus Christ! He censured them for thinking that any god could be confined to an image of stone or gold or silver. But those who "caught his act" did not like being sermonized or put down for their ignorance. So Paul, after only a few conversions, left for Corinth, one of his favorite parishes, to which he would later write two Letters.

Perhaps the lesson is that, whereas we must be aware of how the world thinks, we need not frame the simple message of Jesus with worldly references. In any case, Paul's final success was not in his preaching and writing, his miracles and cures. It was not his fame and popularity that counted in the kingdom of God. It was his final act of faith, his execution as a Christian in Rome. It isn't nearly as important how we live as how we die—although in most lives there is a close correlation! To quote the old Greeks, "Call no person happy until he dies well."

You can be important, yet get proud. You can achieve much, yet fall from grace. You can learn to pray, yet for the wrong things. You can learn how to define God without really knowing him. But to die for the message of Jesus is the proof that you really believed until the end and that you are "real."

Acts 1:1-11; Eph 1:17-23;
(A) Mt 28:16-20 or
(B) Mk 16:15-20 or
(C) Lk 24:46-53

Ascension, A, B, C

It is helpful to read all three Gospels the Church has given us for cycles A, B, and C. They tell essentially the same story, but there are discrepancies. Matthew places the Ascension on an unnamed mountain in Galilee, perhaps because in Chapter 28 the angel at the tomb where Jesus had resurrected told the women to tell his disciples to go to Galilee and meet Jesus there. Mark is non-committal about the location in this text, but Luke clearly places the scene of the Ascension near Bethany, which is just over the top of the Mount of Olives, where tradition has it that Jesus ascended to his Father's right hand. The Acts suggests, moreover, that the disciples were to "remain" in Jerusalem for the descent of the Holy Spirit.

We can leave such dilemmas to the scholars; it is the message and meaning of the Ascension that remains significant for us. The cardinal point of all the readings is that Jesus decided to keep his human nature intact, but glorified and empowered with divinity forever. Before the resurrection Jesus could relate only to others who were in earshot of his voice, like all of us. With his spiritualized and divinized humanity he was able to relate to the millions who might invoke his name simultaneously until the end of time—just as our heavenly Father always has! The Ascension is an important theological statement: the Christian Testament writers emphasize the reality of Jesus' corporeal presence after his death and rising. The ancient authors, even the Jews before Christ, taught that the disembodied or "separated" soul lived a kind of half-life, a twilight existence in Hades or Sheol or the underworld. "It is not the netherworld that thanks you, nor death that praises you; neither do those who go down to the pit wait for your kindness."

Even classical heroes lived in a joyless Elysium, as the authors and philosophers of antiquity wrote. Saint Paul, writing only twenty years after the rising and Ascension of Jesus, shows that Jesus alone holds the key to a desirable afterlife. The body is good, designed originally by God in paradise to be immortal along with the soul. Jesus retained his body, as we shall ours, forever. He promises us no shadowy life, but the "new creation," because he is the "firstborn from the dead." He said that he came that we "might have life and have it to the full." To the Church at Philippi St. Paul remarks that Jesus "will change our lowly body to conform with his glorified body." (This is the great motive for chastity, because "in our flesh we shall see our God.")

We are not to be fearful; Jesus has conquered sin and death. Meanwhile he encounters us through the Church and its sacraments. We get our foot into the door of heaven now. Therefore we ought to reverence our own bodies as God's very temple and likewise reverence the bodies of others. Life is sacred; that is why the Church champions the life of the unborn and the terminally ill, and teaches high morality of sex. Even when the Church is opposed, she must always propose the highest level of morality, although not everyone is equally able at a given moment of his or her life to achieve that height!

The passage Paul wrote to the Ephesians, today's second reading, is one of the most consoling and profound, and deserves to be read over and over again. *"May the eyes of [your] hearts be enlightened, that you may know what is the hope that belongs to his call, what are the riches of glory in his inheritance among the holy ones, and what is the surpassing greatness of his power for us who believe."* The Ascension makes Christ our true and only king—not a democratic president elected by his constituents. *"[God] put all things beneath his feet and gave him as head over all things to the church, which is his body, the fullness of the one who fills all things in every way."*

At his Ascension Jesus reviewed his ministerial life, yet the apostles did not fully comprehend his mission as Messiah. In Acts they asked him, *"Lord, are you at this time going to restore the kingdom to Israel?"* They were still thinking earthbound thoughts about an earthly kingdom that would eradicate Roman rule and give their nation political freedom, rather than the spiritual freedom that is at the heart of the Master's message. It is spiritually profitable for every believer to review his or her own spiritual life, too, as Jesus did with his disciples.

Once more, it is necessary to ask the right questions, not have a pocketful of answers. Will your life's work last beyond you? Your material accomplishments will fade, perish and be forgotten after a time. Has the measure of your life been doing what you found pleasure in—although that is not necessarily evil—or does your satisfaction come from having done what is right and availing to salvation? Will it make a difference in eternity that you were ever born at all? Was your constant search for a fleeting happiness or rather contentment with the kind of person you have become? Have your relationships built up the kingdom of God in others, or have you been stingy with your presence to others on this earth?

Get plugged into the power of Jesus. Invite him into your life. Allow him to be your Savior. Call no sin "small" if it separates you from the perfect love you should have for God. Let it be said of us what was repeated even by the pagans of the early centuries: "Behold, how these Christians love one another!"

Friday of the Sixth Week of Easter

Acts 18:9-18;
Jn 16:20-23

Today's first reading actually covers about two years of St. Paul's missionary life. He had left Athens, where he had not been well accepted, and traveled to Corinth, one of his favorite places. To the parish there he sent his two celebrated letters. Paul remained there for eighteen months, then set out for Syria, which has only about one hundred miles of coastline today, lying between Turkey and Lebanon. "Achaia" is the ancient name for Greece.

There is a modern city of Corinth, plus the deep canal across the isthmus of Corinth that men had attempted to cut for 2,000 years and have finally succeeded in our time. In Paul's time, there were only the remains of feeble attempts to make such a canal and a small city at the base of a cliff, which was crowned by the Corinthian acropolis. Today the pilgrim sees the ruins of a temple, a stadium, and the *agora* or forum. Guides can even point out the platform, a small rectangle of stone, whereon Paul stood when he was being judged by Gallio. The latter dismissed the case, but the irate Jews beat up the leader of the synagogue, who had failed in pressing charges against the "heresy" of Paul.

The Gospels from Ascension to Pentecost continue and conclude the final words of Jesus to his disciples at the Last Supper. Thus we hear Jesus' own evaluation of his ministry, his final instructions to his followers, and their preparation for the coming of the Holy Spirit. No doubt Jesus' references that he would soon be gone then return again were later interpreted as meaning Jesus would soon return in glory to establish his reign on earth. But he was really commenting on his death the next day, then his rising. *"You will weep and mourn, while the world rejoices; you will grieve, but your grief will become joy.... But I will see you again, and your hearts will rejoice, and no one will take your joy away from you."*

The Lord expresses the pain we all feel at times. We ask, "What is the meaning of my life? Does it make a difference to anyone that I'm alive? Why do I feel that I'm trapped?" Yet there is the guarantee of the Master: *"I will see you again."* The shining vision of our future glory is often the only beacon towards which we can look for direction and comfort. Meanwhile the voice of Jesus echoes, "Learn of me, because I am meek and humble of heart. Come to me, you who are heavy laden, and I will refresh you." "Why do you worry about what you are to eat or drink or wear? See the birds of the air and the flowers of the field. Your heavenly Father knows you need these things. Who by worrying can change anything? The very hairs of your head are numbered."

It is necessary to keep questioning ourselves about our lives. In one of his plays, the French dramatist, Jean Anouilh, has a scene played at the last judgment. All the ostensibly "good" people were milling around heaven's gate, impatient to be led through the pearly gates. They were eager to receive their reward and march into glory forever. They were sure that they had reserved places after a life filled with the familiar pieties expected on earth from the religious. But a rumor suddenly starts in one corner of the group and races through the crowd: God has decided to forgive everyone, even those who practiced little or no familiar religion, or who sinned wickedly on earth. They grumbled, they shouted, they cursed God—and they were condemned to hell forever for their lack of charity! This scene is not meant to downplay religiosity, but to underscore that "By this shall all people know that you are my disciples: that you love one another."

Saturday of the
Sixth Week of Easter

Acts 18:23-28;
Jn 16:23-28

In virtually every paragraph of Jesus' final discourse he speaks of love. In today's Gospel he encourages the disciples to ask God's favors in his name, that is, the name of Jesus. He says that he will not even have to petition the Father, because the Father already loves the followers of Jesus. *"The Father himself loves you, because you have loved me and have come to believe that I came from God."* When "love" in some form or another is the theme or feature of popular songs, novels and television shows, the word comes easily to our lips, but the realistic practice of love requires discrimination and effort. Only the theory is easy!

It is the small offenses against love that wear down our spirituality: gossip, harsh judgments, putdowns, sarcasms, witty one-liners, jealousy, smugness, putting labels on people. When we confess these offenses against love of neighbor, it is helpful to discern also the cause of such uncharitable acts. Pride heads the list of motives. When we are self-righteous or "holier-than-thou," we think we have a right to judge others. Sometimes we have a subtle resentment at the success of others and wish to cut them down to size, lest we appear less by comparison with them.

Another unrecognizable motive for uncharitableness is our own low self-esteem. Because we devalue ourselves, we do not wish to admit that others have good points. A strange motive for criticizing an absent person is to show someone our trust, because we share confidences and secrets about others. Then our motive may be that we crave attention. We want to seem to be "in the know," have the "inside track" about others or simply entertain or shock our associates by revealing faults and telling unwholesome stories.

Even if our remarks are truthful, they may very well be sinful. Sometimes those who have a drab emotional life try to live vicariously, as it were, from the lives of others. They delight in the downfall of others and their scandals, which brings excitement to their own dull lives. But this is like poisoning your own drinking water and polluting your own environment. You can even destroy a family, a friendship, a business. Booker T. Washington once said, "You can't hold another person down without staying there yourself." As someone said, a rumor manages to get around, even if it doesn't have a leg to stand on! Everyone enjoys a humorist, but not one who makes others the butt of his or her jokes.

Beware of those who begin a sentence with such phrases: "It's none of my business, but—." "I'm not one to complain, but—." "I don't want to criticize, but—." To be unaware of your sins is a tragedy. That is why the Bible indicates the beginning of conversion is being "convicted" or convinced of one's sins. In these days of popular psychology we are encouraged to "let it all hang out" and express our inmost feelings, even if they are bitter or sarcastic. Candor and assertiveness can be important social skills, but they ought not to be learned and exercised at the expense of others. Charity is a contagious virtue and "covers a multitude of sins."

SEVENTH WEEK OF EASTER

Seventh Sunday of Easter, A

Acts 1:12-14;
1 Pt 4:13-16; Jn 17:1-11

After the Ascension the Church enters into a time of prayer and reflection about the meaning of Jesus' public life. This is part of the waiting for the Holy Spirit, as Jesus had commanded his disciples. The first reading records that they returned to the "upper room." After naming the disciples who were making the first novena of the Church—they *"...devoted themselves with one accord to prayer"*—the author, St. Luke, includes the others present: Mary, Jesus' mother; some women (probably those who stood at the foot of the cross); and Jesus' brothers, that is, his cousins. The "upper room" was evidently the temporary summer structure that Jews built on the flat roof terraces of their homes. They generally ate up there and sometimes slept there during the hot summer months, because the "room" could catch any vagrant breeze that came over the mountains into Jerusalem. This was probably the room of the Last Supper as well. When the apostles had closed themselves into the "upper room" (for fear of the Jews as we read in the Gospel) after the crucifixion, they felt more secure in case the Sanhedrin would try to arrest them. They could escape over the rooftops of the adjacent houses!

The Crusaders built a modest church over the site, which the Saracen conquerors turned into a Moslem mosque. Today it is wholly unoccupied and a place visited by tourists and pilgrims. The point of the reading is to emphasize that the disciples devoted themselves to reflection on the life of Jesus and to prayer in preparation for the descent of the Holy Spirit. It must have been a thrilling time of expectation!

As always, St. John's Gospel contains a deep theological statement. He wrote so long after the earthly mission of Jesus that he took more pains than the other evangelists to accent the divinity of the Lord. His recollections often center on Jesus as the Lord of creation and the Son of God. Let us examine today's reading.

Addressing the Father about himself, Jesus declares, *"You gave him authority over all people, so that he may give eternal life to all you gave him."* Thus Jesus then and now through his Church is designated to teach every human being. Even in this post-Christian world it is the task of the Church to comment on the morality of all nations, Catholic or not, and establish the highest spiritual goals of every living being. Although the Church may and often is disregarded, she is not excused from this divine mandate, expressed in the phrase, "over all people."

The text points out that the Son shares the same divinity with the Father. Therefore it is not some "ego trip" on the part of Jesus when he prays, *"Give glory to your son, so that your son may glorify you."* In fact, he adds, *"Now glorify me, Father, with you, with the glory that I had with you before the world began."* He is eternally equal with the Father. They share the same power and authority: *"And everything of mine is yours and everything of yours is mine."* Whereas we are convinced by faith in the equality of the Persons of the Blessed Trinity, John was writing for the first Christian century, during which heresies and doubts already were arising about the full divinity and humanity of Jesus. But there is a subtle point to be made here. When Jesus asks for glory from the Father, he is evidently referring to his humanity also. Jesus' human nature was to experience resurrection and divinization. His spiritualized body could operate on the level of the spirit, as we see from the post-resurrection narratives. Hence his appeal was for divine glory being conferred on his human nature. This is of great interest to us, because we are slated to share by adoption in the same powers!

With these statements Jesus was letting go of his earthly life, ending his merely human journey. *"And now I will no longer be in the world, but they are in the world, while I am coming to you."* In his earlier high priestly prayer he asked not that his followers be taken out of this world, but that they be guarded from its pernicious influence. As he had already told them, they were to be the leaven of the world, the salt of the earth, the light set on a lampstand, and a city built on a hill—that is, to be visible, to teach, to witness.

The subject of "glory" appears also in the second reading from St. Peter's first letter. *"When his glory is revealed you may also rejoice exultantly."* And when we suffer for our religiosity, *"the Spirit of glory and of God rests upon you."* Perhaps this statement gives us more fortitude than consolation, but the followers of Jesus share his lot. "The slave is not above his master." Peter concludes his text, *"But whoever is made to suffer as a Christian should not be ashamed but glorify God because of the name."* This is reminiscent of the comment early in Acts when the apostles were beaten and chastised by the Sanhedrin for preaching the risen Christ: "They were happy to suffer for the sake of the Name."

Seventh Sunday of Easter, B

Acts 1:15-17, 20-26;
1 Jn 4:11-16;
Jn 17:11-19

After Easter Sunday the liturgical readings keep returning to the Last Supper and Jesus' final words to his disciples. There is a strong emphasis on love, both in the prediction of the Holy Spirit of Love who was to come and in Jesus' speaking on a level of great intimacy with his followers—as if to show the necessary link between human love and the Divine Spirit of Love.

There are the theological implications from the Ascension, the fact that Jesus kept his human nature forever. This means that everything human has value except sin. You can train animals by "operant conditioning" to respond to kindness or to recoil from inflicted pain, but only a human being can experience authentic emotions which identify human values, as we discern in the life of Jesus. He was amazed at the faith of the Roman official who asked him to cure his boy: "I have not found such faith in all Israel." He dared to criticize the Pharisees: "You brood of vipers," snakes! He was gentle with the adulteress: "No one has condemned you? Then neither will I condemn you." He was tender with children: "Suffer the little ones to come to me, for of such is the kingdom of heaven." He was disappointed when some Jews could not accept his hard sayings, and he asked his disciples, "Will you also go away from me?" He wept over Jerusalem, which he knew was going to be destroyed: "Jerusalem, Jerusalem, you stone the prophets and kill those who are sent to you. How often I would have gathered you, as a hen gathers her chicks under her wing, but you refused." His arms flung out, defenseless on the cross, he felt despair: "My God, my God, why have you forsaken me?" We can let the scholars write their dissertations about the emotions of

Jesus; we need only to immerse ourselves into the mystery of Jesus' humanness.

The first chapter of the Letter to the Ephesians outlines Jesus' covenant of love with us: "God chose us in him, before the world began, to be holy and blameless in his sight, to be full of love; he likewise predestined us through Christ." God loved us before we were even born—before he threw galaxies into the corners of the universe, before he drew rings around Saturn, before he punctured the black holes and fired the white stars!

At the moment of our physical conception we could have been assigned by divine providence to parents in the Third World, in Kenya, Egypt, Indonesia, communist China. But God placed our particular configuration of personality factors and intelligence and other gifts and potentials (dimensions of the soul, created directly by God when we were conceived) right here—in this land, with these parents, these assets, with freedom to pursue our faith in Jesus. We would have had a different genetic inheritance and a different nurturing in another country and culture, but our spiritual soul was created directly by the Almighty for his own purposes. (This is one important reason for the foolishness of racial prejudice and bigotry!)

In the divine covenant there is no suggestion of human contract, a 50-50 bargain, a "deal" that God makes with us. "He loved us even when we were in our sins." And St. John writes in his first letter, "The love of God consists in this: not that we have loved God, but that he has loved us and sent his only Son to be our Savior." This is not like a human product or service that is paid for. The covenant of Jesus was his free choice for us even before we were conceived in our mother's womb. "Predestination" gifted us with being God's adopted children, brothers and sisters of Christ, temples of the Spirit, heirs of heaven. The covenant is based on God's giving one hundred percent. Through the Mass and sacraments Jesus makes his original saving and ministerial acts present again. He continues to redeem us and apply the merits of his death on the cross. We are so precious and bought at such a great cost, the blood of the Lamb, that Jesus would have undergone his whole agony for just one person, because this would have been the will of his heavenly Father. God expects that we invest ourselves with equal emotion into his kingdom.

Emotions concern what we cherish and what we despise: on one hand, what brings us enthusiasm, attraction, love; on the other hand, what leads to fear, alienation, hatred. Throughout the Gospels we can observe how Jesus handles such emotions (although his only hatred was for what is evil). The activities of the mind are not to be disparaged, but no one converts to Jesus as the end product of one's logic and reasoning; no one makes a significant decision without the interplay of his emotions.

In fact, integral faith engages the whole person, including the heart and the emotions. The mind can err (that is why we have heresies and schisms). But it is hard to fool the heart over a long time. Jesus never accused the Pharisees of ignorance of theology. Factually he told his contemporaries, "Do as they tell you, but do not imitate them." Jesus accused them of heartlessness, of placing burdens on others that they themselves did not carry. They separated knowledge from love. They gave lip service, but not submission of the heart. They were orthodox in mind, but heretics of the heart.

Ask what emotions arise within you about your faith, your religion, doctrines and moral teachings of the Church, papal authority. Are you hostile or bored at Mass, or just find it irrelevant? Is religion empty ritual?

Are sermons pointless, your priests flawed? How would you feel if your son or daughter said he or she wanted to become a priest or religious? Yet this is undoubtedly the greatest blessing parents can receive from God; their honor in eternity is immeasurable. Do you pray for a vocation in your family or encourage young people? Who will be the facilitators of ministry and agents of salvation in the next generation? Will the Third World have to send missionaries to us? Of course the sacrifices of celibacy and poverty and obedience are difficult; nothing valuable is achieved without sacrifice. There are not enough rewards in this world to make a vocation endurable, because God's method is to take the cracked bell, melt it, remold it into the likeness of his Son. Such a radical commitment requires nerves of steel; chastity demands an armor of bronze; service requires a heart of gold! But the Master has told us, "Do not fear, little flock; I have overcome the world."

Seventh Sunday of Easter, C

Acts 7:55-60;
Rv 22:12-14, 16-17, 20;
Jn 17:20-26

We live in a non-Christian, or rather, in a post-Christian world. The heroes of this culture are "possessors." They possess money, power, clout, fame, pleasure—and sometimes they even possess people, whom they can use and exploit. Our culture tends to applaud those who have "made it" and indulge their greed, ambition, jealousy and lust. We even teach our children to value being competitive; perhaps that is why so many youngsters consider themselves failures and even commit suicide.

In the past, no doubt, the Christian world was often seduced by these same values, even churchmen, perhaps because the Church did need some possessions to operate schools, charities and church buildings. Nevertheless Christians do not take their meaning and find value in being "possessors" but in being "becomers." We find our meaning in giving away, sharing, serving, healing and sometimes dying, as Jesus did and as St. Stephen imitated him in today's first reading. To "become" something that we are not yet requires emptying of self and dying to self—one of the messages of Philippians. "Jesus emptied himself and took the form of a slave...." Therefore our value system is non-competitive, non-manipulative and non-judgmental. Letting go of "possessions," we try to "become" a certain kind of person.

The first disciples, whom we sometimes call the "apostolic college," experienced the fate of Jesus when the world was clearly non-Christian or rather pre-Christian. Andrew was crucified in Greece, Simon the Zealot in Persia, and Simon Peter upside-down in Rome. Bartholomew was skinned alive in Armenia, Judas Thaddeus was shot by archers, and Matthew was cut down with a sword in Ethiopia. The Jews of Jerusalem killed the two Jameses, Jesus' cousin and the son of Zebedee. Philip was hanged in Phrygia, and Thomas suffered martyrdom in India. The latecomer Matthias was beheaded. Only John, the beloved disciple, escaped martyrdom, but he was sent into exile, and other attempts were made on his life. Stephen, of course, replicates the death of Jesus. He also was taken outside the walls of Jerusalem and repeated the sentiments of forgiveness and commendation that Jesus expressed on the cross.

The same Spirit is active now as then. Hence we may assume that God, who never deserts his Church, issues as many calls to his service now as in the first days, when there was no lack of vocations and martyrs. But parents must prepare the soil to receive the seeds of their children's vocations. They cannot gear their children to be "possessors" rather than "becomers." Conversely, parents sometimes try to possess their children as signs of their own success or in the hope that their children will achieve goals that eluded them, the parents.

Many studies reveal that religion is a great aid to mental health, because faith along with religious expressions of faith recast us into the mold of Jesus. Original sin has left all of us like cracked bells that go clunk and whap when they are rung or struck. Yet all the original metal is there. To regain the pure tone, the metal has to be melted and recast—the obvious application means to be recast into the likeness of Jesus. He himself spoke against the "possessors." "Whoever gives up family, home, wife, children and possessions for my sake, will receive a hundredfold and everlasting life as well." This is scary: to let go, to give up, to throw out.

In today's Gospel we hear Jesus praying for us, his disciples, so that we might actually have that unity that comes from being molded in the same way, *"...that they may all be one, as you, Father, are in me and I in you, that they also may be one in us...."* St. Paul in writing to the Philippians used the same simile: "He will refashion our lowly bodies according to his own in glory." This refers, of course, to our resurrected bodies, but the necessary prerequisite is that we are internally molded like him. We hold loosely in our hands whatever is not of eternal value, so that we can easily shake free of "possessions" and "become" another Jesus Christ.

Monday of the Seventh Week of Easter

Acts 19:1-8;
Jn 16:29-33

The Upper Room of the Last Supper is the setting for almost every Gospel of the Easter Season. This may seem curious, because the supper precedes in time the resurrection. Yet this is appropriate, because the Lord is giving "closure" to his ministry. He is summing up, interpreting his past three years of public life, giving the Church, through the apostles, the "bottom lines" of his teaching. He is preparing them also for his absence through the Ascension and the coming of the Holy Spirit.

Throughout his last speech Jesus seems in a human way to be pressed by an urgency that he cannot say everything that the Church needs to know for its future. Hence he promises the Advocate, the Spirit of Truth, to teach them everything. Because we have started the novena to the Holy Spirit, Acts, in the first reading, tells us about another descent of the Spirit. As soon as Paul laid his hands on the newly baptized, the power of the Third Person was manifest in tongues and prophecies.

At the Last Supper Jesus warned his followers of his death and the dispersal, the time *"...when each of you will be scattered to his own home and you will leave me alone."* But he adds a parenthesis about the source of his own strength and determination: *"But I am not alone, because the Father is with me."* He gives them and us this warning: *"In the world you will have trouble, but take courage, I have conquered the world."* It is our burden to live for the Gospel; it would be our glory to die for it!

Meanwhile, as the apostles for these nine days of waiting, we watch and pray in the upper rooms of our souls. We lift our minds and hearts heavenward, forsaking earthly ("carnal") thinking. We interrupt the cycle of original sin (that disability, that inability to love adequately and altruistically), and instead share the love we have from God. We await the return of the Lord in glory and listen to the insistent voice of the Holy Spirit who alone gives us rebirth and a new springtime to the Church.

Perhaps we are still living in the original springtime, the initial thrust of the Spirit, and have not yet experienced the fruitfulness of summer, much less the autumn harvest. Only a small portion of the world is even evangelized; believers are generally weak and perhaps lax. The harvest is still great, but the laborers are yet few, as Jesus had said. We must pray that the Lord of the harvest send laborers into his harvest. The healing of the wound of original sin will not be complete until Jesus returns in glory; then we will understand what the Lord meant by having life to the full. Original sin will be reversed in the elect, whereas the condemned who refuse to believe will feel the full penalty imposed on our first parents.

Tuesday of the Seventh Week of Easter

Acts 20:17-27; Jn 17:1-11

Chapter 19 of Acts tells the story of St. Paul's griefs in establishing the believing community at Ephesus, a city which later was to claim being the residence and place of death of the Blessed Virgin Mary. Ephesus was then a thriving center in Asia Minor, anciently called Anatolia and now Turkey. Founded along the trade routes, it is today a small village. There were in Ephesus believers who had received only the baptism of John the Baptist, not the Baptism in the name of the Trinity. Paul's mission was opposed by practitioners of witchcraft, philosophers, Jewish priests and the pagan silversmiths, who were losing business after Paul's preaching because no one bought any more statuettes of Artemis (or Diana). Finally Paul was accused before the imperial officials.

Following the instruction of Jesus during his public life, Paul shook the dust of Ephesus from his feet and left this important town, famed for one of the Seven Wonders of the Ancient World, the great Temple of Diana, which conserved an image of the goddess which was purported to have fallen from the sky. He visited Macedonia, then set sail for Miletus, which was near Ephesus and where he met with some believers from Ephesus. Just as Jesus made his farewell address to his disciples before he died, Paul makes some predictions about his future chains and hardships, and gives an overview of his ministry.

When I read Acts and Paul's Letters, certain aspects of his life and personality emerge: He feels a radical need to explain, even justify what he has done on his preaching missions. No doubt he feels sorry for himself, but we can forgive him this, because nothing is more satisfying than to wallow in a little self-pity when you've earned it!

Paul could be caustic and unkind, unforgiving and somewhat rigid. In chapter 15 Paul asked Barnabas to accompany him to check on the spiritual progress of the towns which they had already evangelized. "Barnabas wanted to take along John, called Mark. But Paul insisted that as Mark had deserted them at Pamphylia, refusing to join them on that mission, he was not fit to be taken along now. The disagreement which ensued was so sharp that the two separated. Barnabas took Mark along with him and sailed for Cyprus. Paul, for his part, chose Silas to accompany him on his journey." It is difficult to attribute this action to the inspiration of the Holy Spirit!

Paul appeared driven by a great urgency to preach. As his time ran out, as he was repeatedly arrested and punished, he felt that unless he did everything himself, it wouldn't get done. He never lacked courage, but his trust at times seemed weak. Yet the other apostles were busy evangelizing from Spain to India—only they did not have secretaries or scribes to record their missions. At Paul's side Luke was often found, taking notes, as if he intended to write a best-seller—which is actually what he did! It is not as if Paul were bragging, but he did seem to complain, feeling put down, passed over and plain exhausted.

Paul must have been a terror to live with, demanding his own way (and generally being right!), pushing his adversaries to the wall. Yet he is unimpeachable in his desire to live and die for Christ. Rising above trials, sorrows and plots, he never shrank from telling painful truths. He was dedicated and human and a wonderful saint!

Wednesday of the Seventh Week of Easter

Acts 20:28-38;
Jn 17:11-19

The idea of "missions" or "sending" is clear in today's Gospel. This appears in the context of our preparation for Pentecost, which is the "sending" of the Holy Spirit upon the Church. The Trinitarian theology that surfaces is this: The Father sends the Son to earth. At the Last Supper the Son promises to send the Spirit, the Advocate, from himself and his Father, which occurs on Pentecost. On that day the Spirit sends the apostles forth into the world—in fact, the whole Church, the Body of Christ, until the end of time. The Church is still being impelled by the momentum of that first sending.

The Latin word for "sending" is *missio,* whence the English word, "mission." In the documents of Vatican Council II it is written that an essential note of the Church is to be "missionary." We are all sent to evangelize the world. Thus Jesus said to his Father of his apostles in today's Gospel, *"As you sent me into the world, so I sent them into the world."* They were to carry a message: the Father's Word—his self-disclosure—in Jesus Christ: *"I gave them your word, and the world hated them.... Consecrate them in the truth. Your word is truth."*

Jesus does not ask his Father that the Church be removed from the world, because the problem is not the Church in the world, but the world in the Church! Instead Jesus asks his Father to *"...keep them from the evil one,"* whom elsewhere Jesus called the "prince of this world," the antichrist. The apostles were sent to be witnesses of what Jesus said and did in their presence. "Testimony" in ancient Greek is *maturion*, from which we derive the English word, "martyr." Today we associate this word with the shedding of one's blood, suffering and death. However you use this word, which signifies a grace not given to many, the preparation is as important as the consummation. You have to burn in life to go out in a blaze of glory. You have to be willing to be consumed like the sun, which is giving light and heat to our whole solar system as it slowly dies itself.

Yet Jesus called those who suffer "blessed." Sometimes that crucial word from the beatitudes is translated "happy," but this is a substantial error. The Greek word is *makarios*, and it is rather naive to translate, "Happy are the poor, the hungry, the maligned, those persecuted for the sake of justice." They are anything but "happy." But they are "blessed" to suffer for the sake of the Name of Jesus. "Happiness" describes a passing event or a personal perception of something. But "blessedness" comes from God's intervention in our lives; he establishes this state within us.

Nothing suggests happiness, at least not temporal happiness, in the beatitudes. So they do not refer to a transitory feeling, but to faith that generates contentment with what we have and what we have become. Happiness suggests an absence of frustration, which few persons achieve on this earth; there is always something to shake our equanimity. From this viewpoint even suffering and privation can lead to contentment from the imitation of Jesus. In God's eyes no one is a "wimp" because he is meek, nor is anyone a "loser" because he hungers after justice, nor is someone a "dummy" because he is poor in spirit. But if I could second-guess Jesus and take his wisdom a little further, I would tack on one more beatitude: Most blessed of all are they who can achieve happiness in spite of suffering and still keep their mental health! These are the ones who bring the greatest nobility and joy to religion!

Thursday of the Seventh Week of Easter

Acts 22:30, 23:6-11;
Jn 17:20-26

In the reading from Acts today the "plot thickens." Paul applies the Roman proverb of his day: *divide et impera*, "divide [your enemies] and rule [them]." After his last grueling missionary journey, Paul had finally reached Jerusalem, where he was arrested as an agitator. He was probably held in one of the two prisons in which Jesus himself had been detained a few years earlier. Then he had to testify before the seventy-member Sanhedrin, where he applied the Latin proverb to "divide and rule."

There were two schools of theology in Judaism: the conservative Pharisees and the liberal Sadducees. (Does this sound familiar?) The Sadducees rejected an afterlife, the existence of angels, and especially the resurrection from the dead, but the Pharisees were exactly opposed on these points, besides being more faithful adherents of the Law of Moses and liturgical and dietary norms. Therefore Paul divides them on their assessment of his own position by suggesting his belief in the resurrection of Jesus, precisely because Paul had been a Pharisee himself. After a heated debate some Pharisees were inclined to release him, but their opponents evaded issues and tried to tear him to pieces. So the commander of the Roman legions came down from the fortress Antonia and put him into prison for safety's sake.

The exchanges between St. Paul and that commander reveal much about Roman government and the politics of that day—which is recounted in chapter 21 of Acts, left out of this week's readings. It is one of the most dramatic scenes of the Christian Testament and is saved by the liturgists for a feast of St. Paul. After ignoring prophecies that he would come to no good in Jerusalem, Paul was recognized by visitors from abroad who were in the Temple precincts for a feast.

Try to visualize the setting: two huge rectangular structures intersecting along a common side—the Temple Mount with the magnificent structures of Herod, destroyed not long afterwards, and the fortress Antonia, which the Roman garrison occupied. It had water reservoirs, thick walls, and towers that overlooked the Temple square. The remains can yet be identified, and one tower has become the minaret used today for the loudspeakers of the muezzins who call the Islamic faithful to prayer. A Roman guard, posted to watch for riots, saw the fracas around Paul. Soldiers ran down the stairway into the Temple area and rescued Paul, who was "double-chained," hands and feet, so he had to be carried into the fortress! To extract the truth, the commander ordered Paul to be flogged. The latter countered that he was a Roman citizen by birth and it was inadmissible to scourge him! The officer said, "I had to buy my citizenship, but you are a citizen by reason of having been born in Tarsus." (The Roman government generally offered citizenship in the Empire to whole cities who were allies or who aided Roman expansion. Thus there were not many Roman citizens in Palestine, because the Jews resisted the occupation of the Roman army.)

Paul's lesson for us is that we ought to use the world and even its politics for the building of the kingdom of God and take advantage of its laws and privileges, as long as it serves the spiritual betterment of the world. Besides, the Lord revealed to Paul during the night that there was an ulterior design of God: *"Just as you have borne witness to my cause in Jerusalem, so you must also bear witness in Rome."*

Friday of the Seventh Week of Easter

Acts 25:13-21;
Jn 21:15-19

Today's readings provide us with a glimpse into the lives of Sts. Peter and Paul. Paul is in Caesarea, a flourishing seaport built by Herod the Great, who had erected so many other monumental buildings in Palestine, including the Second Temple. Herod started with piling moles into the sea, then added warehouses, markets, a theater, homes and an aqueduct to carry fresh water along the shore from Mt. Carmel. Even in their ruins they are still impressive. The Roman governor subsequently made his residence there in the city with the imperial name of Caesar.

Paul was imprisoned there by Festus, the Roman official, because Paul had appealed to Rome for judgment, knowing his Jewish adversaries wanted him to stand trial in Jerusalem, where he would be more vulnerable to assassination. So Festus was waiting for some decision from Rome. The passages in Acts provide the first hagiography in the history of Christianity. Paul realized how he would finally end up. In his Second Letter to Timothy, chapter 4, he remarked, "I have fought the good fight, I have finished the race; I have kept the faith. From now on a merited crown awaits me."

Little did Peter and Paul realize that the Lord helped them escape death several times, because their "time had not yet come." They were being saved for Rome. Thus God used them even after their deaths to effect his plan to establish his Church at the seat of the Empire. Because both of them expected the imminent return of Jesus, they did not plan far ahead. But God wanted the papacy to be founded there, to become the center of Church activities and the point of unity from the beginning. With the mandate of Jesus to Peter in today's Gospel to guide and feed his sheep, the role of Peter is spelled out. But it is not a city that is the center of the Church; it is a person, who is the "stand-in," the vicar of Christ. Wherever Peter is, one can find the Church. That is why Paul and the other apostles always discussed their ministry with Peter—Paul even engaged in verbal battle!—it was necessary to believe as Peter believed.

At Caesarea Philippi, a much different inland city northwest of Galilee, Jesus told Peter that he was the rock on which the Church was being built by him. A rock is immovable, unchanging, unflinching. Jesus added, "I will entrust to you the keys of the kingdom of heaven. Whatever you declare bound and loosed on earth shall be bound or loosed in heaven." The touching scene of the Gospel contains interesting inferences. Peter was familiar only with fishing; now he was supposed to switch gears and become a shepherd, the Lord's favorite metaphor, and a doorkeeper. Of course, men like Peter and Paul, no matter how charismatic their preaching, are able to convert no one. This is the Lord's work; only he is the Savior. Nevertheless all Christians are supposed to sow the seed of the Gospel, but the harvest is the Lord's. In processing the grain, we are not to lace it with sugar, raisins and fruits. The plain-spoken truth is what finally prevails.

To Peter's response of love Jesus said, *"Feed my lambs.... Tend my sheep.... Feed my sheep."* Knowing that Jesus never said nor did anything casually, interpreters have tried to understand the specific meanings of "feed," "tend," "lambs," "sheep." Why these distinctions? We can only guess that the meaning is to provide spiritual nourishment for both the inexperienced and the leaders, who would be the sheep. An extra admonition to "tend" the sheep may indicate the need to provide guidance as well for the experienced or mature sheep.

Men like Peter and Paul represent the totality of the Church's work in the world: Peter is the rudder, and Paul is the wind in the sail. We need both to arrive at the harbor of truth and port of salvation. We pray that the Pope keeps a steady hand and discerns who is blowing a favorable wind!

Saturday of the
Seventh Week of Easter
(Morning Mass)

Acts 28:16-20, 30-31;
Jn 21:20-25

We pick up on the story of St. Paul again today; this is also the end of the Book of Acts. Backtracking a little, we saw that Paul was spirited out of Jerusalem to avoid his assassination by the Sanhedrin and, with the help of 470 soldiers, brought to Caesarea Maritima ("on the shore"), headquarters of Felix the governor. The high priest himself, Ananias, came with others to press charges of sedition (as had been done with Jesus). Felix could not decide, but kept Paul in safety in prison and spoke with him often during two years. A new governor, Porcius Festus, was appointed. Tired of this dilatory process, which prevented him from preaching, Paul appealed to Caesar. (There is a hiatus of three chapters between yesterday's and today's readings.) King Agrippa and his wife, Bernice, came to call on Festus and were asked by the governor to question Paul; they were residents of Palestine, but from a petty kingdom to the northwest. Festus wanted to collect evidence for a statement to be sent to Rome. Paul recounts his personal history and conversion with such eloquence that Agrippa admits, "A little more, Paul—and you will convert me!"

Festus said he would have freed Paul, but the latter had appealed to Caesar. Actually, Festus was "passing the buck," so as not to irritate the Jews; he remembered how Pontius Pilate fared! So a small party set sail for Italy, but the seas were unruly and dangerously stormy. Nevertheless an angel appeared to Paul to say that everyone's life would be spared (there were 276 persons aboard) so Paul could bear witness in Rome. They were shipwrecked on a sandbar off Malta and made it to shore—a favorite theme on Maltese stamps. After adventures with a poisonous snake, cures in the name of Jesus, and some evangelization, they took ship in spring for southern Italy. At this point we reach today's text.

Paul is allowed to rent his own house, where a guard lives with him to keep watch, lest he escape. Arrangements were casual, because no one could escape Roman justice anyway. He preached to Jews and Gentiles fearlessly for two years, as we read today. The text ends here abruptly. Perhaps Luke, the author, had to leave Rome. The rest of Paul's brief history derives from earlier documents and legends. It was said that his decapitated head bounced three times, and three springs of water gushed out of the ground. This is hard to believe: the fountains are about twenty feet apart! In any case, they dried up in 1958, due to the building of high-rises in the EUR zone of Rome.

The end of St. John's Gospel alludes to some interesting facts. The dialogue between Jesus and Peter, especially in light of John's long life, led to the idea that the Beloved Disciple would not die.

Far more significant is the writer's statement that Jesus said and performed so many things, that not all the books of the world could contain those facts and events! We can allow this hyperbole to the author, but we are left with the suggestion that these unrecorded facts will continue in the history of salvation under the rubric of Tradition!

PENTECOST

Gn 11:1-9 or Ex 19:3-8,
16-20 or Ez 37:1-14 or
Jl 3:1-5; Rom 8:22-27;
Jn 7:37-39

The Vigil
of Pentecost, A, B, C

Each of the four choices for the first reading, Genesis, Exodus, Ezekiel and Joel, illustrates a suggestion of the presence of the Third Person already in the Jewish Bible, or some relationship with Pentecost. The Tower of Babel, a sign of arrogance of mankind which tried to pierce the heavens and contend with God himself, led to the confusion of languages. (We use the phrase, "babbling brook" or child, to signify pointless chatter.) At Pentecost the apostles reversed this process and were able to be understood by each listener in his or her own tongue.

The scene from Exodus, the second option, recalls Moses' ascent to Mt. Sinai to encounter God and receive the Decalogue, attended by thunder, lightning, smoke and trembling. This is suggestive of the upper room shaking when the Holy Spirit descended upon the group awaiting and praying for his arrival. Ezekiel's vision, the third option, is the subject of a Negro spiritual: "Dry bones, hear the word of the Lord!" God told his prophet to proclaim, *"From the four winds come,*

O spirit, and breathe into these slain that they may come to life." The Holy Spirit gives life when we are "born of water and the Holy Spirit," and is the soul of the Mystical Body. Finally, in Joel, the fourth option, we read, "*I will pour out my spirit upon all mankind. Your sons and daughters shall prophesy, your old men shall dream dreams, your young men shall see visions....*" This is an allusion to the Holy Spirit, of whom we recite in the Sunday Nicene Creed, "who spoke through the prophets." Thus these four readings carry an extensive theological message.

The second reading indicates how the Holy Spirit enters into individual lives. *"We ourselves, who have the firstfruits of the Spirit, we also groan within ourselves as we wait for adoption, the redemption of our bodies."* We agonize until our bodies, too, are spiritualized and divinized through our personal resurrection. *"The Spirit too comes to the aid of our weakness; for we do not know how to pray as we ought, but the Spirit itself intercedes with inexpressible groanings."* When we are at a loss for specific words and are not sure what the will of God might be, or when we lack the proper dispositions in addressing our heavenly Father, the Holy Spirit presents us to God and lifts us up to him with unspoken desires and longings to please him. *"And the one who searches hearts knows what is the intention of the Spirit, because it intercedes for the holy ones according to God's will."* The Father nevertheless understands these "groanings," because, being one with the Father in the Trinity, the Spirit speaks up for us as Advocate in the manner and substance that the Father expects.

The context of today's Gospel is the Feast of Booths. Jesus delayed going up to Jerusalem, because the time had not yet come for his apprehension. But driven by an inner urgency, he dialogues with the crowds in the Temple area. His final words, today's text, sharply divided his hearers, including the Sanhedrin. He quoted scriptures, *"Rivers of living water will flow from within him."* (Here he was referring to the Spirit, whom those who came to believe in him were to receive. There was, of course, no Spirit as yet, since Jesus had not yet been glorified.) Naturally the Holy Spirit existed from before time began, but he was not yet manifest—which would occur after the Ascension on Pentecost. The point of living waters is made about life itself: the life that is given in Baptism and afterwards by the sacraments. There is one condition: *"Let anyone who thirsts come to me and drink."* To receive the Spirit we must desire him in us after we have accepted the teachings of Jesus. This is the only enduring relationship!

Civilizations and cultures rise and fall; each one thought it would endure forever—from the ancient hegemonies to the Third Reich of Hitler. They are all gone, but the Church continues until the end of time, because its destiny is not linked to political structures. Most of us have similarly lived through many pastors and in many parishes; we have seen many kinds of popes and bishops. We have heard leftist and rightist, liberal and conservative homilies and tirades. We passed from Latin to English, from organs to guitars, from altars turned around to denuded sanctuaries. We have seen scandals and abuses. Yet we are not "Catholics" because of personalities, music, sanctuary furniture or even sermons. We profess the Catholic religion because Jesus said, "I am with you all days," and the Holy Spirit of Truth teaches us to observe whatever Jesus commanded. This is the only truth that sets us free, although the truth may also make us uncomfortable. Monuments of brick and stone will finally decay; our monuments of virtue and truth are everlasting.

Sometimes it seems as if the Church is slow to act, but this is necessary for her to stand back, disengage herself from controversy, and pass judgment on this world. Even though St. Paul said this world is "fast passing away," it has its own philosophy and age-old values. It maintains its competence in technology, moneymaking and war. Jesus reproached us, "This world is wiser than the children of light." We must assert our values and through ourselves make Jesus more visible, more "incarnate" in this world. It is the Holy Spirit that makes us achieve divinity itself! St. Basil, a Greek Father of the Church, wrote in his work, *On the Holy Spirit:* "Through the Spirit we acquire a likeness to God; indeed, we attain what is beyond our most sublime aspirations—we become God." If your fantasy is to be "superman" or "superwoman" or even "divine," this can take place only when we are "clothed with the power" of the Holy Spirit.

Pentecost Sunday, A, B, C

Acts 2:1-11; 1 Cor 12:3-7, 12-13; Jn 20:19-23

It seems that only once a year do we remember the Holy Spirit: when his solemnity arrives in the liturgy at the end of the Easter Season. Most of the time we take him for granted. Yet the original believing community was very conscious of the Holy Spirit. The Gospels concluded the physical life of Jesus with the ascension. Jesus told his disciples to remain in Jerusalem until they were "clothed in power." On Pentecost the mystical life of Jesus begins; his Spirit is the active principle, the enlivening force, the soul of the Mystical Body—who we are!

Preachers often call Pentecost the "birthday" of the Church. This is the springtime of the Church, yet not its beginning. The Church began with Mary, its first member who believed in Jesus, when at the annunciation she conceived him in her womb. Pope Pius XII, however, wrote that the Church was "born out of the side of Christ" on Calvary, when Jesus triumphed over sin. It is correct to say that on Pentecost the Church reached maturity with all the gifts and insights and presence of the Holy Spirit to carry it successfully until the end of time. Yet there will remain a certain incompleteness until the Day of the Lord, the endtime when the Father will restore all things in Christ.

Although the Spirit sounded noisy on Pentecost, he is rather the "Silent Partner" of the Trinity. He will not contend with the distracted and distracting world. You have to listen and concentrate—which is a good description of prayer. The first novena of prayer in the Church was the nine days while they were awaiting the coming of the Third Person with listening and concentration. When the Holy Spirit "fell on them" all heaven broke loose. We call Christ the Word of God, the self-disclosure of the Father spoken in time in Jesus. But the Holy Spirit is rather the Whisper of God; you have to listen patiently. His whispers are those sudden inspirations to good, an understanding of the Scriptures, good resolutions, reconciliation with one's enemies, reaching a difficult decision.

In the Gospel we read that Jesus *"breathed on them and said to them, 'Receive the holy Spirit.'"* This is a subtle reference to the creation of Adam, when God breathed life into Adam, then Eve. Jesus, the new Adam, gives his own Breath of Life to his followers. Therefore the action was not a new experience on Pentecost, when he came upon the whole Church. In the Gospel this was a personal gift for the forgiveness of sin or the refusal of absolution, given only to ordained ministers.

Commentators on the theological meaning of Pentecost call it the reversal of Babel (Genesis 11). All the ancients believed that the earth was covered with a kind of concave dish, called the "firmament." The stars were holes poked through the firmament that allowed the light of God's glory to shine through at night. The purpose of the tall ziggurat or Tower of Babel was to pierce the firmament and steal the power of God from heaven. God dealt with such arrogance by confusing their tongues, so they had to divide into groups which shared a common tongue. (That is the story the sacred author devised to explain the diversity of languages of mankind.) But on Pentecost people understood the sermons of the apostles each in his or her own tongue. The Holy Spirit began to heal the discord of the nations. Some scholars think that the specific names of nations enumerated in Acts are meant to signify universality: the various nations were symbolized by animals and signs that were in the zodiac, such as aquarius for Egypt (the Nile River). Put together, the whole astrological circle was represented. In ancient Latin, too, the *orbis terrarum*, "circle of lands," meant the whole earth! Every word of the Bible carries some message. A river ran around the lands—*okeanos*—from which comes "ocean."

The second reading, the first Letter to the Corinthians, reminds us of the unity of all believers, whatever their background, in the body of Christ, the Church. We have different gifts, works and ministries, but only one Spirit of whom we have been given to drink. He empowers us to make two outcries. In Corinthians Paul said, *"No one can say, 'Jesus is Lord,' except by the holy Spirit."* This means it is a grace to understand and acknowledge that Jesus is a Divine Person. Elsewhere Jesus relates that by the Spirit we can cry out, "Abba," which means "Papa," or "Daddy," or "Father" in a loving and familiar way. Once more, this is the action of grace, God's life in a person. "Abba" suggests not only the loving familiarity of a child, but also sharing in the same life as our Father in heaven. In St. Peter's second Letter we read that the Spirit makes us "sharers in the divine nature." The Creed sums it all up: he is God, the Third Person, the Spirit, the Enabler. "We believe in the Holy Spirit, the Lord, the Giver of Life."

The Christian Testament compares the Spirit to the river of living (not stagnant) water that brings life to a thirsty land. Water has a thousand uses: to irrigate, to wash, to cool a nuclear reactor, to raise goldfish, to wash the shores of a lake, to make saltwater taffy! Water is adaptable to everyone's need. *"To each individual the manifestation of the Spirit is given for some benefit."* All creation is passive before the Holy Spirit; we cannot contain nor possess the Divine Person. What he meant is that we remain open to being enclosed by him—"clothed with the Holy Spirit." In fact, because God is Pure Act, all of creation is subject to him. Ask the Holy Spirit to reveal what your special gift is for the Church and for the world.

Appendix

Preparation
for the Sacrament
of Reconciliation, I

Ezekiel 18:1-5,
7-9, 20-23

Upon hearing Jesus' parables and reading the events of his life and ministry, I have always felt sympathetic to someone whom the Master reproved and rebuked. There was Martha, who was slaving to show hospitality to Jesus, cooking and making beds, yet Mary was praised for having chosen "the better part." Then there were those who bore the burden of the day's heat in the vineyard, who thought they deserved a little more pay than those who came in the eleventh hour, but the owner (Jesus in the tale) chided them for not being satisfied with the agreed payment. There was the older, faithful son, brother of the prodigal son, who was miffed that his kid brother was indulged by their father.

Probably our indignation is a sign of how far we are from the generosity and mercy of God our Father. God closes his eyes to the sins for which we have repented and from which we have turned away. He integrates our wounded faculties with his graces so as to remove the layers of guilt that encapsulate our souls. We know something is wrong in our lives, but cannot always quite put our finger on the trouble; God's inspiration helps us to be more decisive in making resolutions. At other times in our sudden fervor we set spiritual goals beyond our abilities; we have a feeling that we are not doing enough for God. To overcome all these unproductive and negative feelings we must first admit that we are crippled spiritually and need God's help in getting free not only from real guilt, but also from the phony guilt we lay on ourselves.

The reading from Ezekiel clarifies the notion of guilt. In the context, the prophet alludes to the prior Jewish notions that the sins of parents are visited on their children, and that parents are responsible for the wrong-doing of their children. This latter notion is so common among parents whose children have strayed from the Church, drink too much, or take drugs. The proverb from the past is quoted by Ezekiel: *"Fathers have eaten green grapes, thus their children's teeth are on edge."*

But the prophet tells us that everyone is responsible for his or her own life and relationship with God. Each adult knows the law or can study it. Of course, there are those false teachers, even priests, who are out of step with the law of God and tell Catholics that omitting Mass on Sundays consistently and having premarital sex are permissible. These are false prophets and will receive a false prophet's condemnation.

Did you ever eat a bunch of unripe grapes or a premature persimmon when you were a child? Or drink a glass of lemonade into which someone forgot to mix the sugar? It takes your taste buds a while to recover. Ezekiel uses the metaphor that one's children's teeth are set on edge—up to the third or fourth generation, with respect to the effects of sin in the lives of our offspring. In the tribal concepts of Jewish morality, often there were social effects of sin, affecting the whole tribe and family. We can see this factor in the lives of the children of alcoholics, criminals and the promiscuous. Even unborn babies can become addicts in the womb if their mothers use drugs.

Today's bible reading clarifies, however, that God does not impute guilt to the offspring of sinners. Each person is responsible for his or her own sins. Pause to consider your sins and failings. Emphasize the more serious sins or those you have to confess the most or those of which you are the most ashamed or those you have been trying the hardest to overcome. You must confess at least the serious or mortal sins. Ask the confessor to help you if you are in doubt.

"The virtuous man's virtue shall be his own, as the wicked man's wickedness shall be his."

Preparation for the Sacrament of Reconciliation, II

Lv 19:1-18 and
Mt 25:31-46

Both texts provide an examination of conscience. Although the Jewish Testament text was part of the legal covenant between God and his people, the text is not legalistic. The text ends: *"You shall love your neighbor as yourself."* Of course, a "neighbor" meant another member of your tribe or nation or an ally of your nation.

When Jesus answered the question, "Who then is my neighbor?" he told the story of the Good Samaritan. A member of the detested sect from Samaria rescued a Jew (his enemy), took the injured man to an inn, and paid for his care—with no hope of repayment, because robbers had taken the victim's possessions. The essential definition of a "neighbor" in Jesus' words is someone with whom you have face-to-face contact, and (in this case) for whom you can supply a need. The Master therefore goes beyond the Jewish Bible concept.

According to this New Testament measuring-stick Jesus delineates a picture of the Final Judgment and the "code of Christian honor" by which we are to be judged. He names the specific persons whom you might meet or know about, who have specific needs: hunger, privation, lack of shelter or clothes, the sick and imprisoned. To bring the message home to yourself, you might have to smell the urine of the incontinent in an old folks' home; hear the clang of the jail gates locking you in when you visit prisoners; feel the cold of unheated apartments because a family cannot afford the cost; see the elderly sit in the dark because the electric bill is too high for only a Social Security check—and see them eat dog food because it is cheaper and requires no refrigeration!

Christianity is not simply a moral code, not even the works of mercy mentioned in Matthew today. Christianity means accepting Jesus. When we examine our conscience, we should ask whether we have found Jesus in others. He himself said, *"whatever you did"*—or neglected to do—*"for one of these least brothers of mine, you did"*—or neglected to do—*"for me."*

Solemnity
of the Annunciation
# of Our Lord, March 25

Is 7:10-14; Heb 10:4-10;
Lk 1:26-38

The Annunciation was made to Mary, but its message concerned Jesus; hence this solemnity is called the "Annunciation of our Lord." It is like the overture to a grand opera. The Divine Composer is establishing the themes to be developed in their entirety, in lyrics and melodies, throughout the musical drama. At this time Mary was the first Christian as such. The essential doctrine of Christianity is the mystery of the Trinity. Now

Mary was the first to receive this revelation, as she, indeed, was first to receive every Christian revelation. Hence we may even say that the Church began with her as she conceived Jesus in her womb. For nine months she was the whole "Church." The angel's salutation describes what the Church should be: full of grace and with the Lord.

Now is the time for fulfillment of prophecies. In Matthew's version Jesus is said to have been reared in Nazareth; in fulfillment of the prophecies he would be known as a Nazarene. Yet factually there is no such prophecy in the Jewish Bible. Still the "mystery hidden from all ages" and "God's secret plan" is being set into action. Matthew's Gospel tends to be stark, even gloomy: the bare stable, the massacre of the Innocents, the flight into Egypt, and the loss of Jesus in the Temple. But in Luke the childhood of Jesus is bathed in joyous light and song: the canticles of Mary, Zechariah and Simeon!

Such marvels are implicit in the Annunciation, when heaven meets the earth. Nazareth was a small town then of perhaps three hundred residents. The Archangel Gabriel passes the homes of more influential citizens: the priest, rabbi, the entrepreneurs, the Pharisee and doctor of the Law. God is not impressed by affluence and status. Joseph was "only" a carpenter, and Mary called herself the "handmaid of the Lord." When God sets out to turn the world upsidedown, he begins with the helpless, poor, barren and sterile (as Elizabeth)—in a forgettable village of a second-rate nation under foreign domination.

Centuries of hearing the same stories and Gospels leave our inner ears deaf and insensitive to the startling Good News. The coming of Jesus heralds the time when all men will be enabled to share the very divine love life of the Trinity. That is why this mystery had to be revealed at the Annunciation! Sometimes we fantasize about our own response, had we been present for these sacred events. Actually, there are ways to assess such a response. The liturgical readings are intended to make present the saving events of Jesus' life. What did Mary do immediately? She went to help—or rather to evangelize—her cousin Elizabeth with the Good News of her Son.

The Gospel is not a biography of Jesus and Mary and Joseph, nor are we to seek for merely pious stories. The Gospels are invitations to accept Jesus after the examples of the Bible characters. Mary responded, *"May it be done to me according to your word,"* and we also say, "Yes!" to God. The consequence of our "Yes" is to go out and evangelize others. Christ is not using coercion, authority and superiority, but influences us by the attractiveness of his life and message. He invites us to become his "other selves."

In the response to the Isaian text we see how people found their way to God by rituals of Judaism, "Sacrifice or oblation you wished not, but ears open to obedience you gave me"—which shows that God sees the inner person. This is fulfilled in the Letter to the Hebrews, *"But a body you prepared for me."* Jesus is the spiritual revolutionary as clearly stated by the writer: *"He takes away the first [covenant] to establish the second."* The "body" refers to the Incarnation, whereby we need no rituals from Judaism, but go directly to the Father through Jesus.

Ask yourself whether God is visiting you today through some messenger to elicit a "Yes" from you—to change your life, to accept some task in the Church, to be reconciled to someone with whom you are at odds, to understand some new insight in the Scriptures. Your "Yes" would be the opportunity to be filled with grace and have the Lord be with you in a special way!

*VISIT, WRITE or CALL your nearest ST. PAUL BOOK &
MEDIA CENTER today for a wide selection of Catholic books,
periodicals, cassettes, quality video cassettes for children and
adults! Operated by the Daughters of St. Paul.
We are located in:*

ALASKA
750 West 5th Ave., Anchorage, AK 99501 **907-272-8183.**
CALIFORNIA
3908 Sepulveda Blvd., Culver City, CA 90320 **213-202-8144.**
1570 Fifth Ave. (at Cedar Street), San Diego, CA 92101
619-232-1442.
46 Geary Street, San Francisco, CA 94108 **415-781-5180.**
FLORIDA
145 S.W. 107th Ave. Miami, FL 33174 **305-559-6715; 305-559-6716.**
HAWAII
1143 Bishop Street, Honolulu, HI 96813 **808-521-2731.**
ILLINOIS
172 North Michigan Ave., Chicago, IL 60601
312-346-4228; 312-346-3240.
LOUISIANA
423 Main Street, Baton Rouge, LA 70802 **504-343-4057; 504-336-1504.**
4403 Veterans Memorial Blvd., Metairie, LA 70006 **504-887-7631;**
504-887-0113.
MASSACHUSETTS
50 St. Paul's Ave., Jamaica Plain, Boston, MA 02130 **617-522-8911.**
Rte. 1, 450 Providence Hwy., Dedham, MA 02026 **617-326-5385.**
MISSOURI
9804 Watson Rd., St. Louis, MO 63126 **314-965-3512; 314-965-3571.**
NEW JERSEY
561 U.S. Route 1; No. C6, Wicks Plaza, Edison, NJ 08817
201-572-1200; 201-572-1201.
NEW YORK
150 East 52nd Street, New York, NY 10022 **212-754-1110.**
78 Fort Place, Staten Island, NY 10301
718-447-5071; 718-447-5086.
OHIO
616 Walnut Street, Cincinnati, OH 45202 **513-421-5733; 513-721-5059.**
2105 Ontario Street (at Prospect Ave.), Cleveland, OH 44115
216-621-9427.
PENNSYLVANIA
168 W. DeKalb Pike, King of Prussia, PA 19406 **215-337-1882;**
215-337-2077.
SOUTH CAROLINA
243 King Street, Charleston, SC 29401 **803-577-0175.**
TEXAS
114 Main Plaza, San Antonio, TX 78205 **512-224-8101.**
VIRGINIA
1025 King Street, Alexandria, VA 22314 **703-549-3806.**
CANADA
3022 Dufferin Street, Toronto, Ontario, Canada M6B 3T5
416-781-9131.